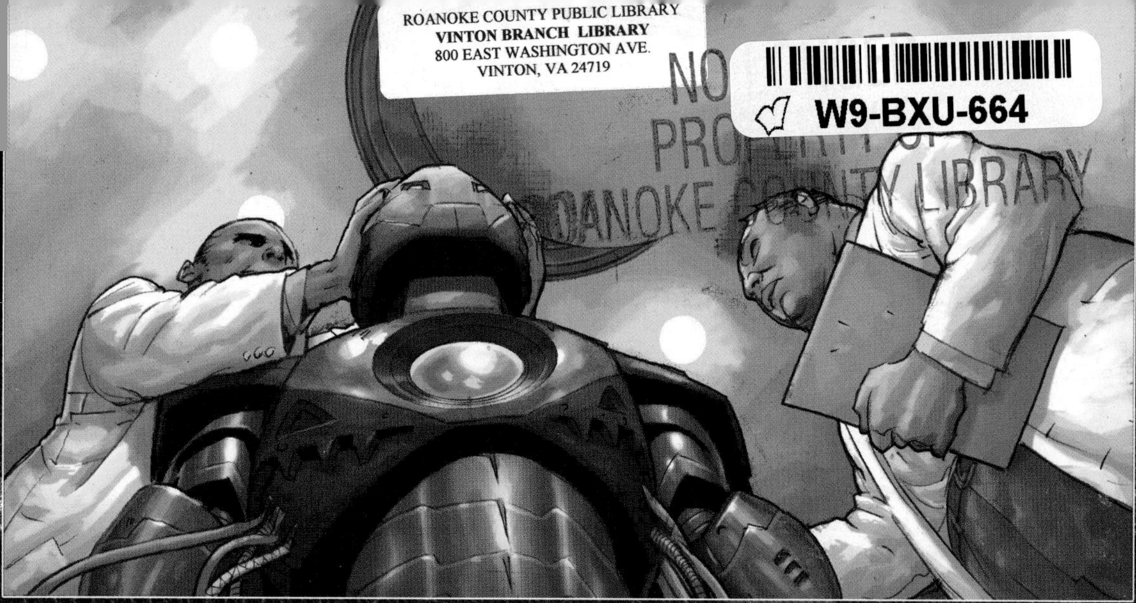

ULTIMATE HULK VS. IRON MAN_

ULTIMATE HUMAN

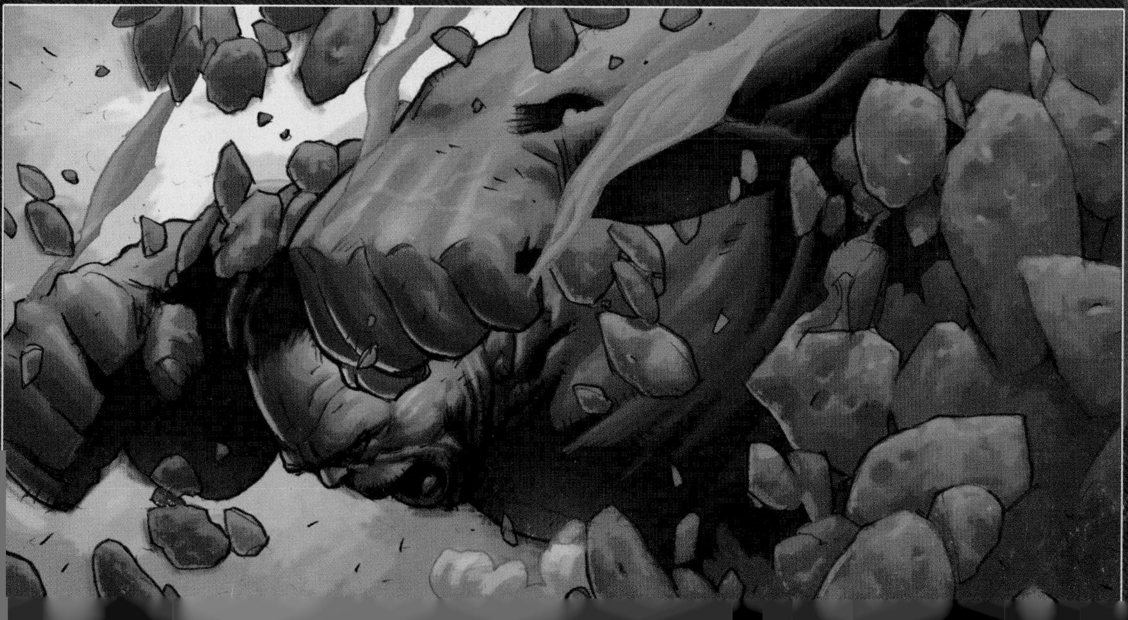

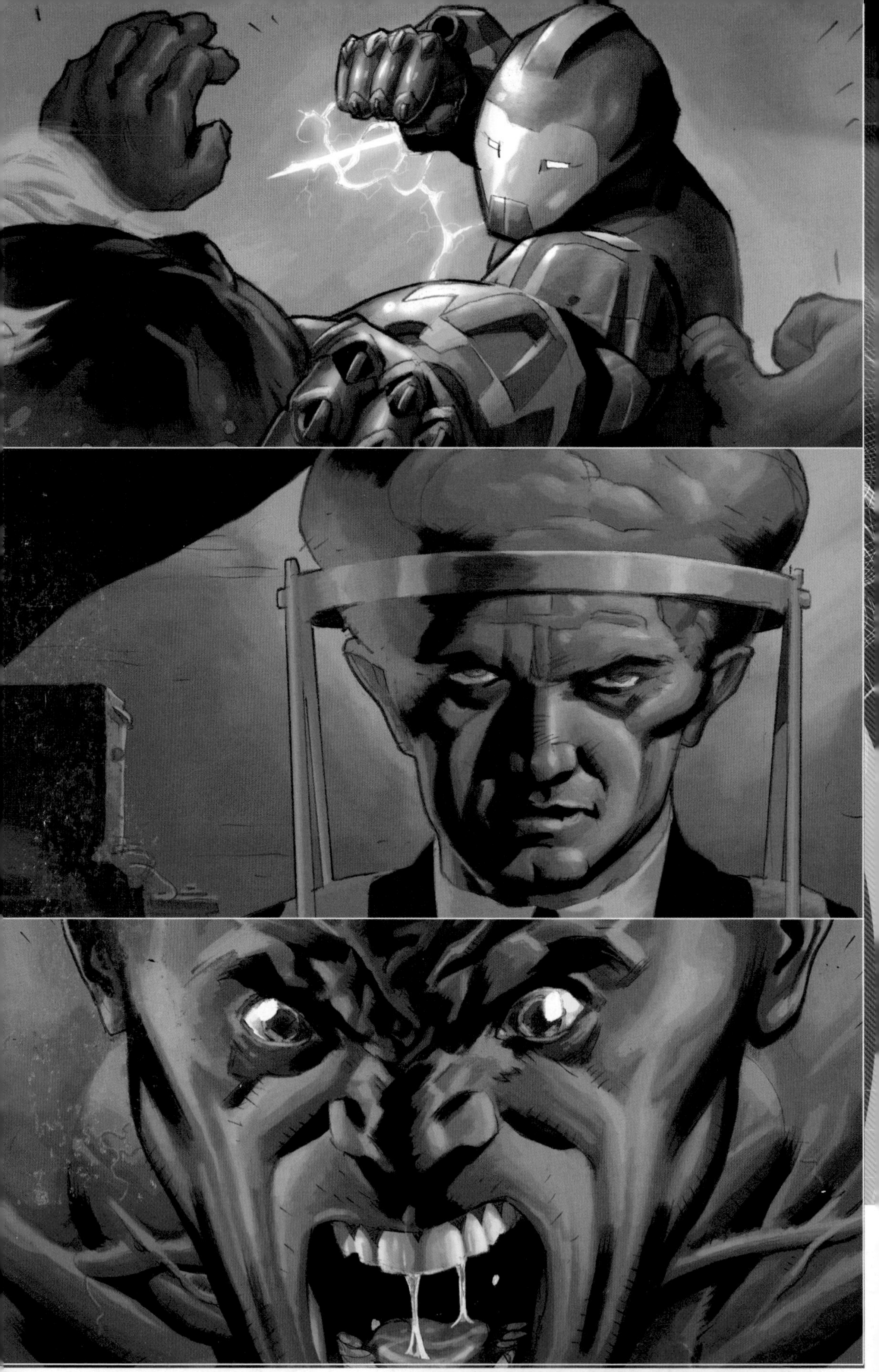

ULTIMATE HULK VS. IRON MAN_

ULTIMATE HUMAN

WRITER: **WARREN ELLIS**
ARTIST: **CARY NORD**
COLORIST: **DAVE STEWART**
LETTERER: **DAVE SHARPE**
COVER ARTISTS: **CARY NORD** & **RICHARD ISANOVE**
ASSISTANT EDITOR: **LAUREN SANKOVITCH**
EDITOR: **BILL ROSEMANN**
SENIOR EDITOR: **RALPH MACCHIO**

COLLECTION EDITOR: **JENNIFER GRÜNWALD**
EDITORIAL ASSISTANT: **ALEX STARBUCK**
ASSISTANT EDITORS: **CORY LEVINE** & **JOHN DENNING**
EDITOR, SPECIAL PROJECTS: **MARK D. BEAZLEY**
SENIOR EDITOR, SPECIAL PROJECTS: **JEFF YOUNGQUIST**
SENIOR VICE PRESIDENT OF SALES: **DAVID GABRIEL**
PRODUCTION: **JERRY KALINOWSKI**
BOOK DESIGNER: **RODOLFO MURAGUCHI**

EDITOR IN CHIEF: **JOE QUESADA**
PUBLISHER: **DAN BUCKLEY**

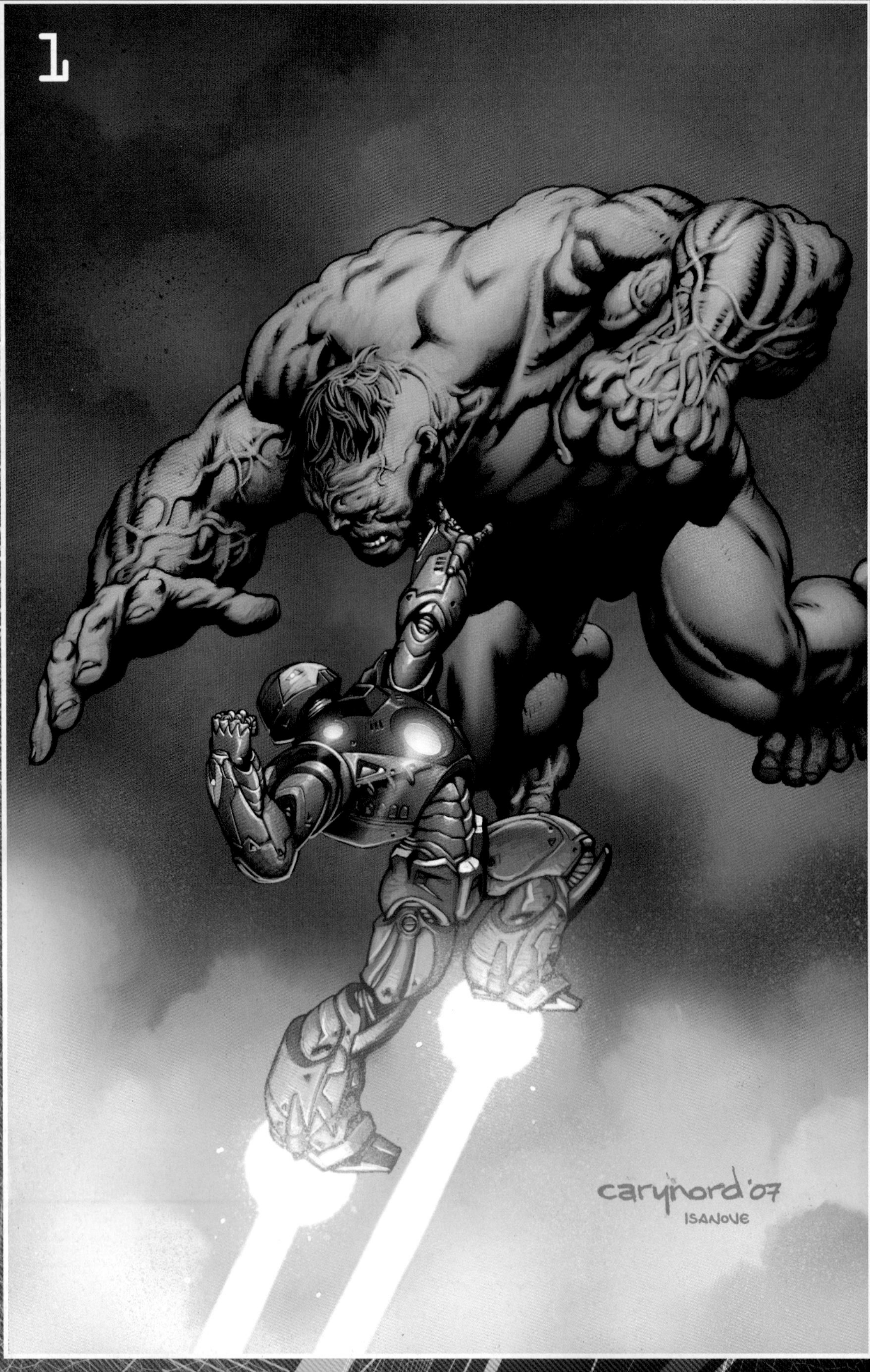
1
carynord'07
ISANOVE

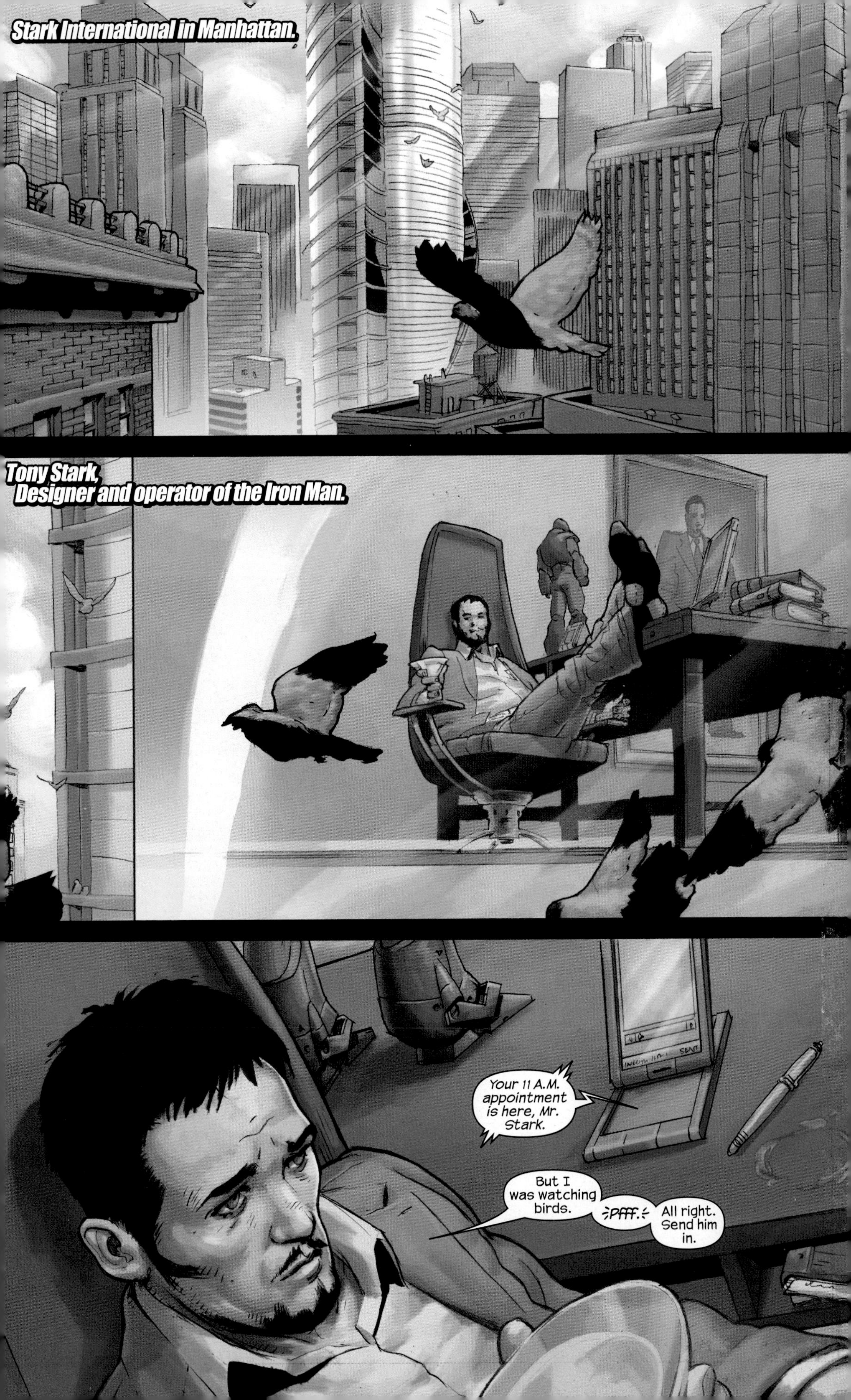
Stark International in Manhattan.
Tony Stark, Designer and operator of the Iron Man.
Your 11 A.M. appointment is here, Mr. Stark.
But I was watching birds.
PFFF.
All right. Send him in.

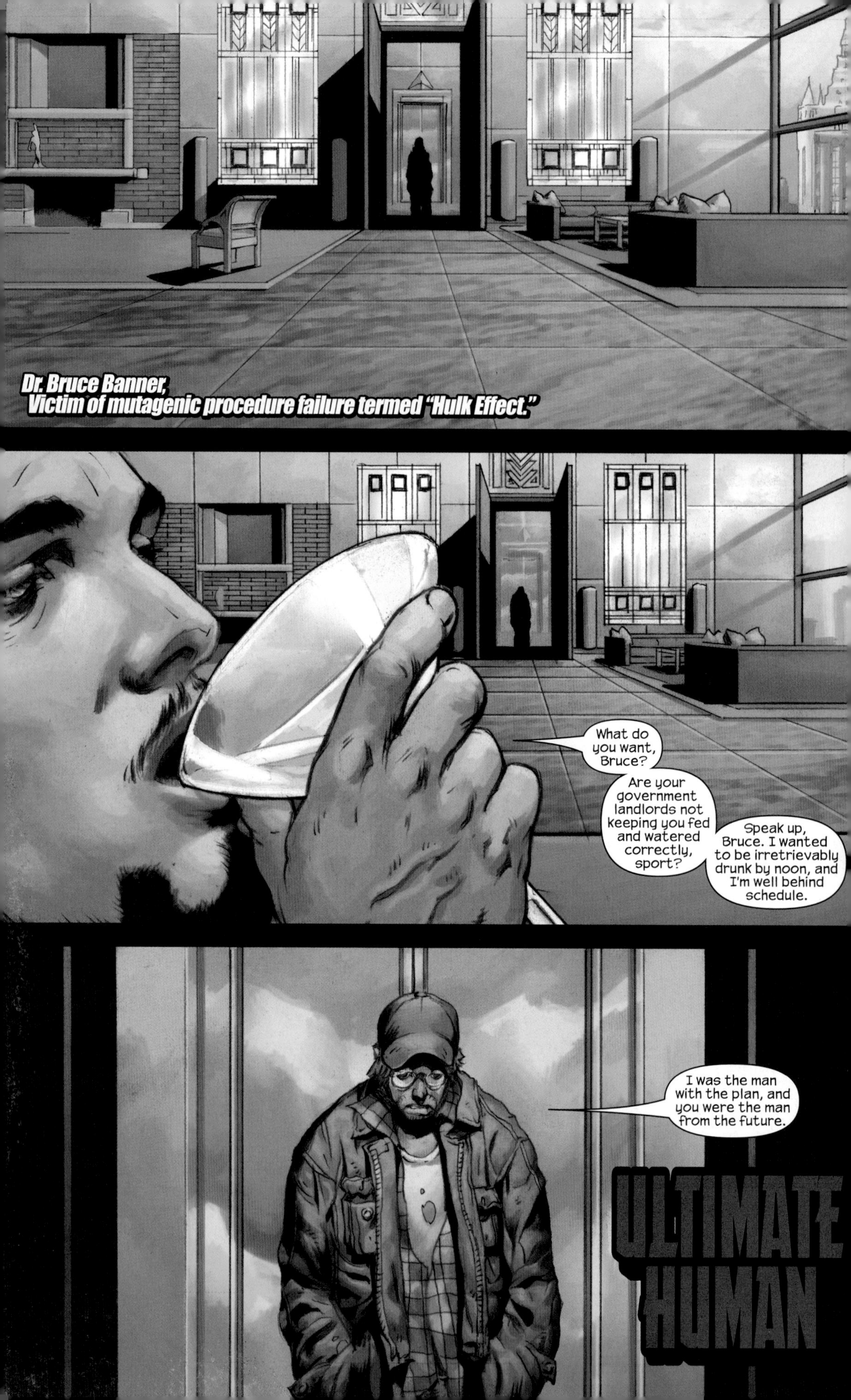
Dr. Bruce Banner,
Victim of mutagenic procedure failure termed "Hulk Effect."
What do you want, Bruce?
Are your government landlords not keeping you fed and watered correctly, sport?
Speak up, Bruce. I wanted to be irretrievably drunk by noon, and I'm well behind schedule.
I was the man with the plan, and you were the man from the future.
ULTIMATE HUMAN

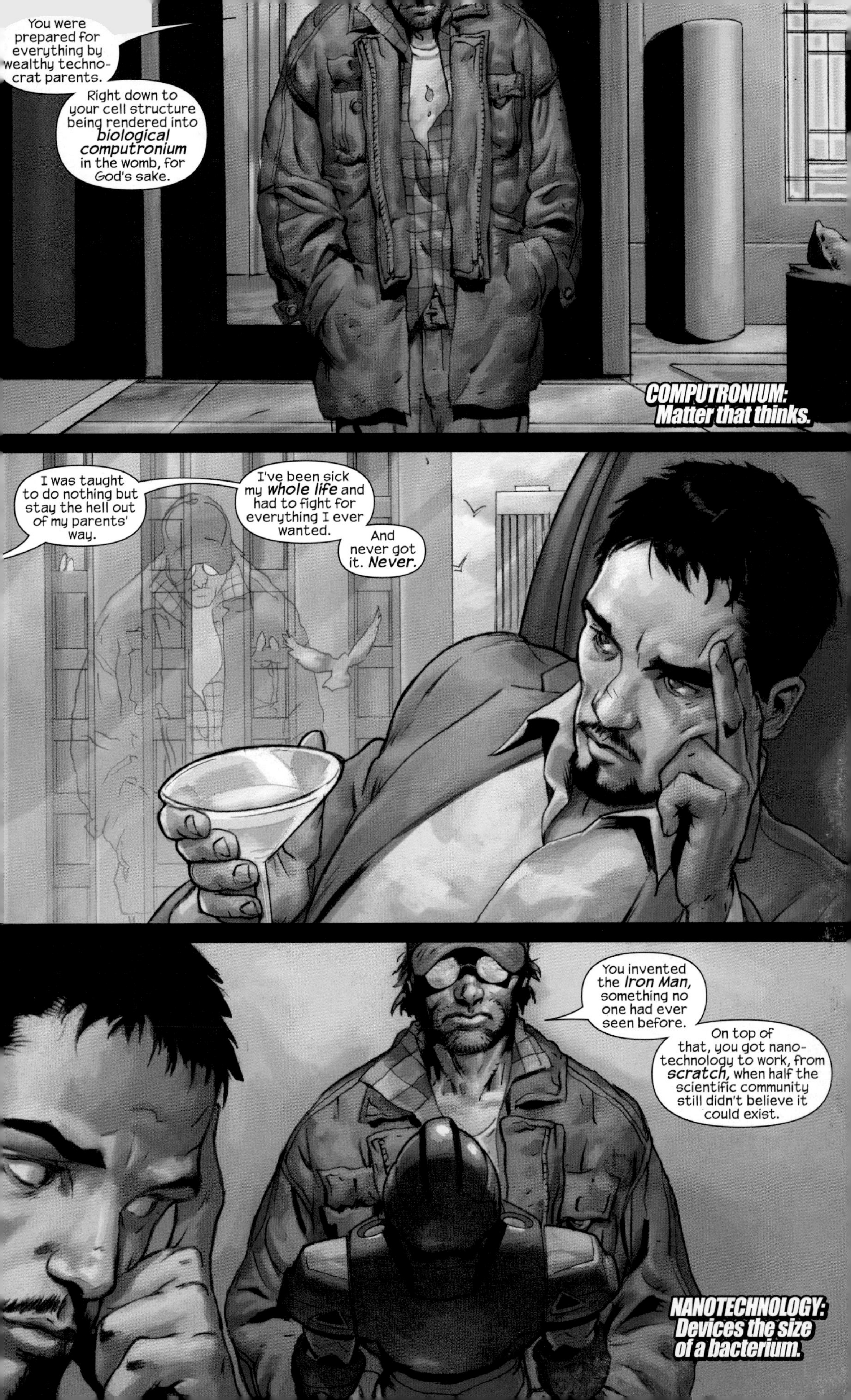
You were prepared for everything by wealthy techno-crat parents.
Right down to your cell structure being rendered into *biological computronium* in the womb, for God's sake.
COMPUTRONIUM: Matter that thinks.
I was taught to do nothing but stay the hell out of my parents' way.
I've been sick my *whole life* and had to fight for everything I ever wanted.
And never got it. *Never.*
You invented the *Iron Man,* something no one had ever seen before.
On top of that, you got nano-technology to work, from *scratch,* when half the scientific community still didn't believe it could exist.
NANOTECHNOLOGY: Devices the size of a bacterium.

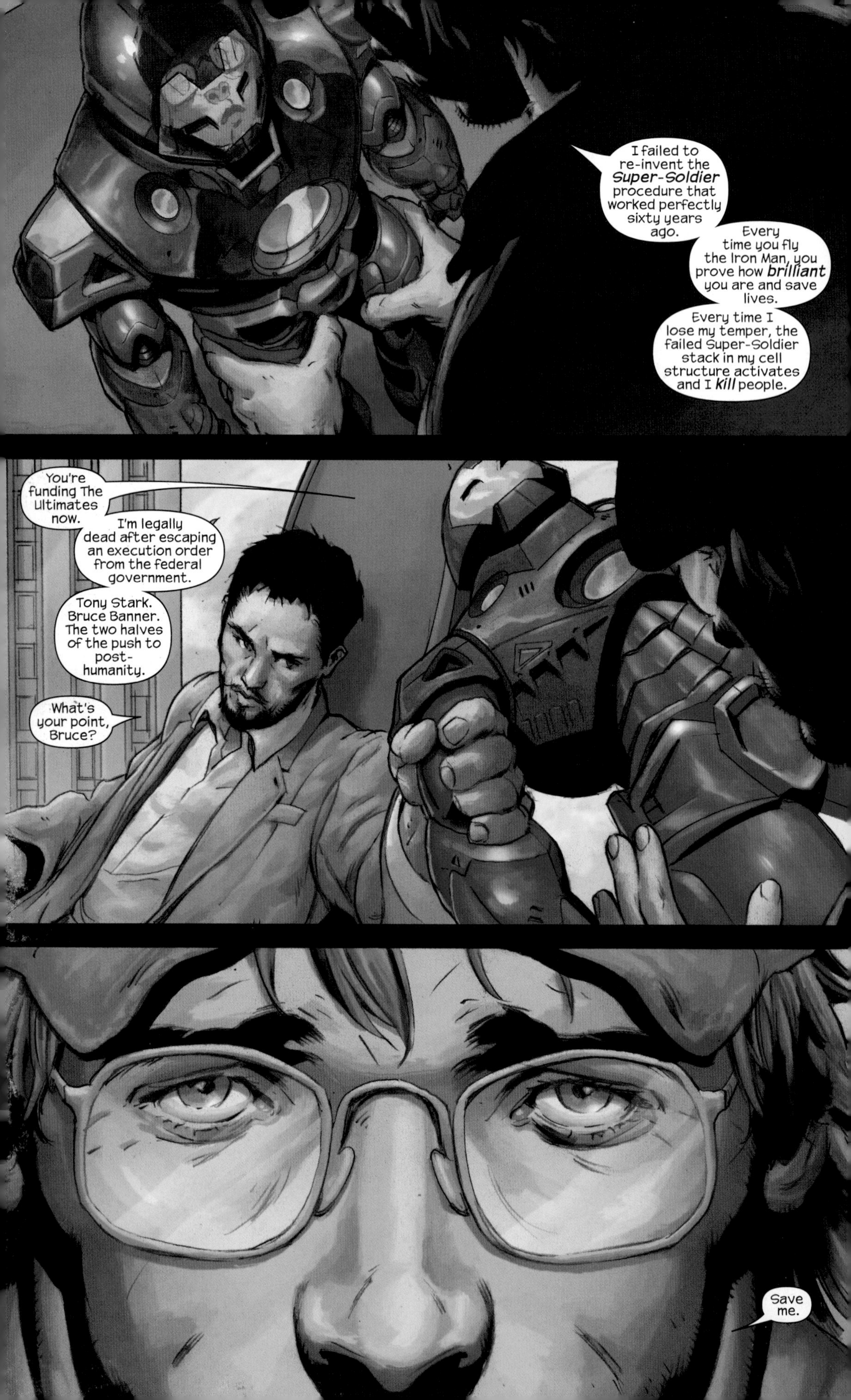

I failed to re-invent the Super-Soldier procedure that worked perfectly sixty years ago.
Every time you fly the Iron Man, you prove how brilliant you are and save lives.
Every time I lose my temper, the failed Super-Soldier stack in my cell structure activates and I kill people.
You're funding The Ultimates now.
I'm legally dead after escaping an execution order from the federal government.
Tony Stark. Bruce Banner. The two halves of the push to post-humanity.
What's your point, Bruce?
Save me.

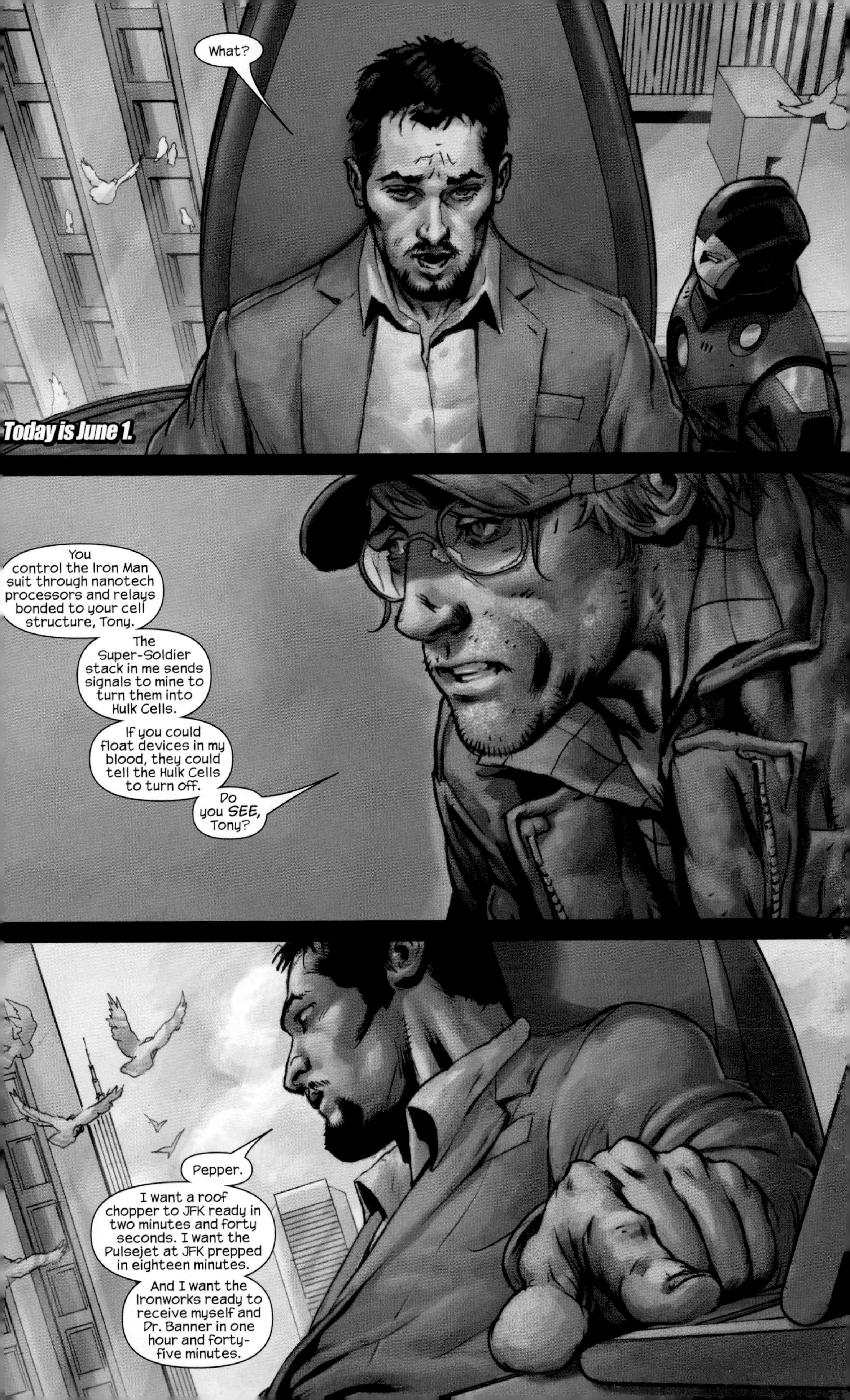
What?
Today is June 1.
You control the Iron Man suit through nanotech processors and relays bonded to your cell structure, Tony.
The Super-Soldier stack in me sends signals to mine to turn them into Hulk Cells.
If you could float devices in my blood, they could tell the Hulk Cells to turn off.
Do you SEE, Tony?
Pepper.
I want a roof chopper to JFK ready in two minutes and forty seconds. I want the Pulsejet at JFK prepped in eighteen minutes.
And I want the Ironworks ready to receive myself and Dr. Banner in one hour and forty-five minutes.

Southern England. June 1.

BLACKCROSSVALE
REGIONAL GOVT
SHELTER
(DECOMMISSIONED)

PRIVATE PROPERTY
NO TRESPASS

1000
123 B

WAR RO...
BLOC...
CONST...
1979

Stark's on the move, sir.

He's en route to the Ironworks. And apparently has Banner in tow, sir.

Oh, that's good. That's very good.

Do I greenlight *Operation Gamma*, sir?

General Quarters, this is *James Larner* speaking for the *Leader.*

Operation Gamma is go at this time. Commence operational prep. Section chiefs report to the War Room in one hour.

Absolutely, Mr. Larner.

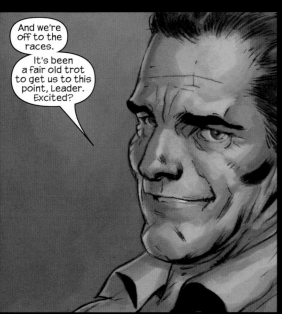

And we're off to the races.

It's been a fair old trot to get us to this point, Leader. Excited?

"Leader." Do you remember when I was Sergeant, James? And then Agent?

And then the youngest D/Ops MI6 had ever seen?

Remember when the old C said, "Peter Wisdom, you are the future of British Intelligence"?

Excited? No. I think I lost the capacity for that the day they threw me out of the service.

Perhaps even the day they threw the British Super-human Initiative to *James Braddock* and his flock of sheep.

Or the day I proved that my British Enhancile Programme worked.

And they looked at me like I was a bloody monster.

Excited? No. *Angry?* Oh, yes.

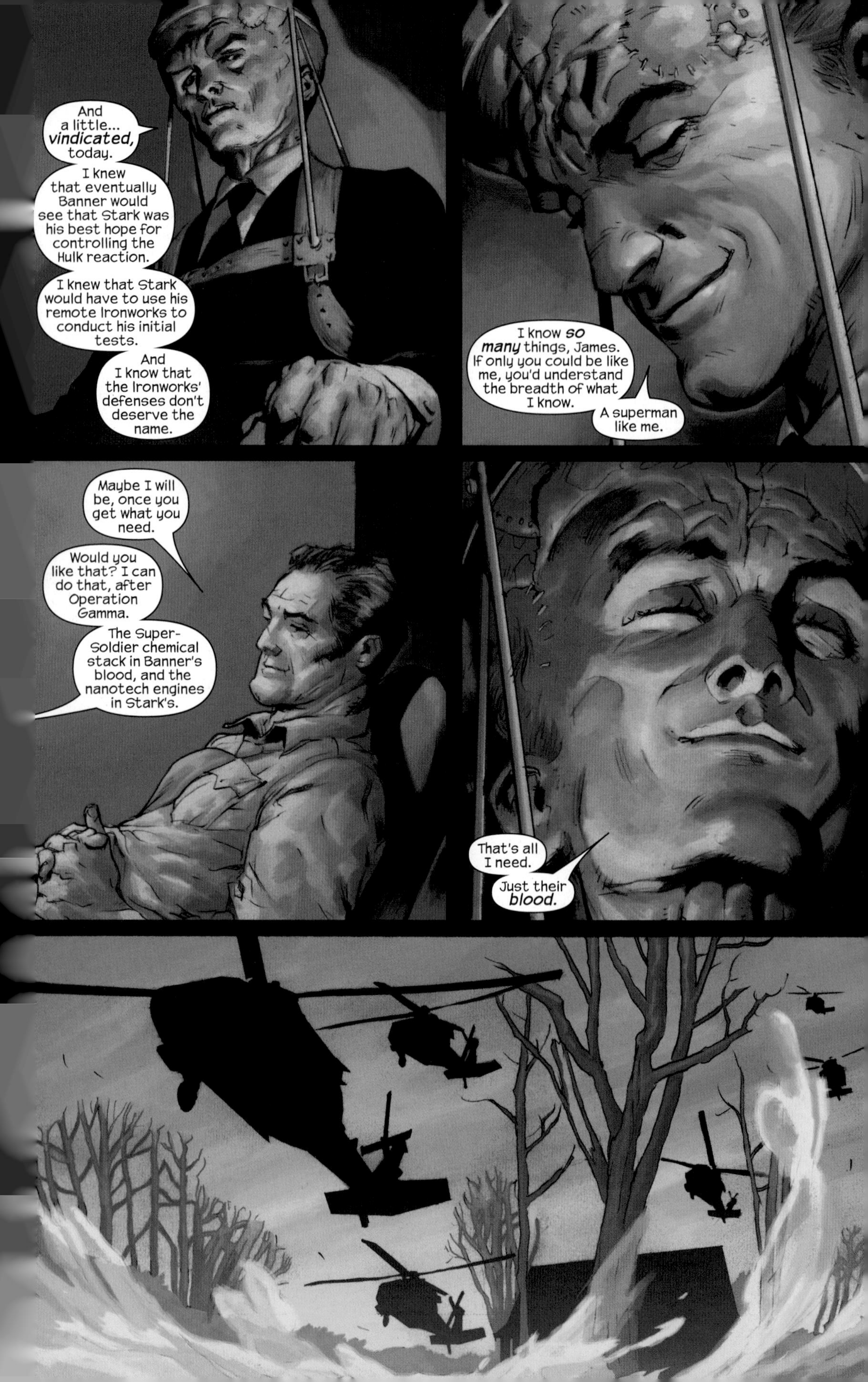
And a little... *vindicated,* today.
I knew that eventually Banner would see that Stark was his best hope for controlling the Hulk reaction.
I knew that Stark would have to use his remote Ironworks to conduct his initial tests.
And I know that the Ironworks' defenses don't deserve the name.
I know *so many* things, James. If only you could be like me, you'd understand the breadth of what I know.
A superman like me.
Maybe I will be, once you get what you need.
Would you like that? I can do that, after Operation Gamma.
The Super-Soldier chemical stack in Banner's blood, and the nanotech engines in Stark's.
That's all I need.
Just their *blood.*

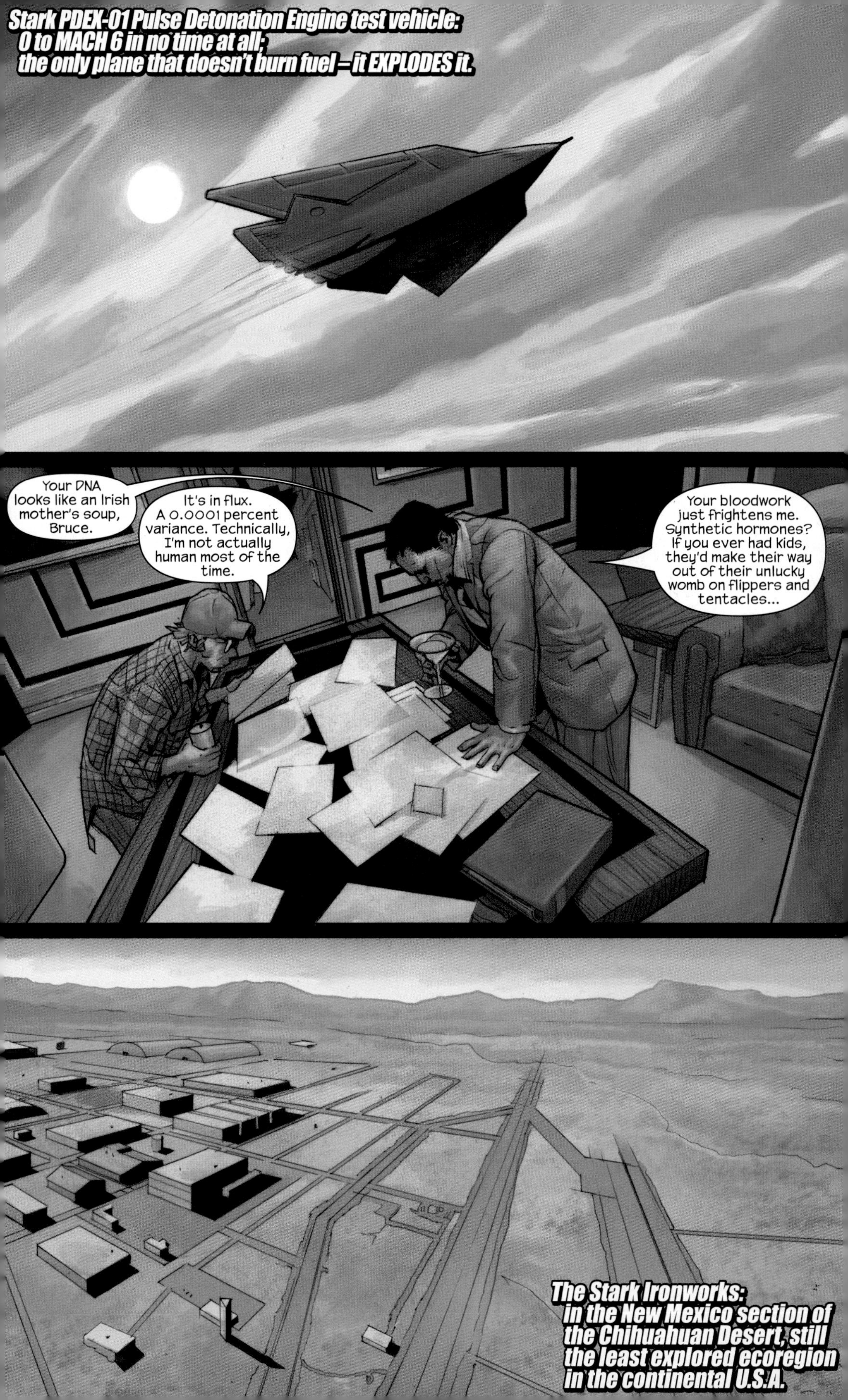

Stark PDEX-01 Pulse Detonation Engine test vehicle:
0 to MACH 6 in no time at all;
the only plane that doesn't burn fuel – it EXPLODES it.
Your DNA looks like an Irish mother's soup, Bruce.
It's in flux. A 0.0001 percent variance. Technically, I'm not actually human most of the time.
Your bloodwork just frightens me. Synthetic hormones? If you ever had kids, they'd make their way out of their unlucky womb on flippers and tentacles...
The Stark Ironworks:
in the New Mexico section of the Chihuahuan Desert, still the least explored ecoregion in the continental U.S.A.

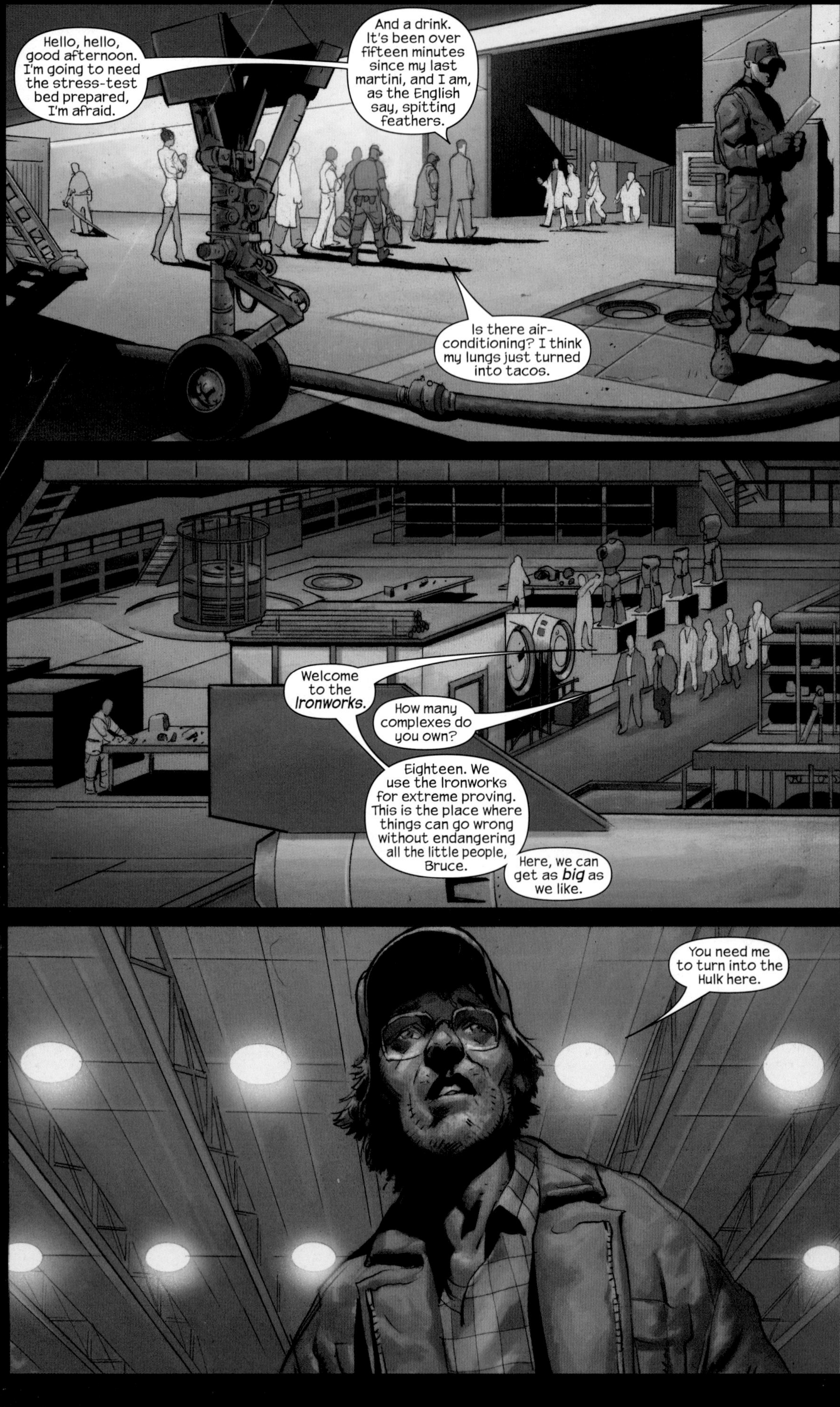

Hello, hello, good afternoon. I'm going to need the stress-test bed prepared, I'm afraid.
And a drink. It's been over fifteen minutes since my last martini, and I am, as the English say, spitting feathers.
Is there air-conditioning? I think my lungs just turned into tacos.
Welcome to the *Ironworks.*
How many complexes do you own?
Eighteen. We use the Ironworks for extreme proving. This is the place where things can go wrong without endangering all the little people, Bruce.
Here, we can get as *big* as we like.
You need me to turn into the Hulk here.

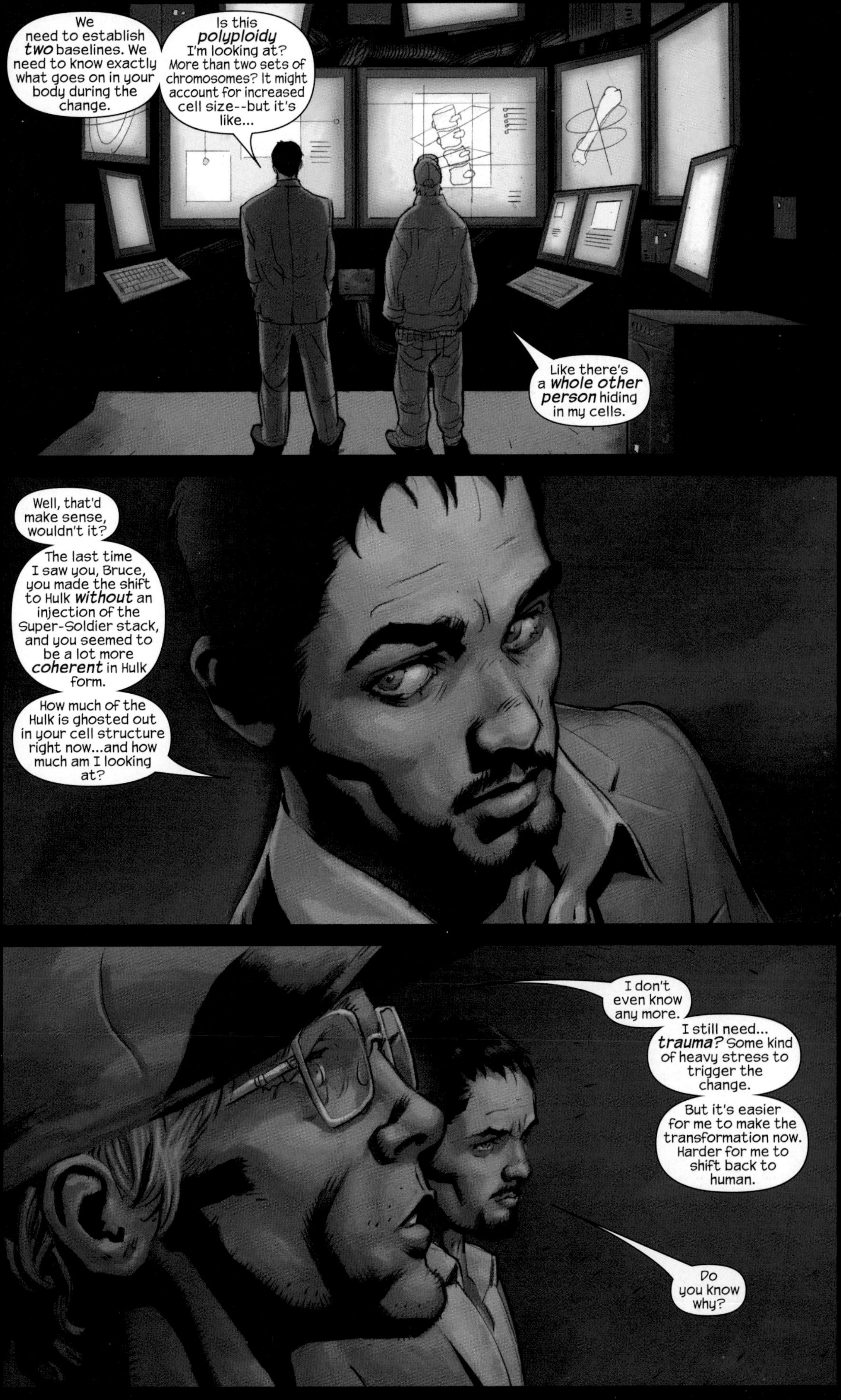
We need to establish *two* baselines. We need to know exactly what goes on in your body during the change.
Is this *polyploidy* I'm looking at? More than two sets of chromosomes? It might account for increased cell size--but it's like...
Like there's a *whole other person* hiding in my cells.
Well, that'd make sense, wouldn't it?
The last time I saw you, Bruce, you made the shift to Hulk *without* an injection of the Super-Soldier stack, and you seemed to be a lot more *coherent* in Hulk form.
How much of the Hulk is ghosted out in your cell structure right now...and how much am I looking at?
I don't even know any more.
I still need... *trauma?* Some kind of heavy stress to trigger the change.
But it's easier for me to make the transformation now. Harder for me to shift back to human.
Do you know why?

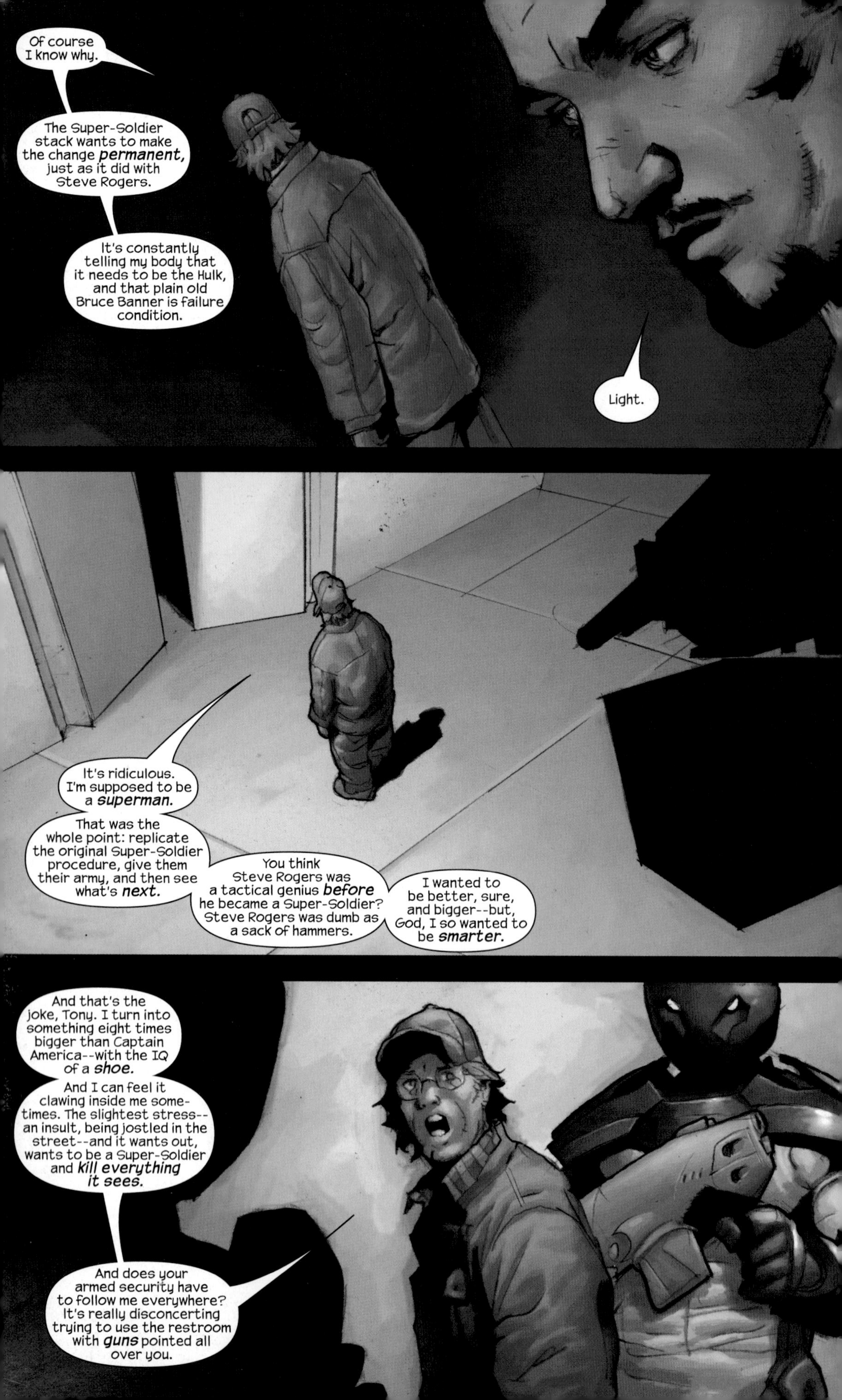

Of course I know why.
The Super-Soldier stack wants to make the change *permanent*, just as it did with Steve Rogers.
It's constantly telling my body that it needs to be the Hulk, and that plain old Bruce Banner is failure condition.
Light.
It's ridiculous. I'm supposed to be a *superman*.
That was the whole point: replicate the original Super-Soldier procedure, give them their army, and then see what's *next*.
You think Steve Rogers was a tactical genius *before* he became a Super-Soldier? Steve Rogers was dumb as a sack of hammers.
I wanted to be better, sure, and bigger--but, God, I so wanted to be *smarter*.
And that's the joke, Tony. I turn into something eight times bigger than Captain America--with the IQ of a *shoe*.
And I can feel it clawing inside me some-times. The slightest stress--an insult, being jostled in the street--and it wants out, wants to be a Super-Soldier and *kill everything it sees*.
And does your armed security have to follow me everywhere? It's really disconcerting trying to use the restroom with *guns* pointed all over you.

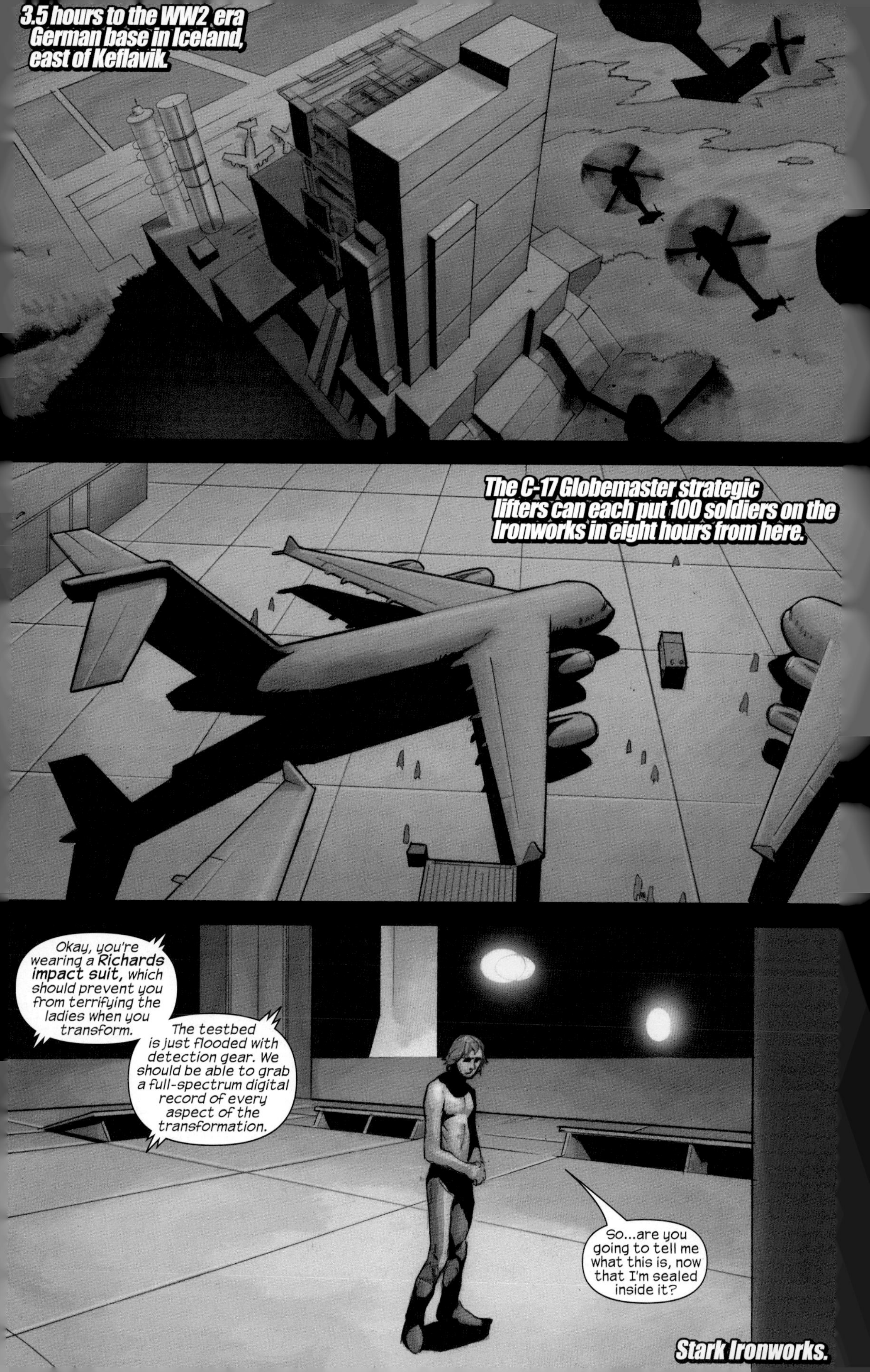
3.5 hours to the WW2 era German base in Iceland, east of Keflavik.
The C-17 Globemaster strategic lifters can each put 100 soldiers on the Ironworks in eight hours from here.
Okay, you're wearing a Richards impact suit, which should prevent you from terrifying the ladies when you transform.
The testbed is just flooded with detection gear. We should be able to grab a full-spectrum digital record of every aspect of the transformation.
So...are you going to tell me what this is, now that I'm sealed inside it?
Stark Ironworks.

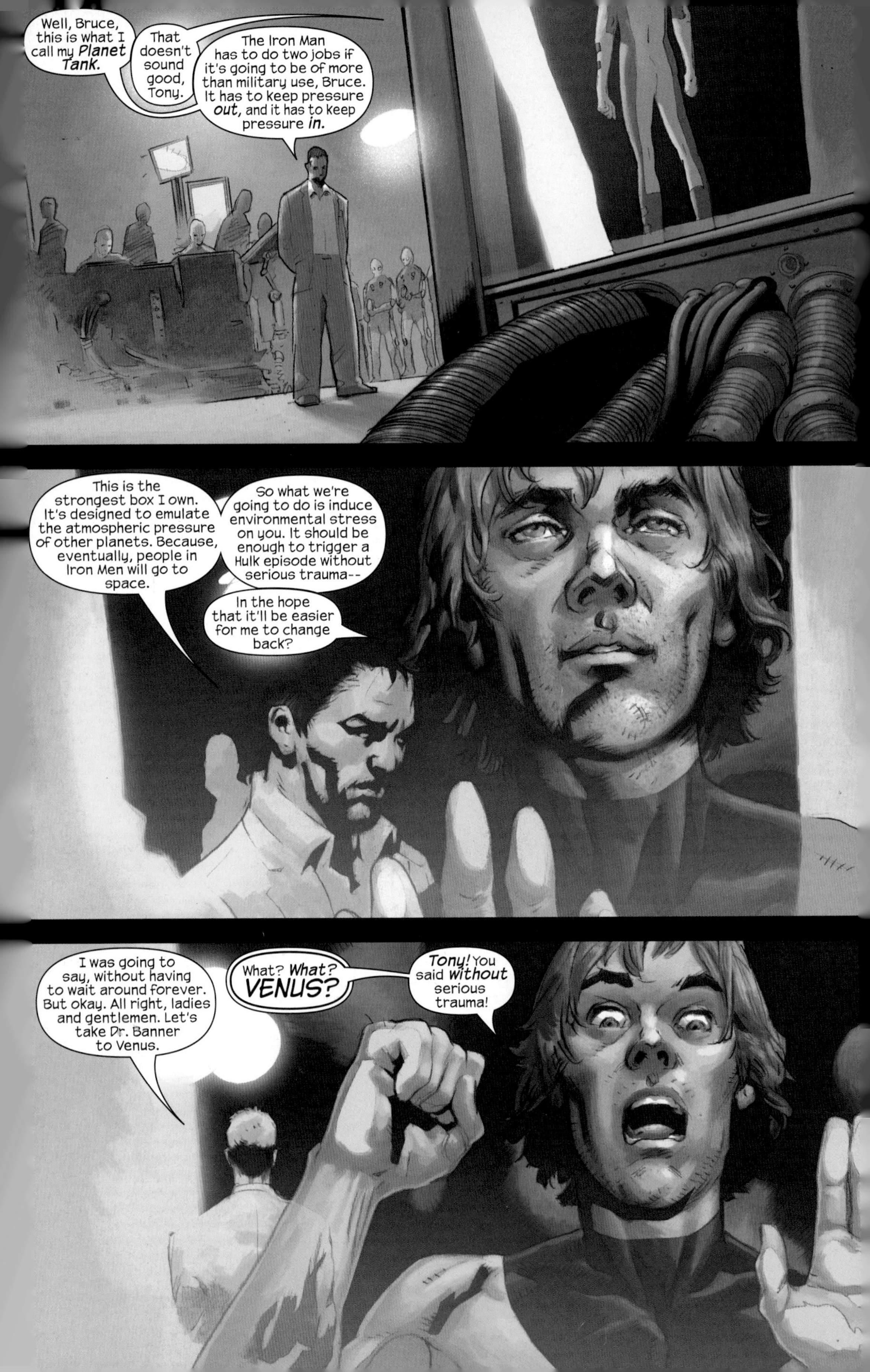
Well, Bruce, this is what I call my Planet Tank.
That doesn't sound good, Tony.
The Iron Man has to do two jobs if it's going to be of more than military use, Bruce. It has to keep pressure out, and it has to keep pressure in.
This is the strongest box I own. It's designed to emulate the atmospheric pressure of other planets. Because, eventually, people in Iron Men will go to space.
So what we're going to do is induce environmental stress on you. It should be enough to trigger a Hulk episode without serious trauma--
In the hope that it'll be easier for me to change back?
I was going to say, without having to wait around forever. But okay. All right, ladies and gentlemen. Let's take Dr. Banner to Venus.
What? What? VENUS?
Tony! You said without serious trauma!

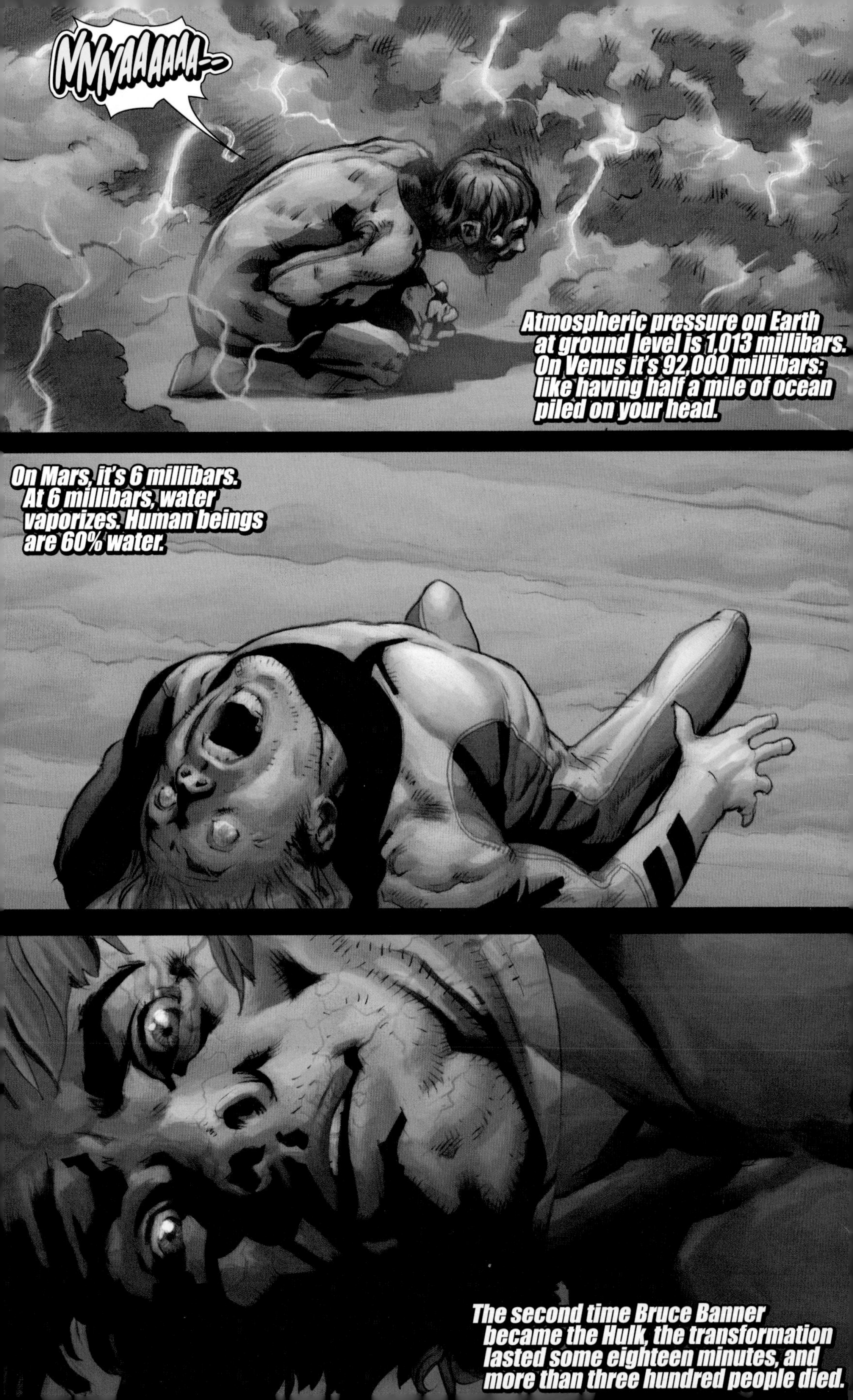
NNNAAAAAA--
Atmospheric pressure on Earth at ground level is 1,013 millibars. On Venus it's 92,000 millibars: like having half a mile of ocean piled on your head.
On Mars, it's 6 millibars. At 6 millibars, water vaporizes. Human beings are 60% water.
The second time Bruce Banner became the Hulk, the transformation lasted some eighteen minutes, and more than three hundred people died.

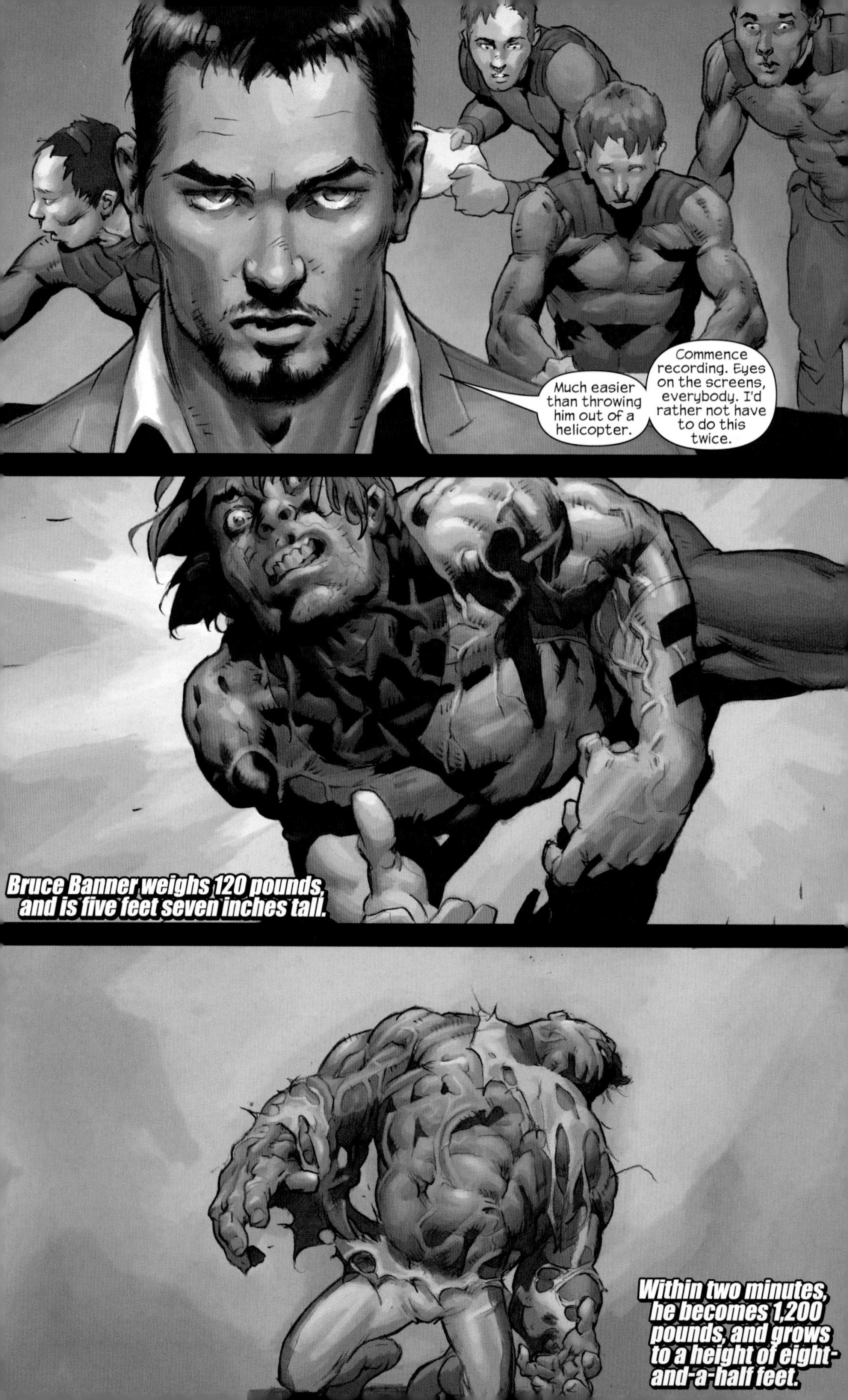

Much easier than throwing him out of a helicopter.
Commence recording. Eyes on the screens, everybody. I'd rather not have to do this twice.
Bruce Banner weighs 120 pounds, and is five feet seven inches tall.
Within two minutes, he becomes 1,200 pounds, and grows to a height of eight-and-a-half feet.

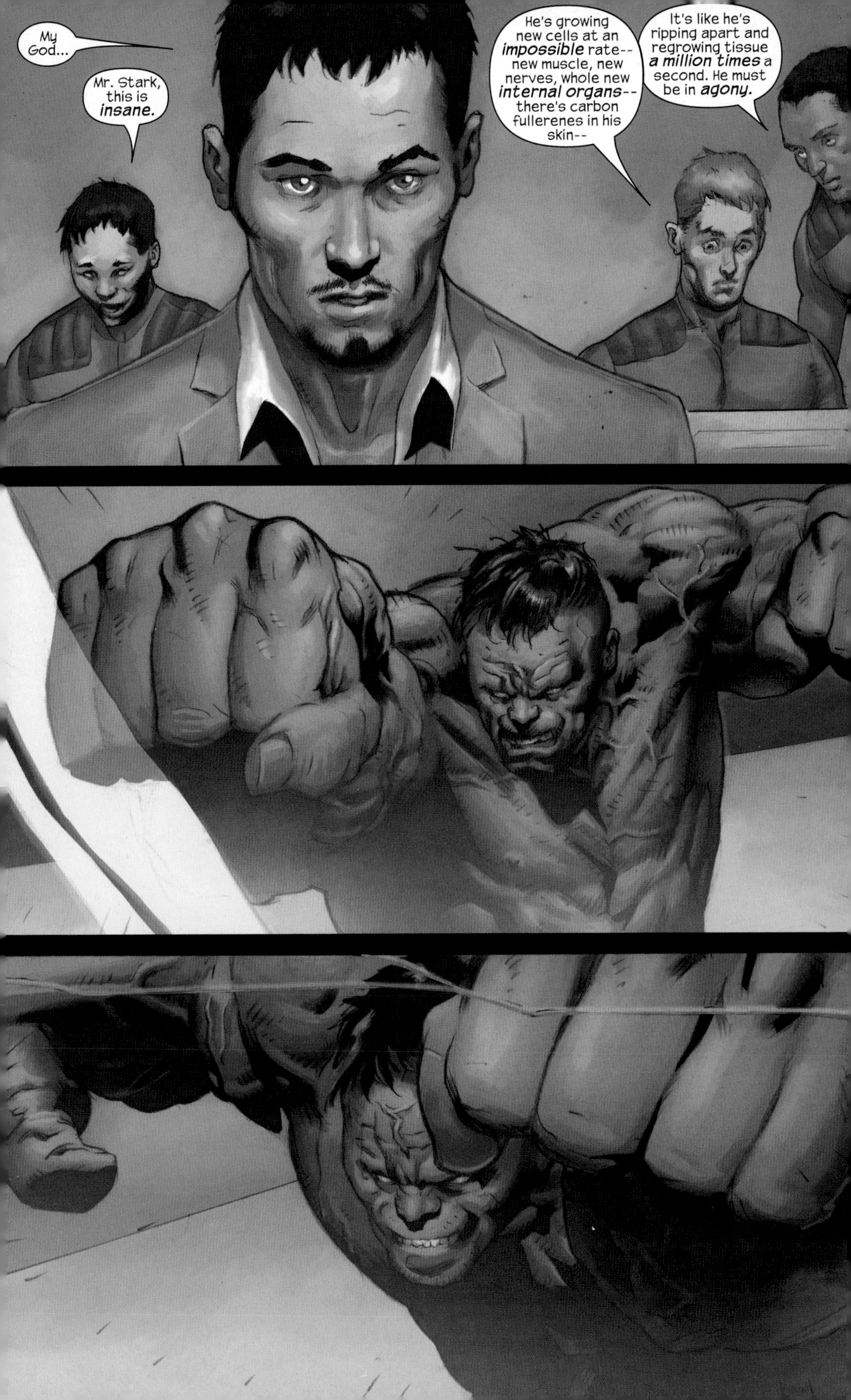
My God...
Mr. Stark, this is *insane.*
He's growing new cells at an *impossible* rate-- new muscle, new nerves, whole new *internal organs*-- there's carbon fullerenes in his skin--
It's like he's ripping apart and regrowing tissue *a million times* a second. He must be in *agony.*

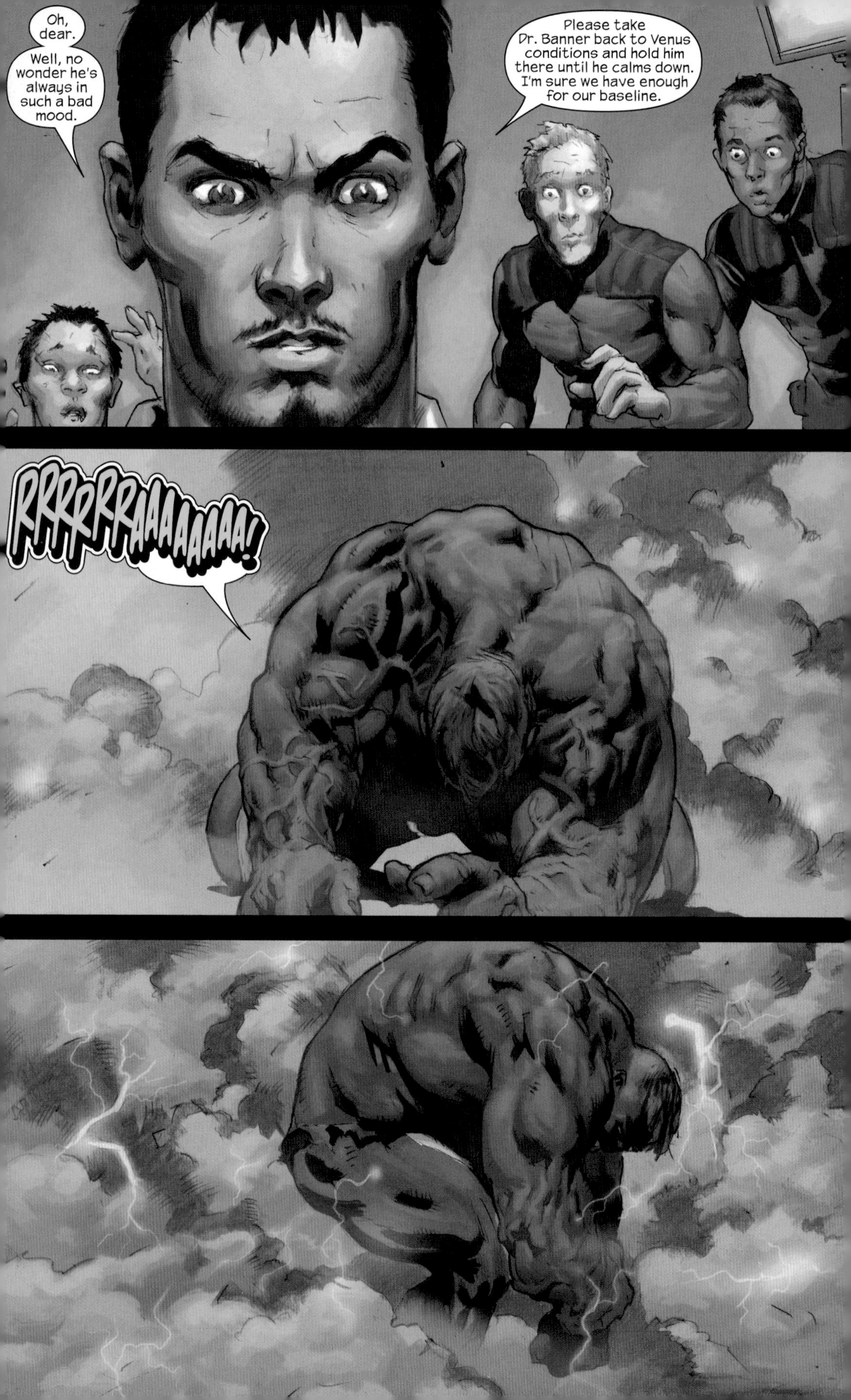
Oh, dear.
Well, no wonder he's always in such a bad mood.
Please take Dr. Banner back to Venus conditions and hold him there until he calms down. I'm sure we have enough for our baseline.
RRRRRRAAAAAAAA!

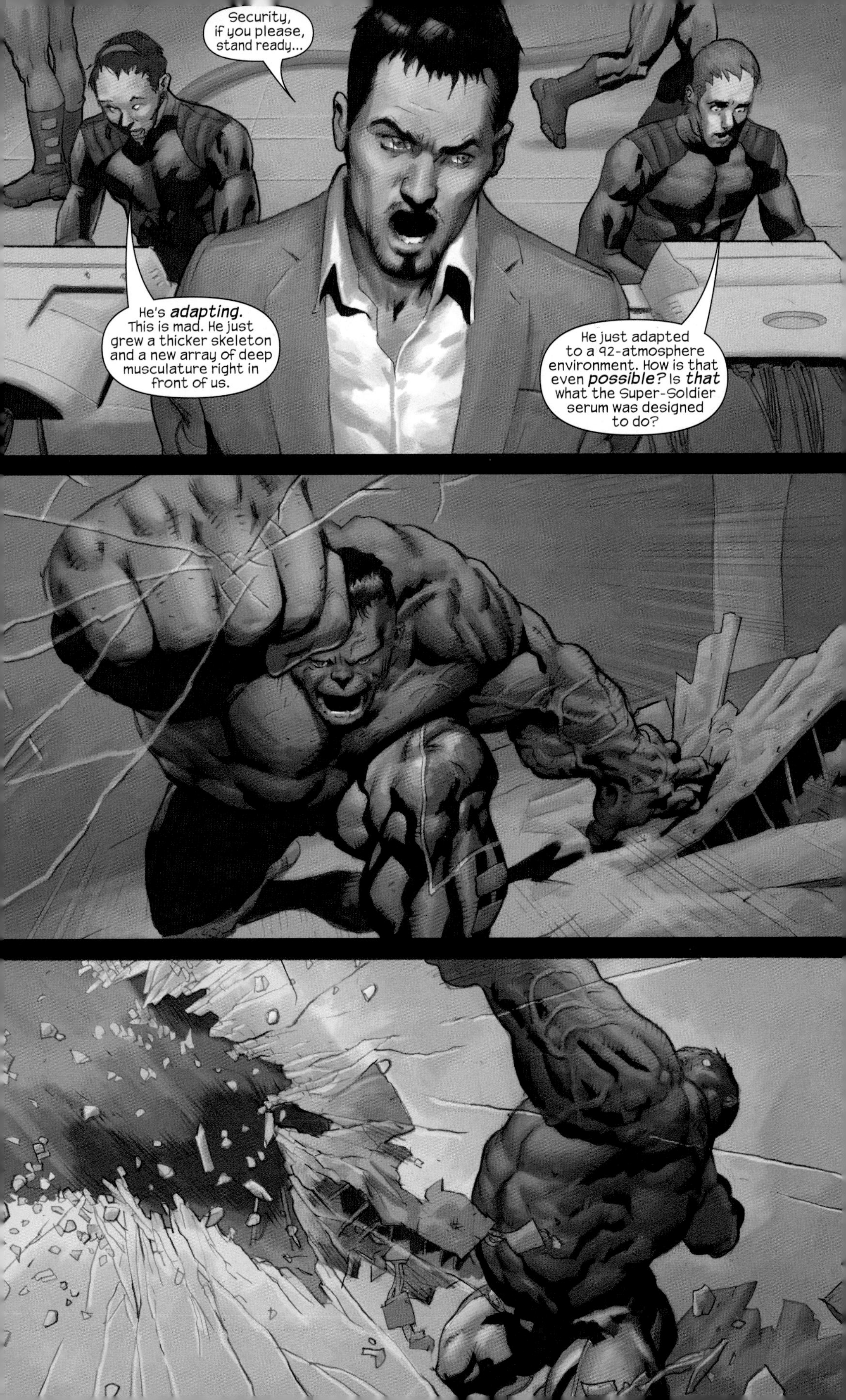
Security, if you please, stand ready...
He's adapting. This is mad. He just grew a thicker skeleton and a new array of deep musculature right in front of us.
He just adapted to a 92-atmosphere environment. How is that even possible? Is that what the Super-Soldier serum was designed to do?

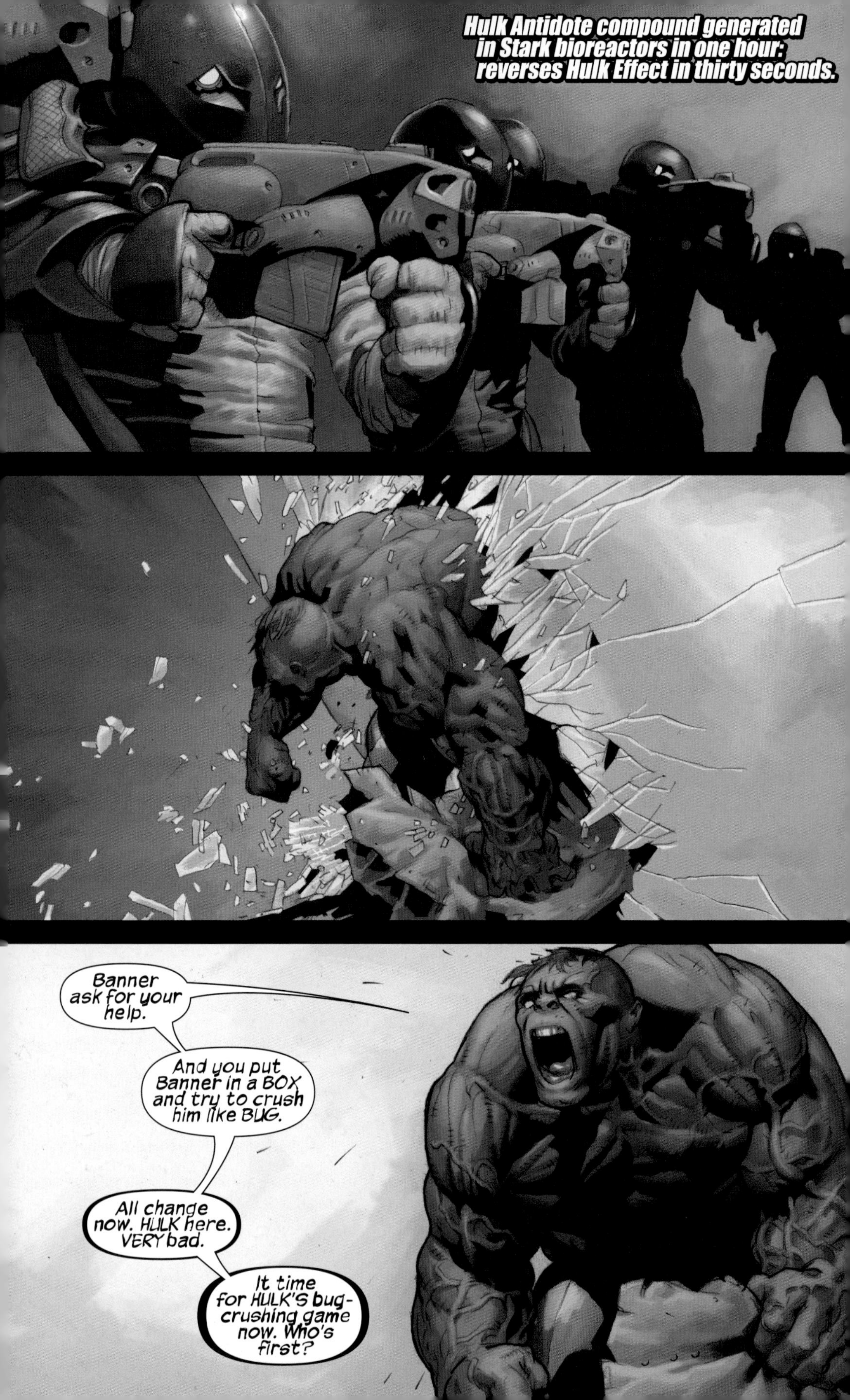
Hulk Antidote compound generated in Stark bioreactors in one hour: reverses Hulk Effect in thirty seconds.
Banner ask for your help.
And you put Banner in a BOX and try to crush him like BUG.
All change now. HULK here. VERY bad.
It time for HULK'S bug-crushing game now. Who's first?

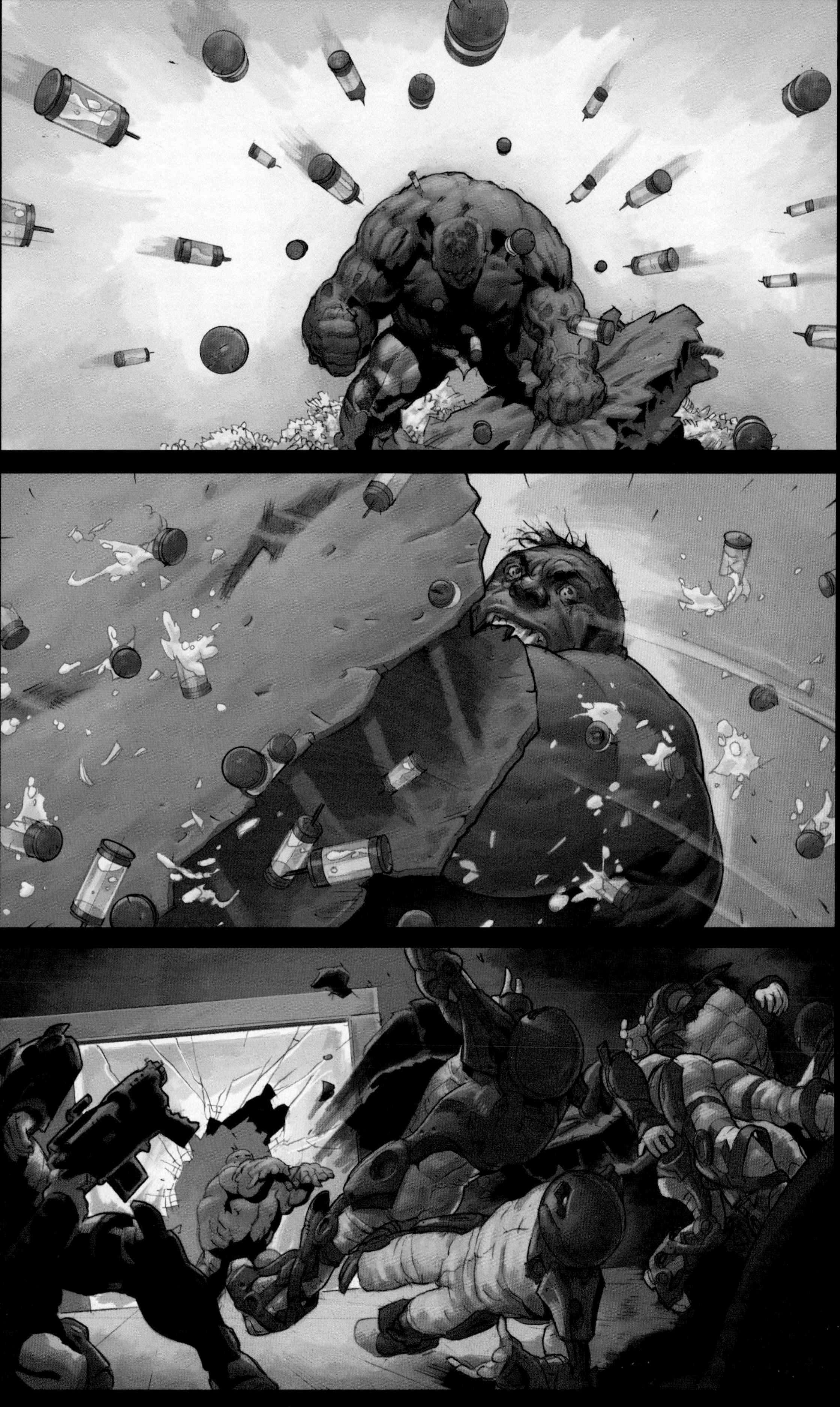

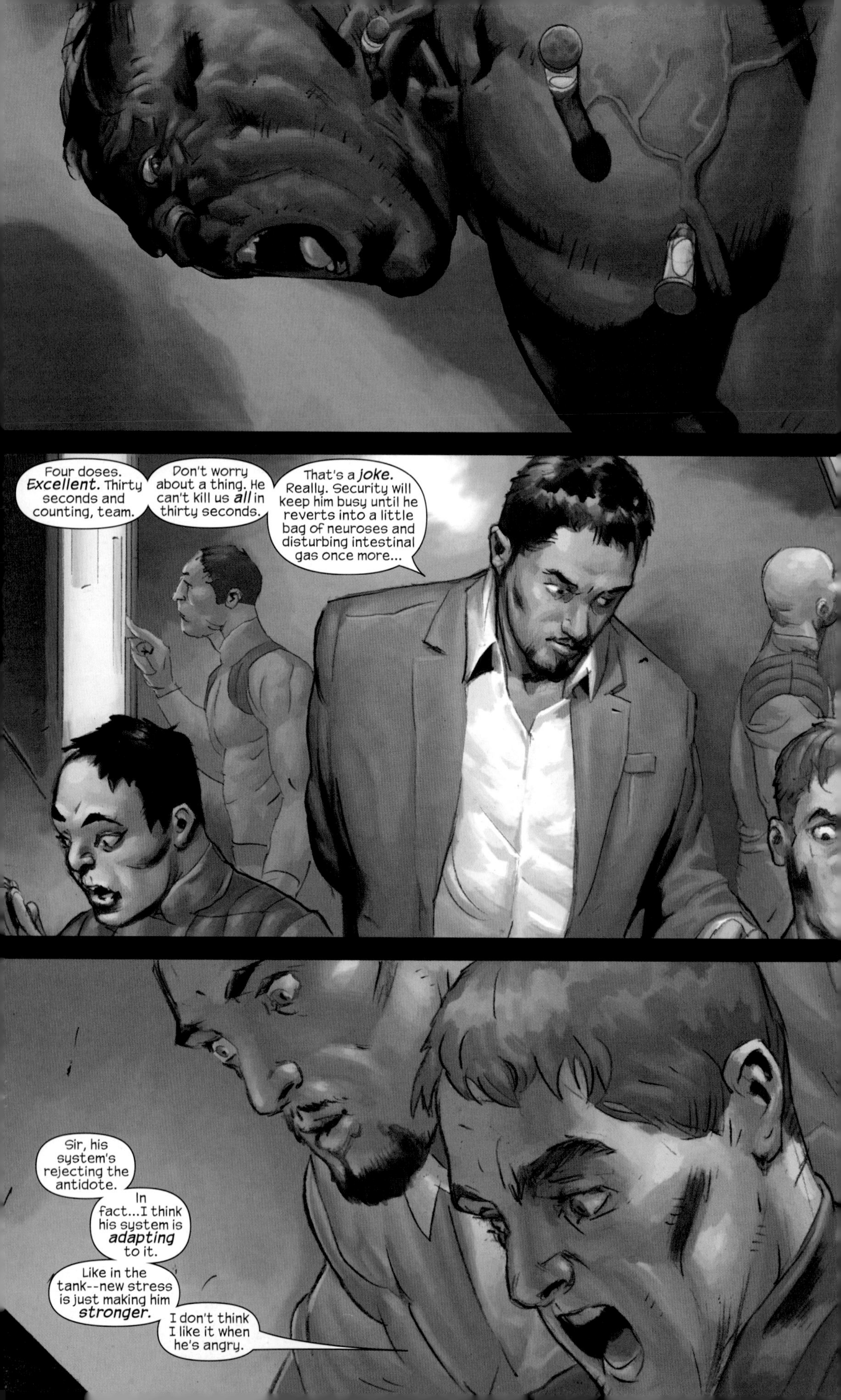

Four doses. Excellent. Thirty seconds and counting, team.
Don't worry about a thing. He can't kill us all in thirty seconds.
That's a joke. Really. Security will keep him busy until he reverts into a little bag of neuroses and disturbing intestinal gas once more...
Sir, his system's rejecting the antidote.
In fact...I think his system is adapting to it.
Like in the tank--new stress is just making him stronger.
I don't think I like it when he's angry.

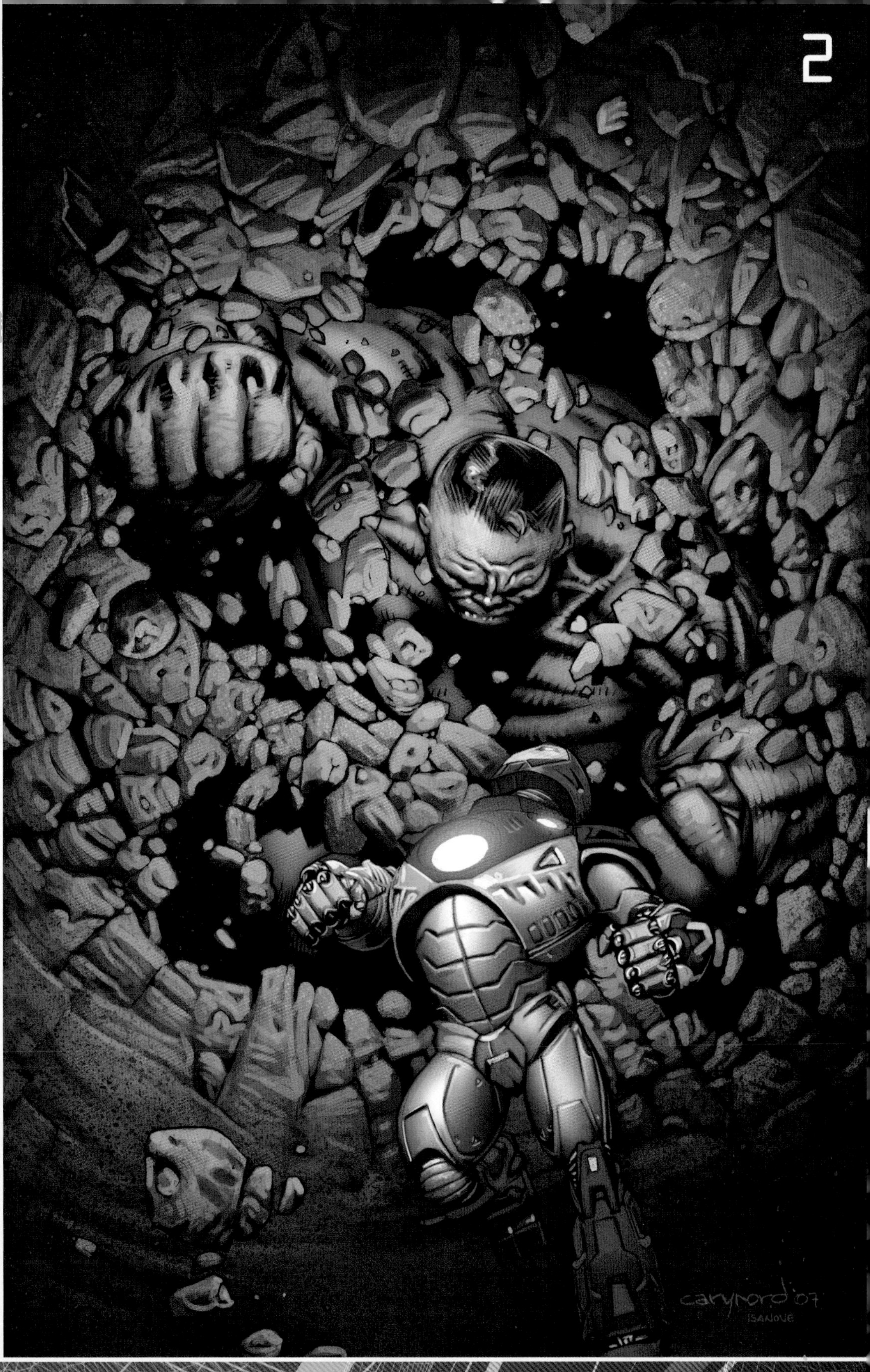
2
carynord '07
ISANOVE

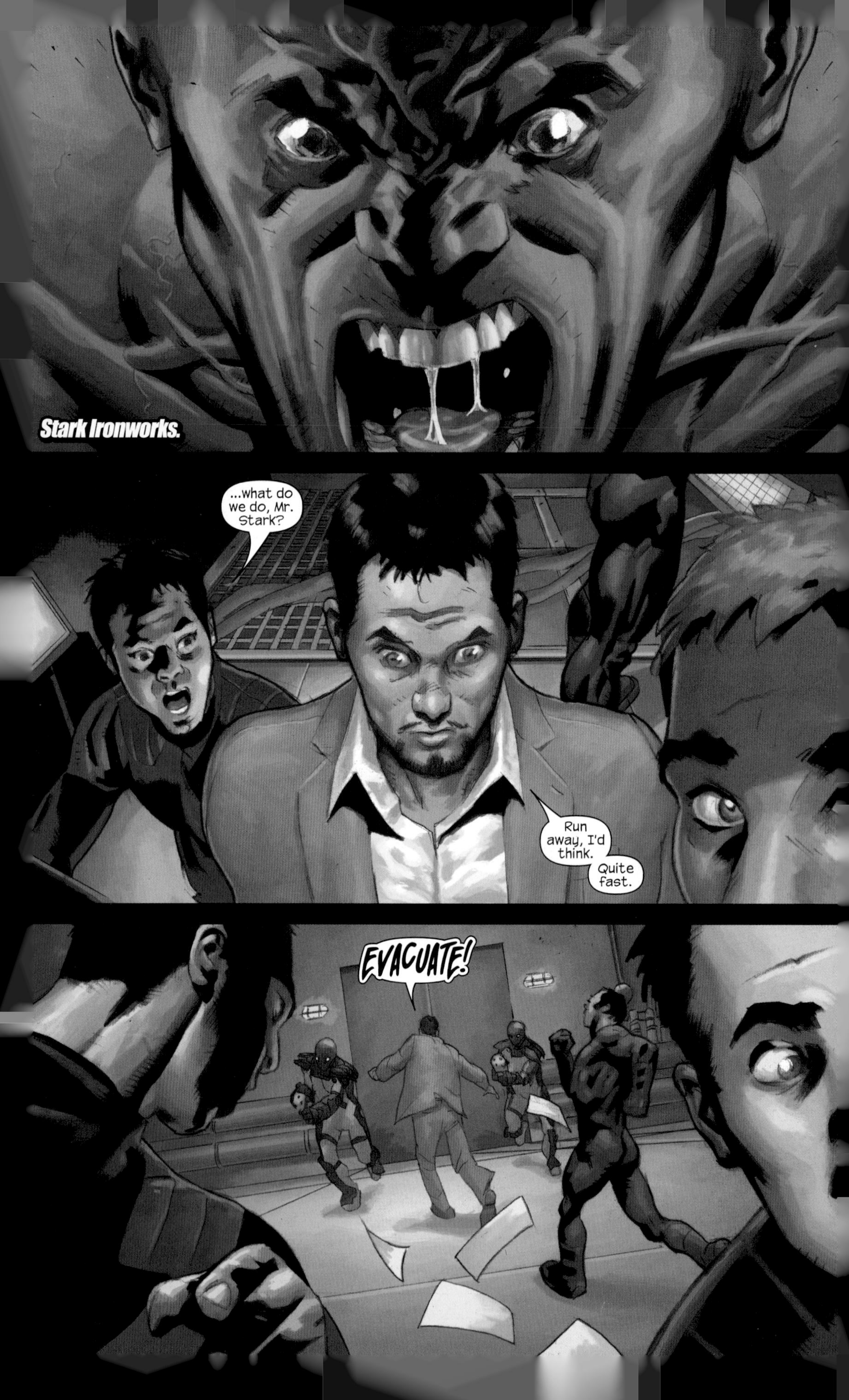
Stark Ironworks.
...what do we do, Mr. Stark?
Run away, I'd think.
Quite fast.
EVACUATE!

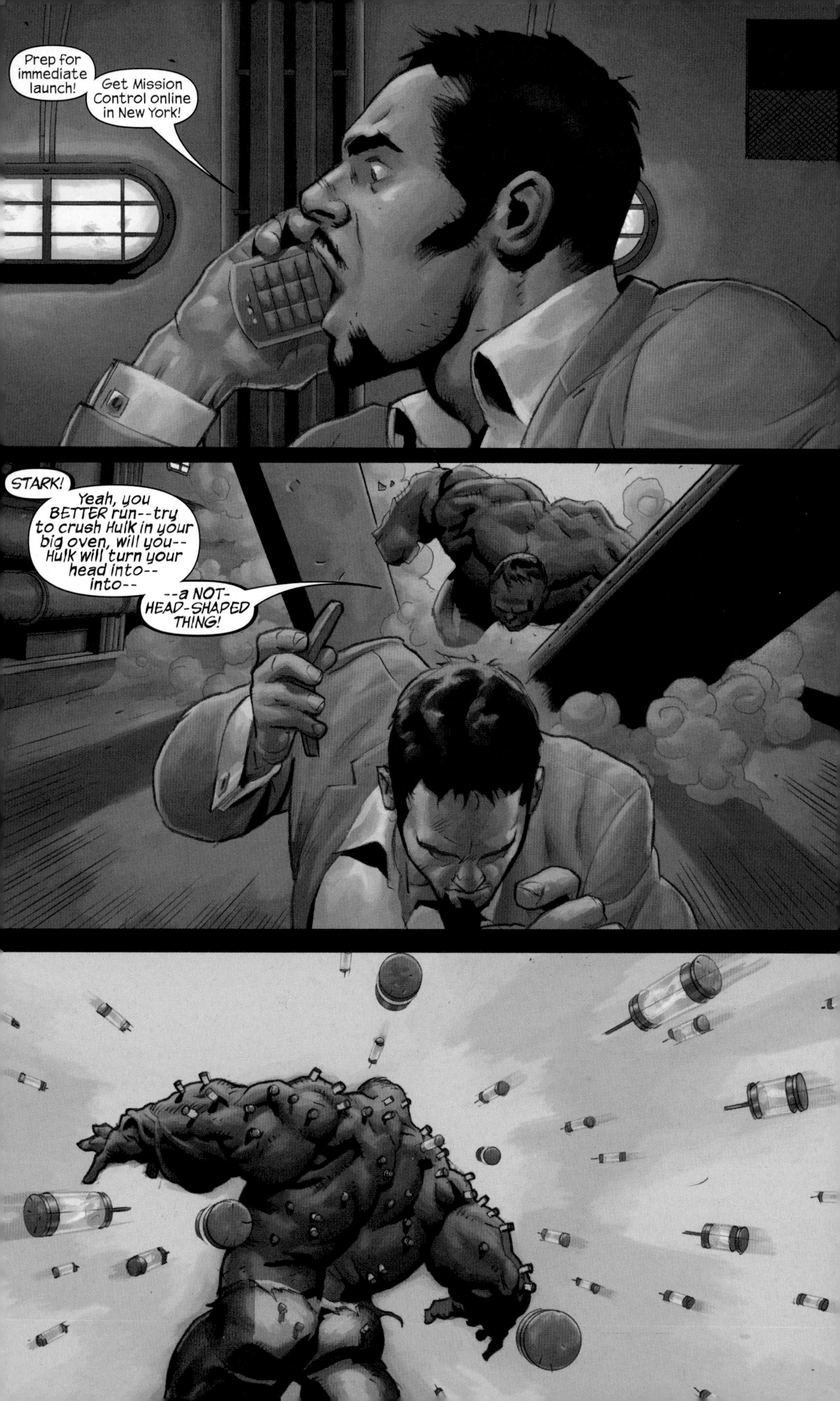

Prep for immediate launch!
Get Mission Control online in New York!
STARK!
Yeah, you BETTER run--try to crush Hulk in your big oven, will you-- Hulk will turn your head into-- into--
--a NOT-HEAD-SHAPED THING!

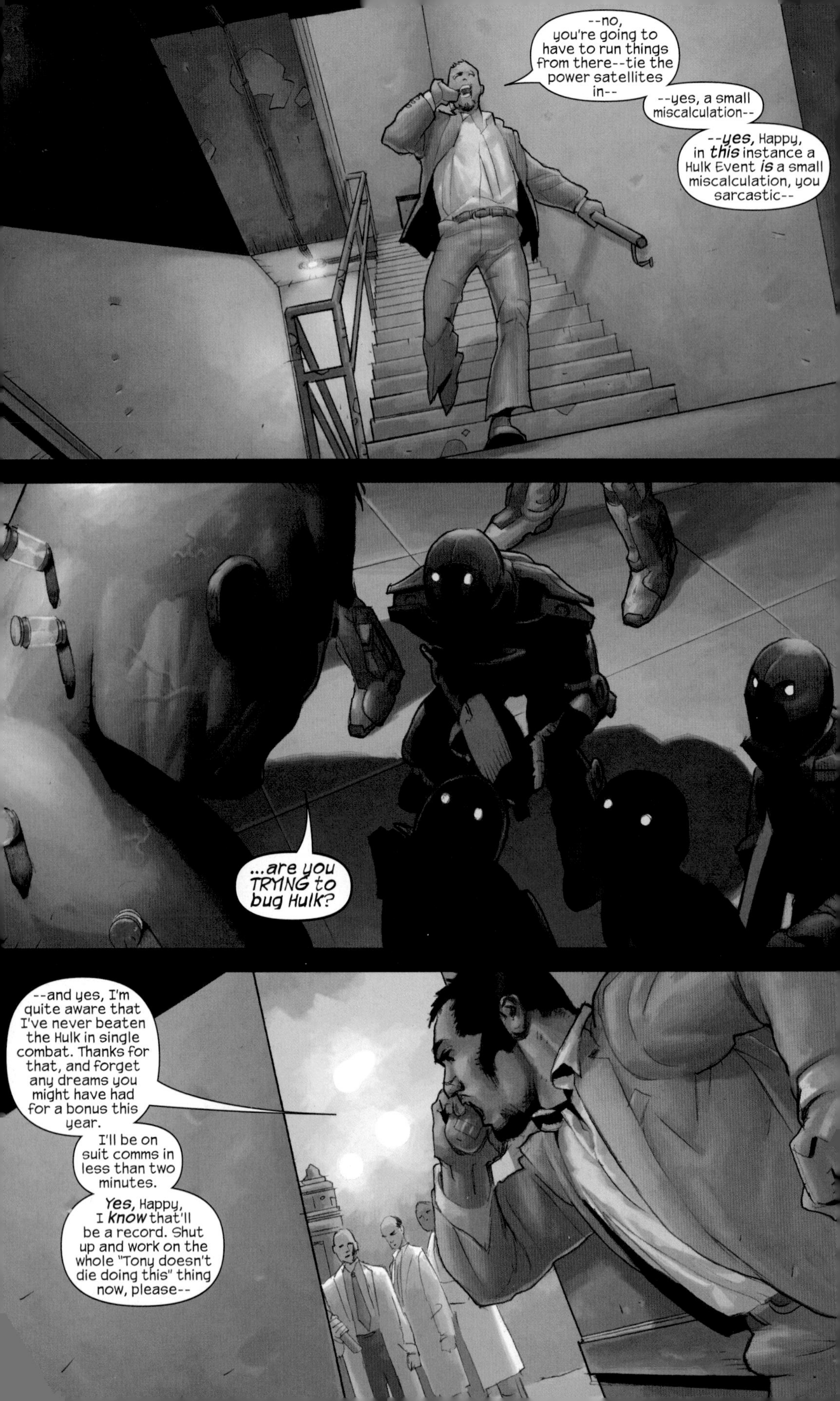
--no, you're going to have to run things from there--tie the power satellites in--
--yes, a small miscalculation--
--*yes,* Happy, in *this* instance a Hulk Event *is* a small miscalculation, you sarcastic--
...are you TRYING to bug Hulk?
--and yes, I'm quite aware that I've never beaten the Hulk in single combat. Thanks for that, and forget any dreams you might have had for a bonus this year.
I'll be on suit comms in less than two minutes.
Yes, Happy, I *know* that'll be a record. Shut up and work on the whole "Tony doesn't die doing this" thing now, please--

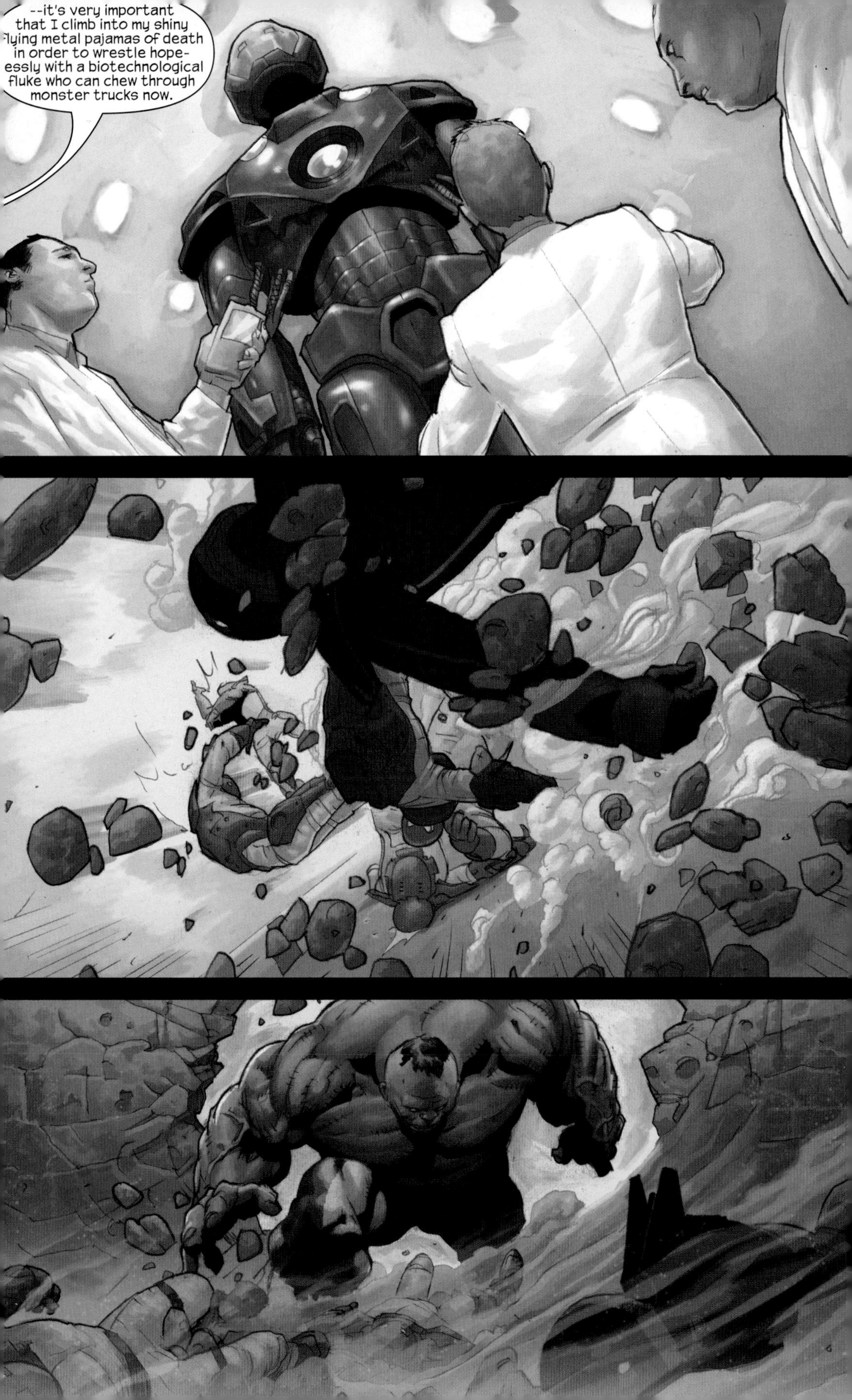
--it's very important that I climb into my shiny flying metal pajamas of death in order to wrestle hope-essly with a biotechnological fluke who can chew through monster trucks now.

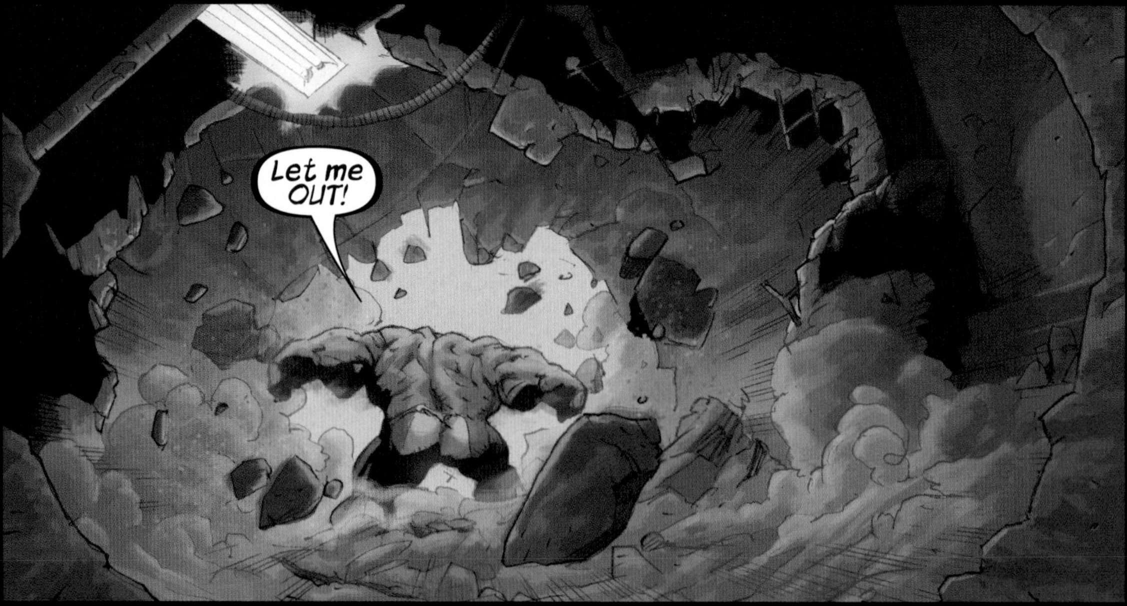
Let me OUT!

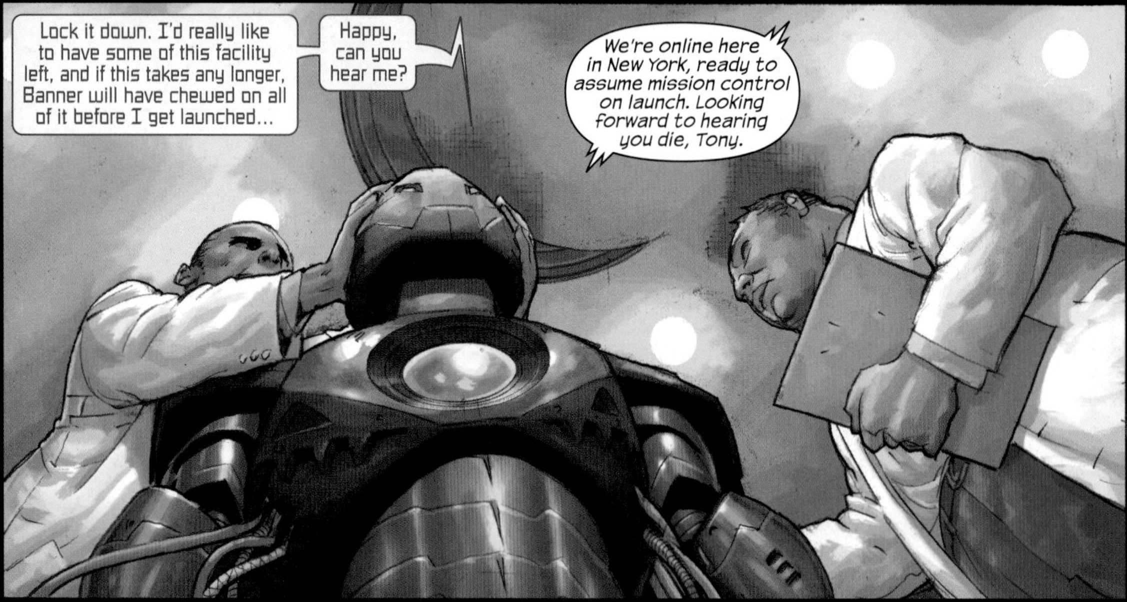
Lock it down. I'd really like to have some of this facility left, and if this takes any longer, Banner will have chewed on all of it before I get launched...
Happy, can you hear me?
We're online here in New York, ready to assume mission control on launch. Looking forward to hearing you die, Tony.

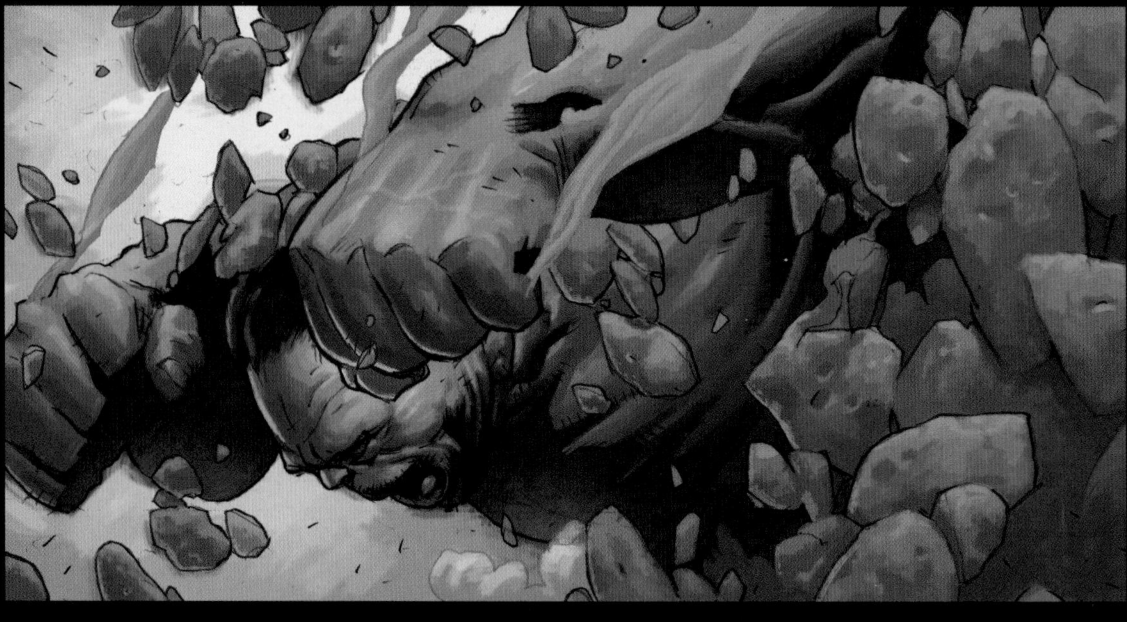

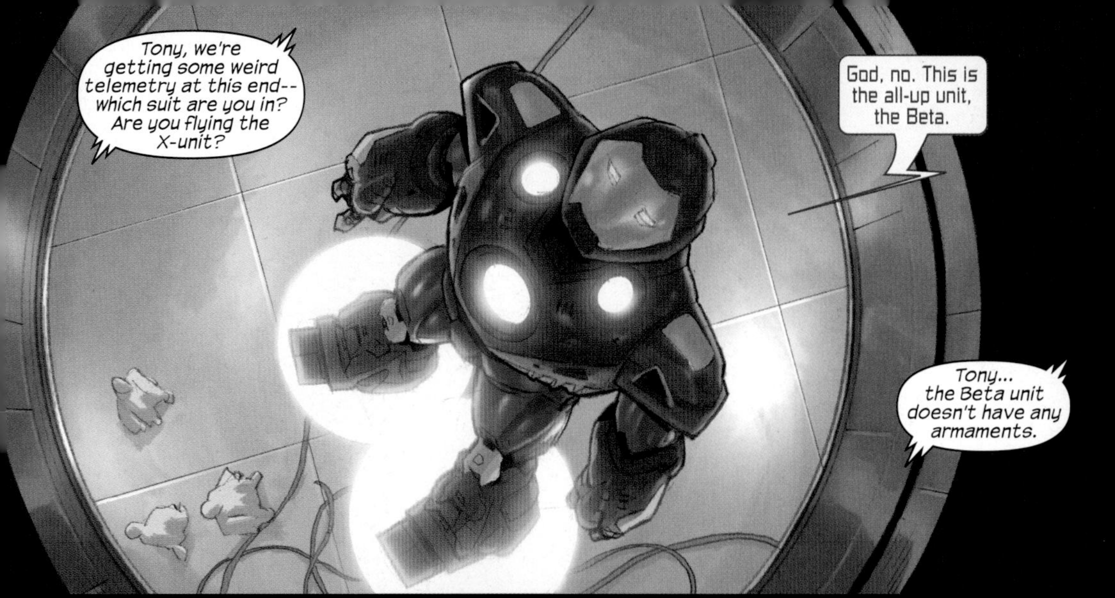
Tony, we're getting some weird telemetry at this end--which suit are you in? Are you flying the X-unit?
God, no. This is the all-up unit, the Beta.
Tony... the Beta unit doesn't have any armaments.

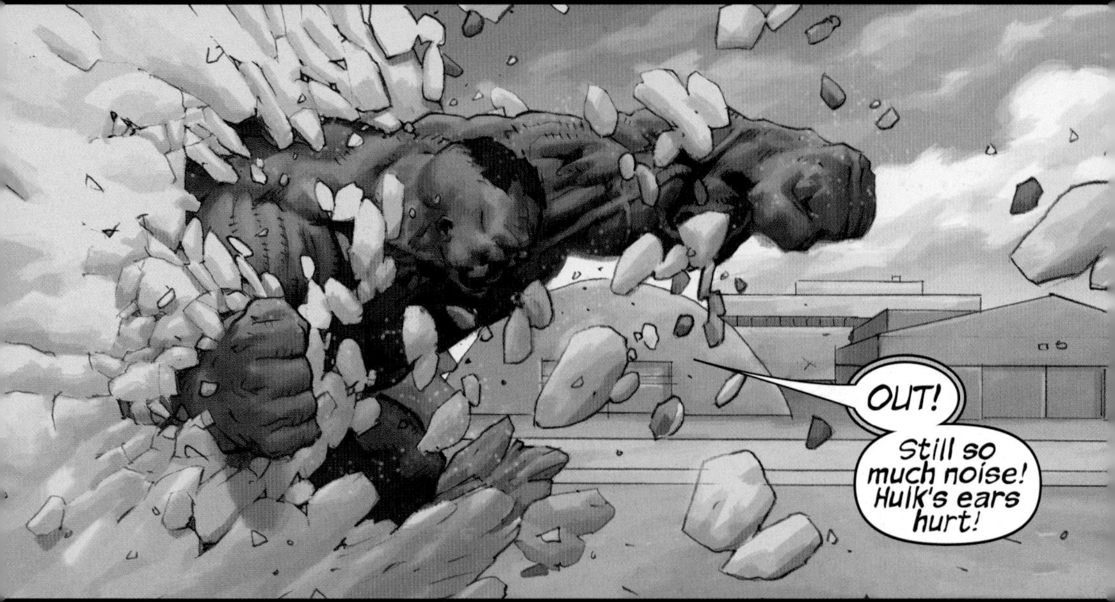
OUT!
Still so much noise! Hulk's ears hurt!

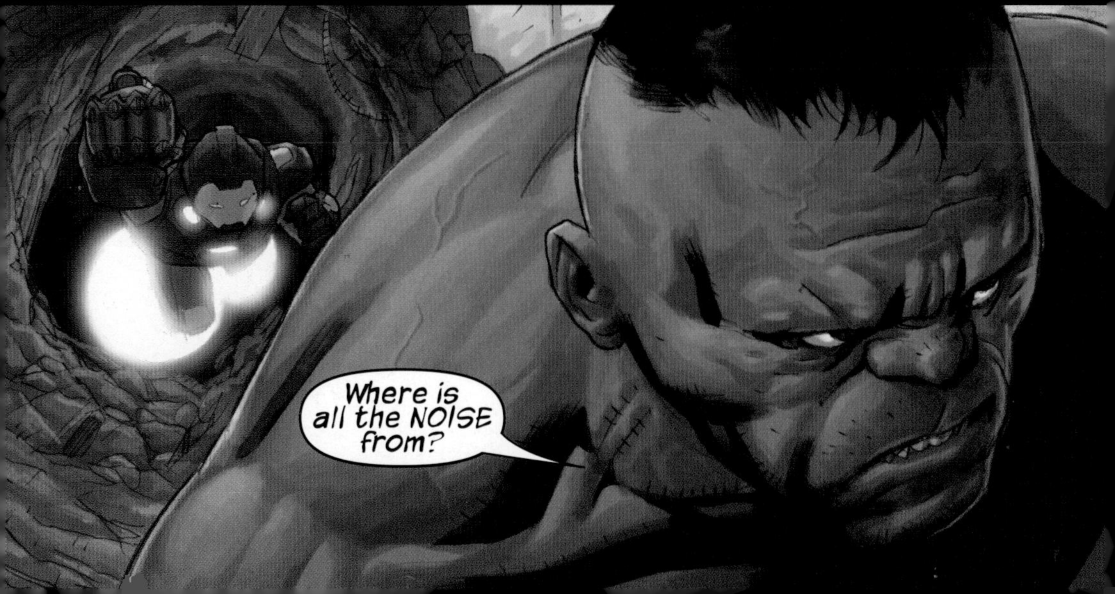
Where is all the NOISE from?

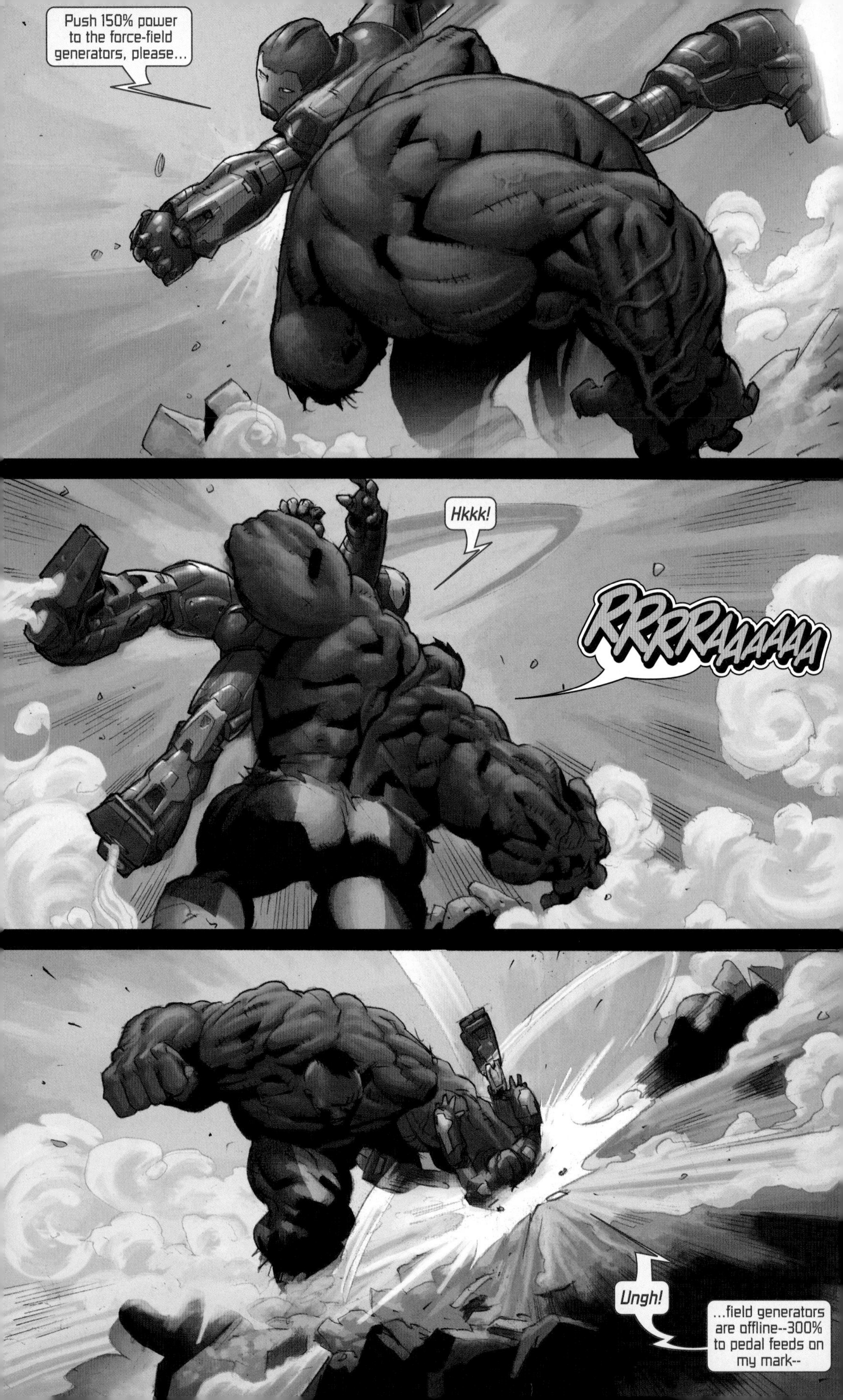

Push 150% power to the force-field generators, please...
Hkkk!
RRRRAAAAAA
Ungh!
...field generators are offline--300% to pedal feeds on my mark--

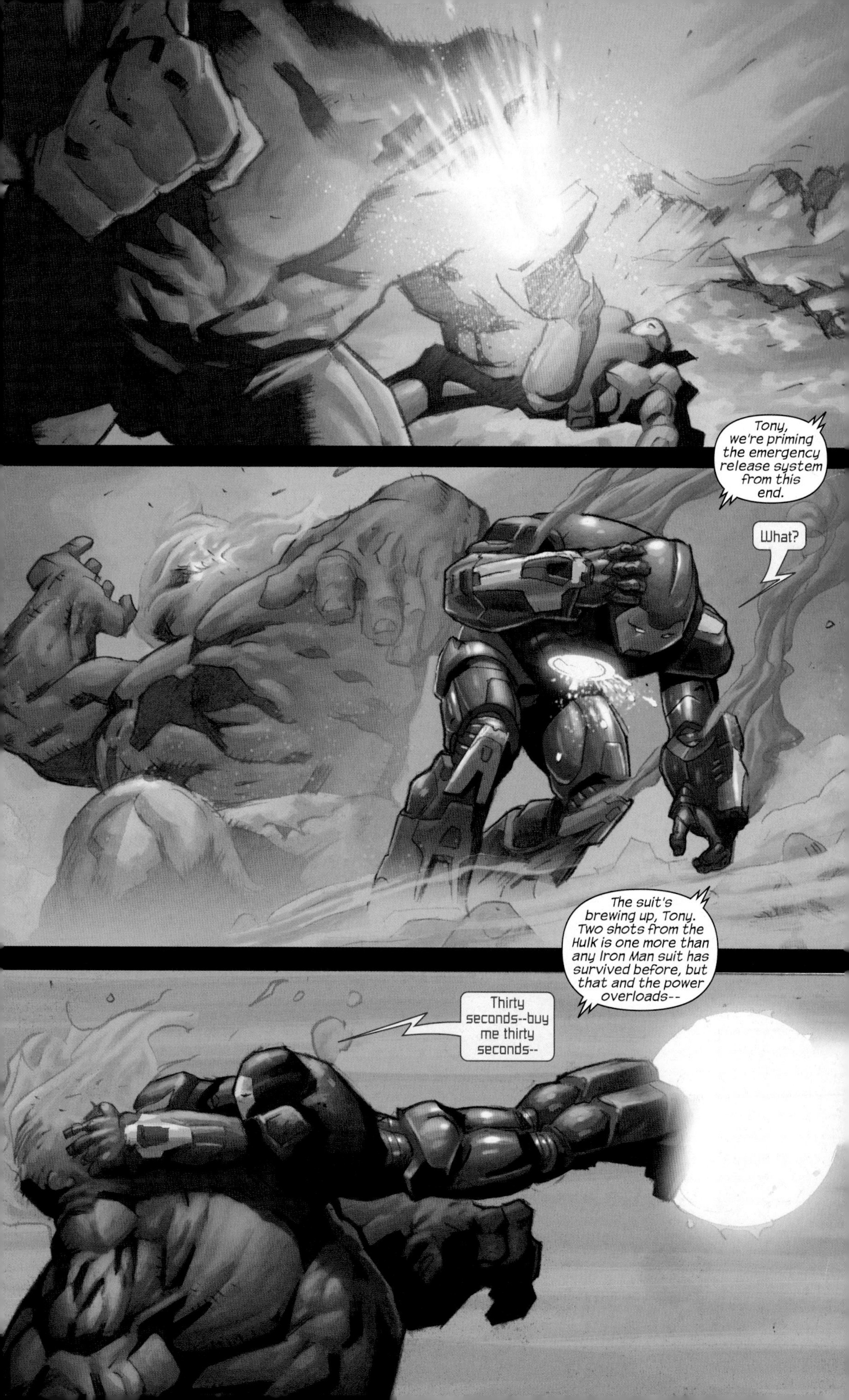
Tony, we're priming the emergency release system from this end.
What?
The suit's brewing up, Tony. Two shots from the Hulk is one more than any Iron Man suit has survived before, but that and the power overloads--
Thirty seconds--buy me thirty seconds--

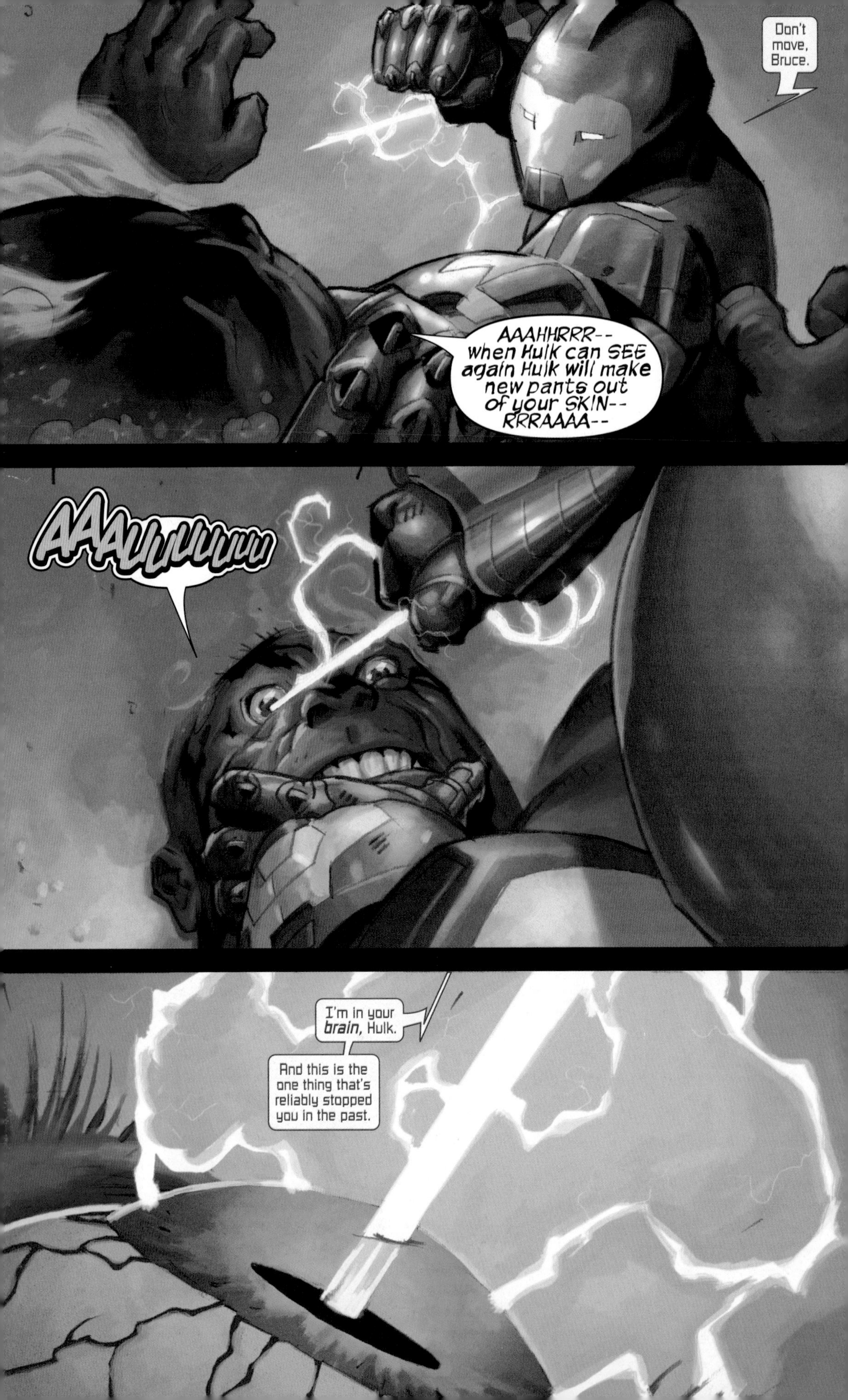
Don't move, Bruce.
AAAHHRRR-- when Hulk can SEE again Hulk will make new pants out of your SKIN-- RRRAAAA--
AAAUUUUUU
I'm in your *brain*, Hulk.
And this is the one thing that's reliably stopped you in the past.

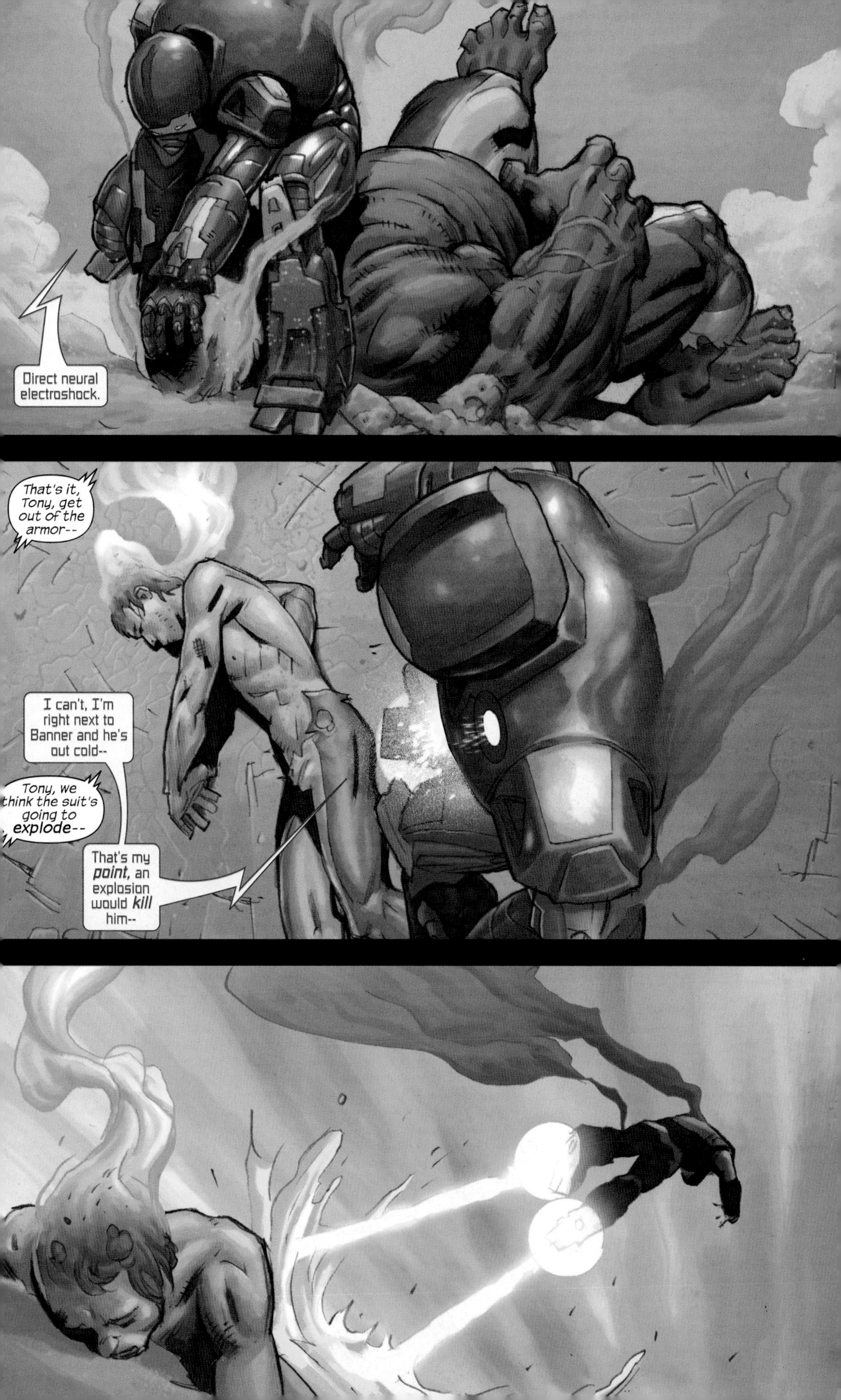
Direct neural electroshock.
That's it, Tony, get out of the armor--
I can't, I'm right next to Banner and he's out cold--
Tony, we think the suit's going to explode--
That's my point, an explosion would kill him--

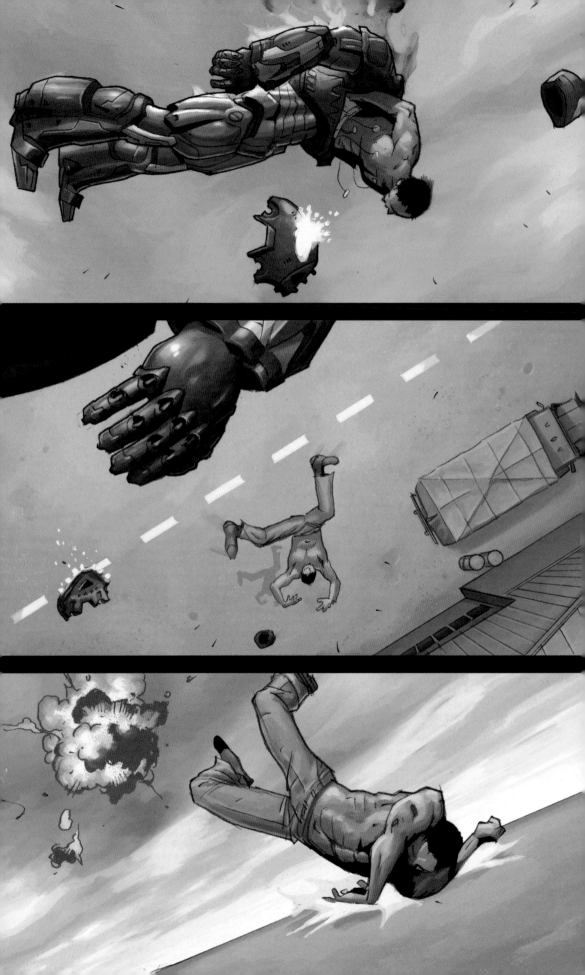

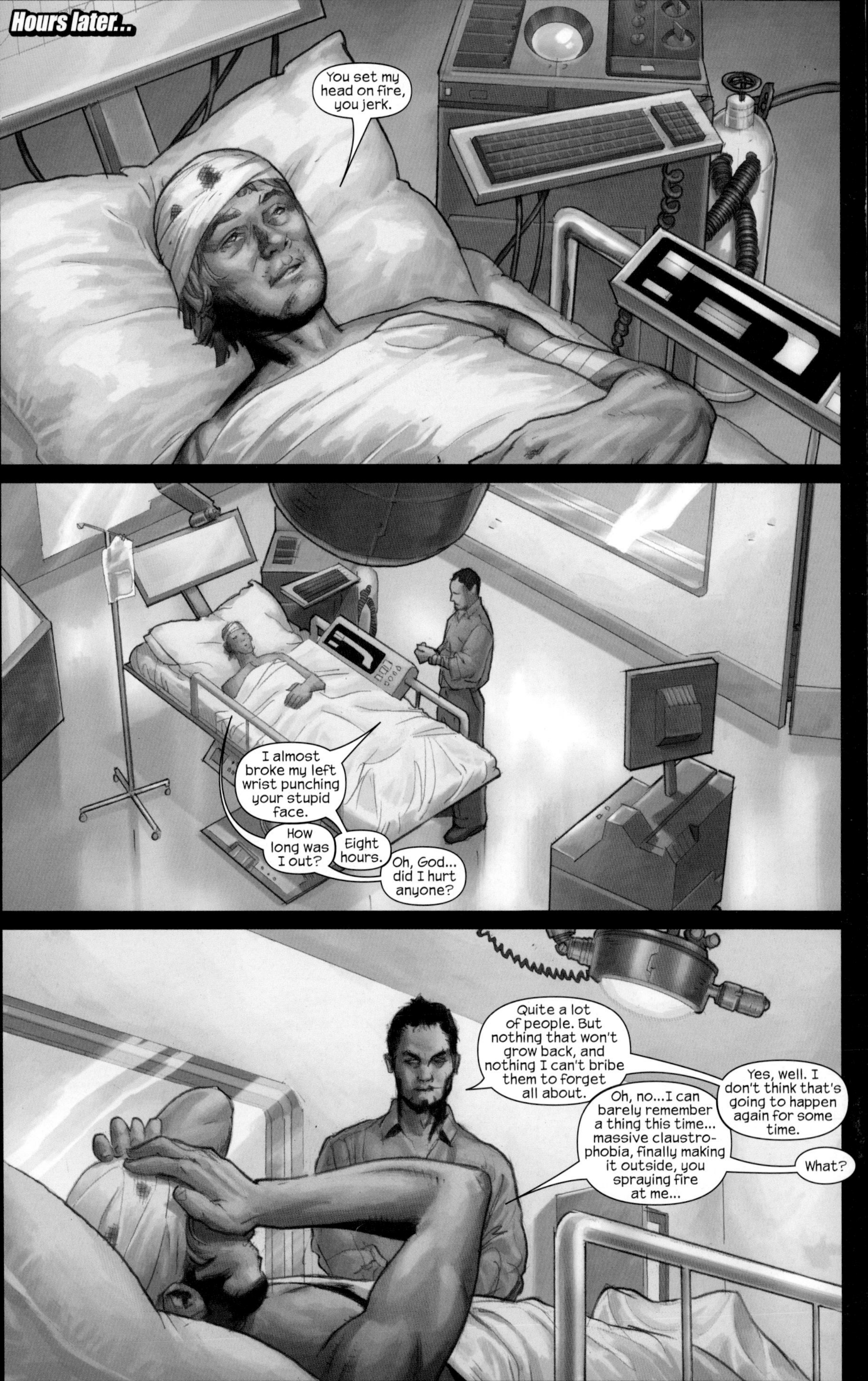
Hours later...
You set my head on fire, you jerk.
I almost broke my left wrist punching your stupid face.
How long was I out?
Eight hours.
Oh, God... did I hurt anyone?
Quite a lot of people. But nothing that won't grow back, and nothing I can't bribe them to forget all about.
Oh, no...I can barely remember a thing this time... massive claustrophobia, finally making it outside, you spraying fire at me...
Yes, well. I don't think that's going to happen again for some time.
What?

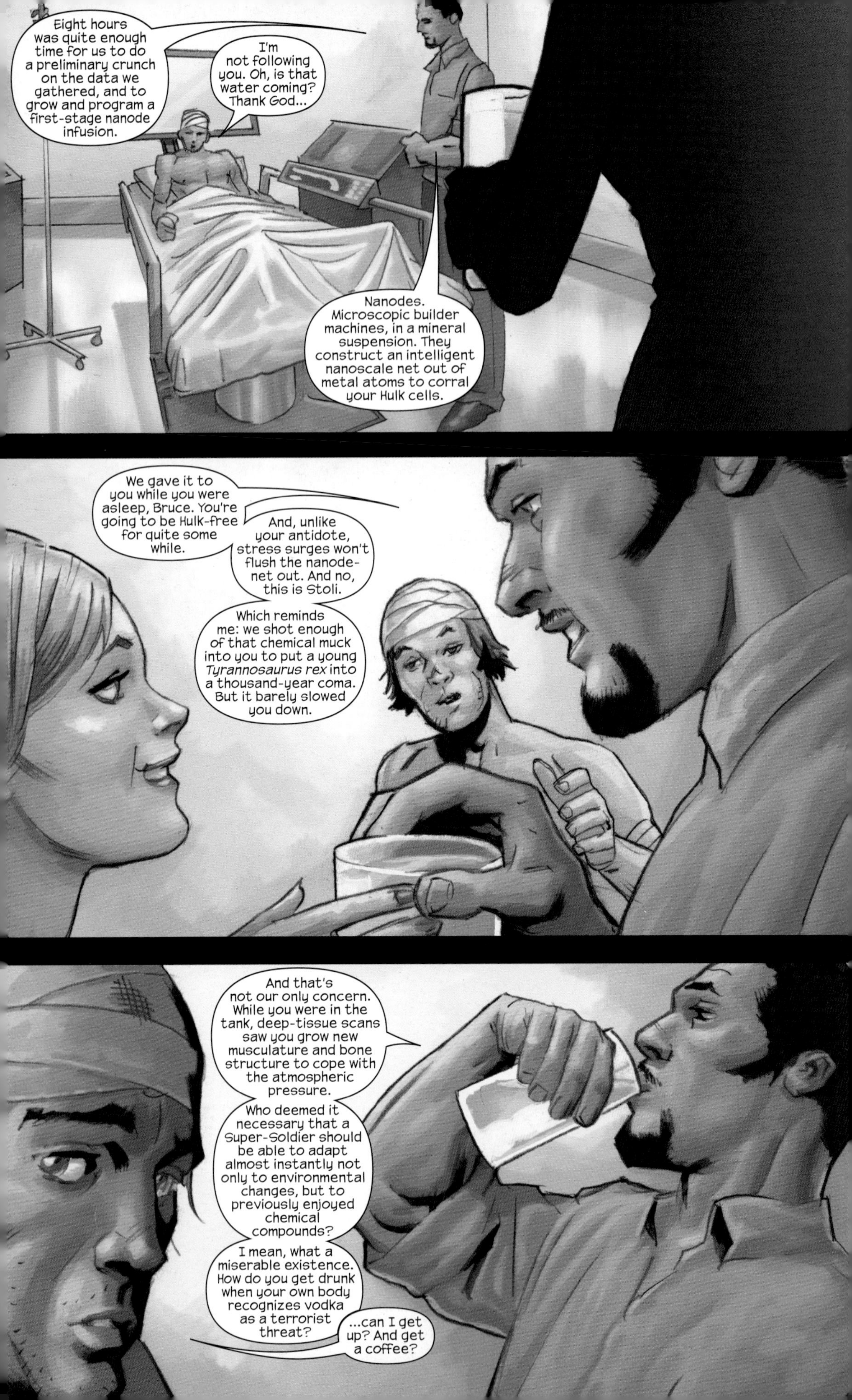
Eight hours was quite enough time for us to do a preliminary crunch on the data we gathered, and to grow and program a first-stage nanode infusion.
I'm not following you. Oh, is that water coming? Thank God...
Nanodes. Microscopic builder machines, in a mineral suspension. They construct an intelligent nanoscale net out of metal atoms to corral your Hulk cells.
We gave it to you while you were asleep, Bruce. You're going to be Hulk-free for quite some while.
And, unlike your antidote, stress surges won't flush the nanode-net out. And no, this is Stoli.
Which reminds me: we shot enough of that chemical muck into you to put a young *Tyrannosaurus rex* into a thousand-year coma. But it barely slowed you down.
And that's not our only concern. While you were in the tank, deep-tissue scans saw you grow new musculature and bone structure to cope with the atmospheric pressure.
Who deemed it necessary that a Super-Soldier should be able to adapt almost instantly not only to environmental changes, but to previously enjoyed chemical compounds?
I mean, what a miserable existence. How do you get drunk when your own body recognizes vodka as a terrorist threat?
...can I get up? And get a coffee?

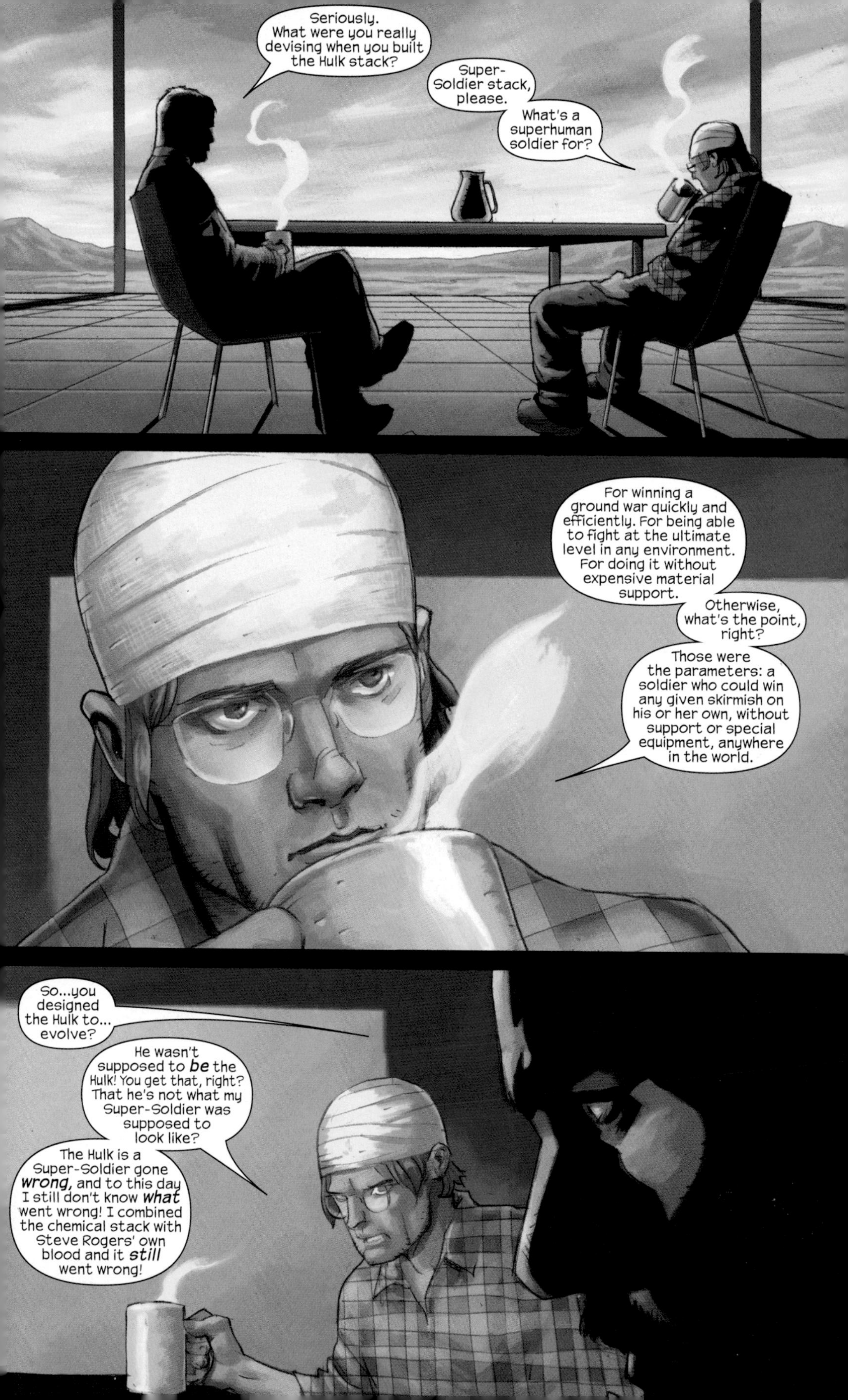

Seriously. What were you really devising when you built the Hulk stack?
Super-Soldier stack, please.
What's a superhuman soldier for?
For winning a ground war quickly and efficiently. For being able to fight at the ultimate level in any environment. For doing it without expensive material support.
Otherwise, what's the point, right?
Those were the parameters: a soldier who could win any given skirmish on his or her own, without support or special equipment, anywhere in the world.
So...you designed the Hulk to... evolve?
He wasn't supposed to be the Hulk! You get that, right? That he's not what my Super-Soldier was supposed to look like?
The Hulk is a Super-Soldier gone wrong, and to this day I still don't know what went wrong! I combined the chemical stack with Steve Rogers' own blood and it still went wrong!

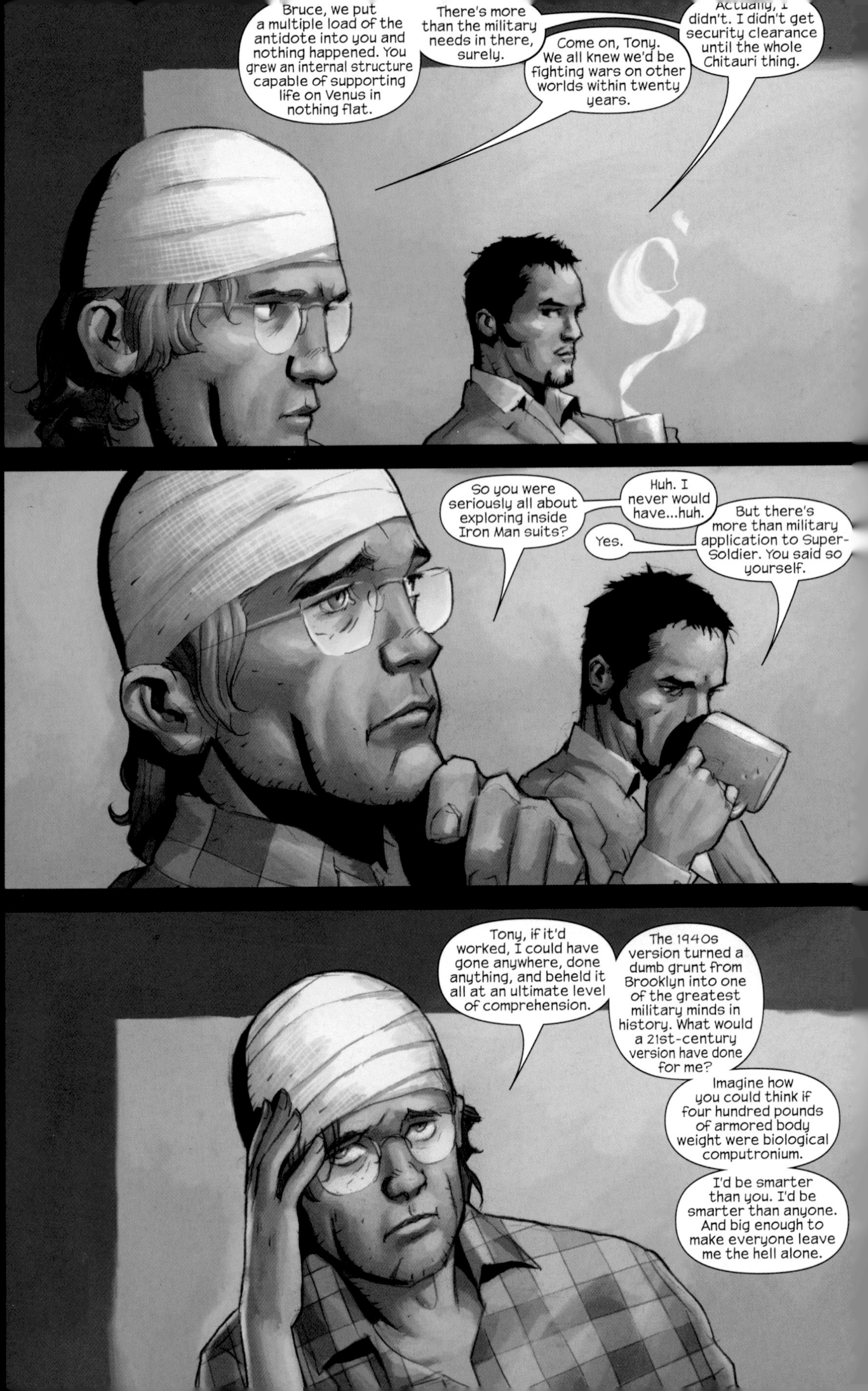
Bruce, we put a multiple load of the antidote into you and nothing happened. You grew an internal structure capable of supporting life on Venus in nothing flat.
There's more than the military needs in there, surely.
Actually, I didn't. I didn't get security clearance until the whole Chitauri thing.
Come on, Tony. We all knew we'd be fighting wars on other worlds within twenty years.
So you were seriously all about exploring inside Iron Man suits?
Yes.
Huh. I never would have...huh.
But there's more than military application to Super-Soldier. You said so yourself.
Tony, if it'd worked, I could have gone anywhere, done anything, and beheld it all at an ultimate level of comprehension.
The 1940s version turned a dumb grunt from Brooklyn into one of the greatest military minds in history. What would a 21st-century version have done for me?
Imagine how you could think if four hundred pounds of armored body weight were biological computronium.
I'd be smarter than you. I'd be smarter than anyone. And big enough to make everyone leave me the hell alone.

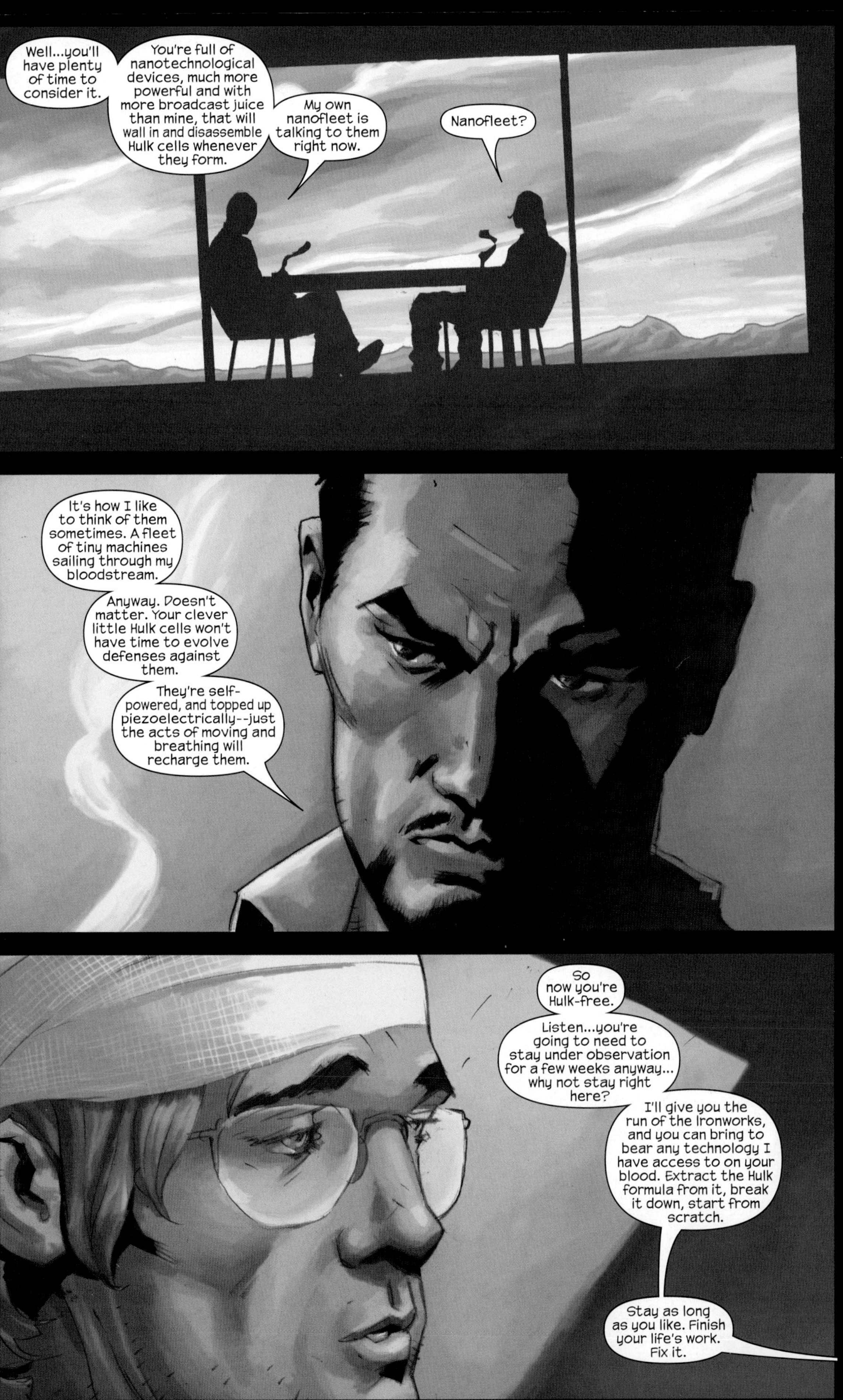
Well...you'll have plenty of time to consider it.
You're full of nanotechnological devices, much more powerful and with more broadcast juice than mine, that will wall in and disassemble Hulk cells whenever they form.
My own nanofleet is talking to them right now.
Nanofleet?
It's how I like to think of them sometimes. A fleet of tiny machines sailing through my bloodstream.
Anyway. Doesn't matter. Your clever little Hulk cells won't have time to evolve defenses against them.
They're self-powered, and topped up piezoelectrically--just the acts of moving and breathing will recharge them.
So now you're Hulk-free.
Listen...you're going to need to stay under observation for a few weeks anyway... why not stay right here?
I'll give you the run of the Ironworks, and you can bring to bear any technology I have access to on your blood. Extract the Hulk formula from it, break it down, start from scratch.
Stay as long as you like. Finish your life's work. Fix it.

Excellent. Excellent work, Larner.

Thank you, Leader.

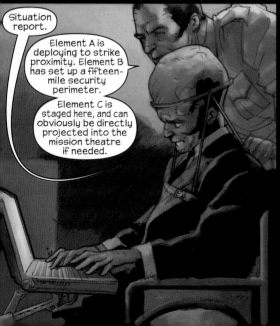

Situation report.

Element A is deploying to strike proximity. Element B has set up a fifteen-mile security perimeter.

Element C is staged here, and can obviously be directly projected into the mission theatre if needed.

I designed the force-projection system, you know.

I know that, Leader.

I sit here, an authentic superhuman. "Man is something to be overcome," said Nietzsche. And yet here I sit, a superman who cannot hold up his own head.

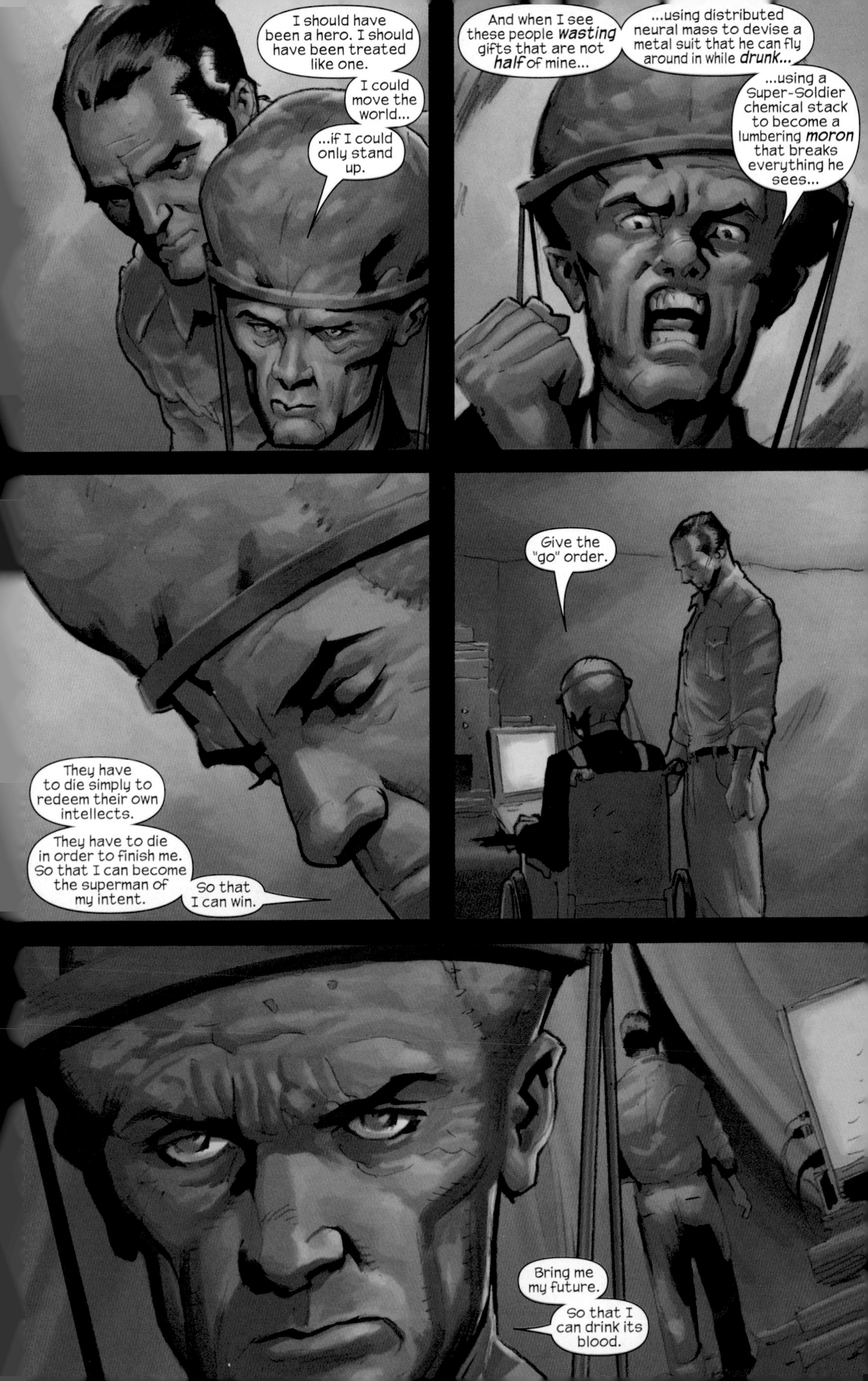

I should have been a hero. I should have been treated like one.
I could move the world...
...if I could only stand up.
And when I see these people *wasting* gifts that are not *half* of mine...
...using distributed neural mass to devise a metal suit that he can fly around in while *drunk*...
...using a Super-Soldier chemical stack to become a lumbering *moron* that breaks everything he sees...
They have to die simply to redeem their own intellects.
They have to die in order to finish me. So that I can become the superman of my intent.
So that I can win.
Give the "go" order.
Bring me my future.
So that I can drink its blood.

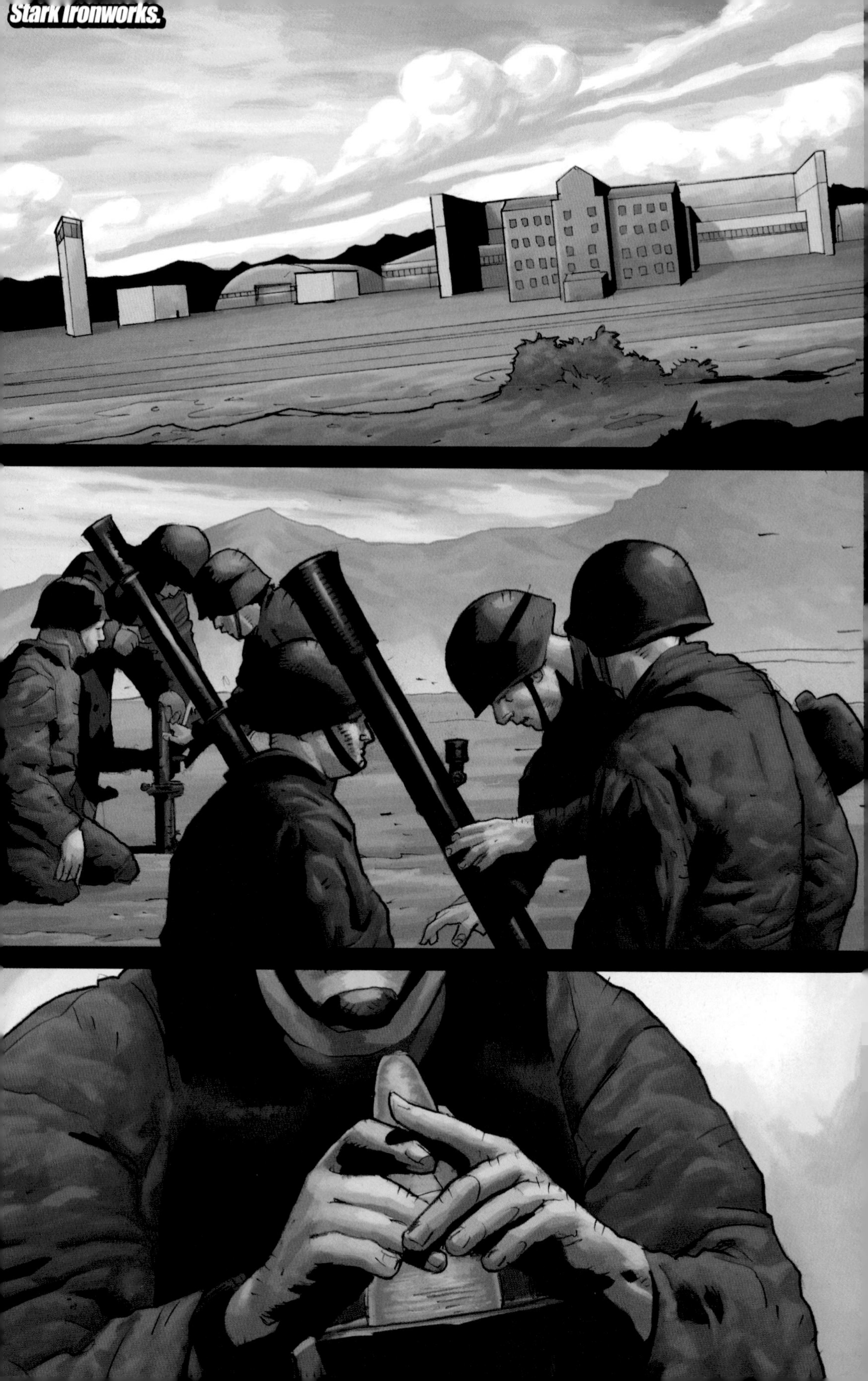
Stark Ironworks.

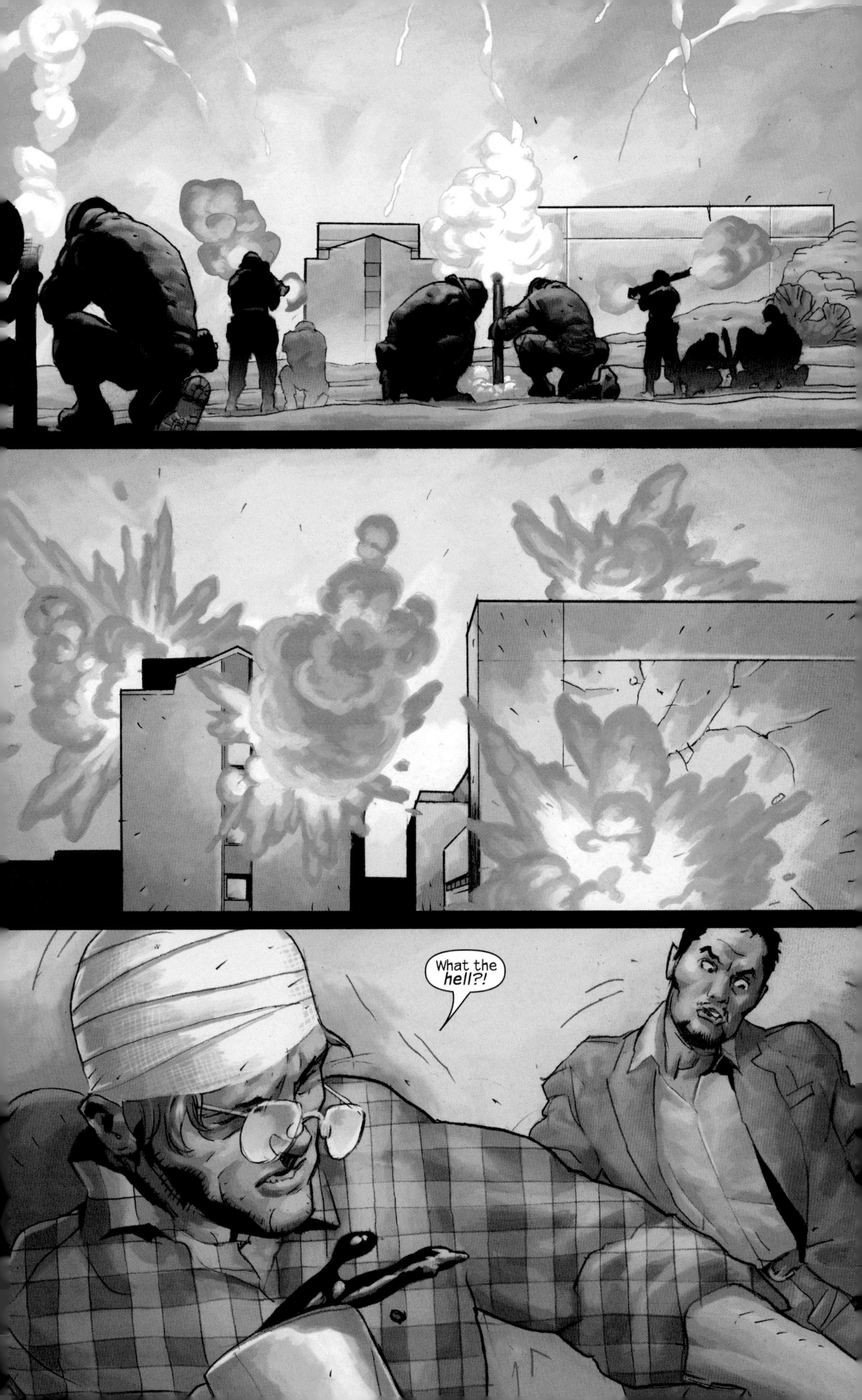
What the *hell?!*

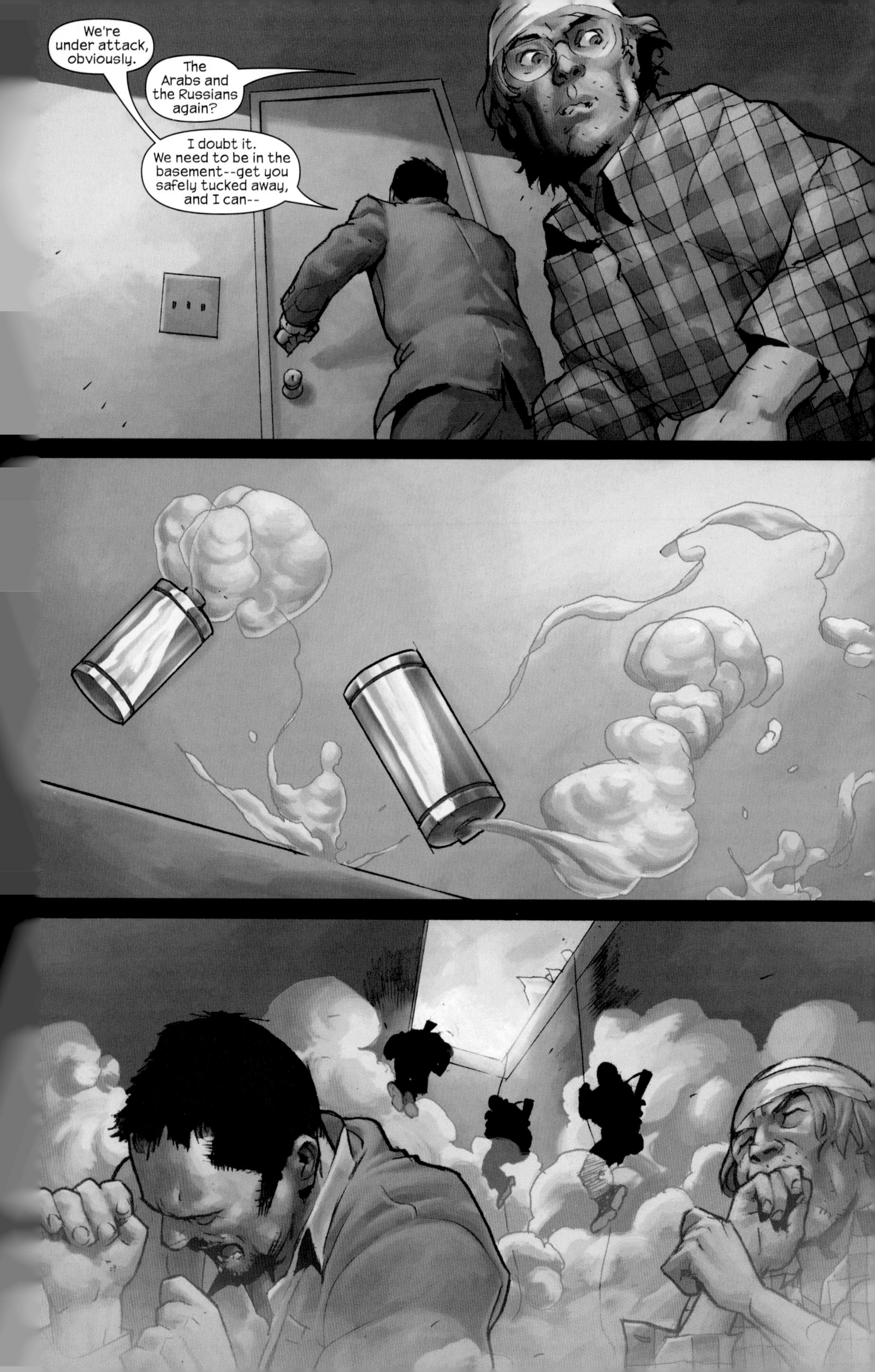
We're under attack, obviously.
The Arabs and the Russians again?
I doubt it. We need to be in the basement--get you safely tucked away, and I can--

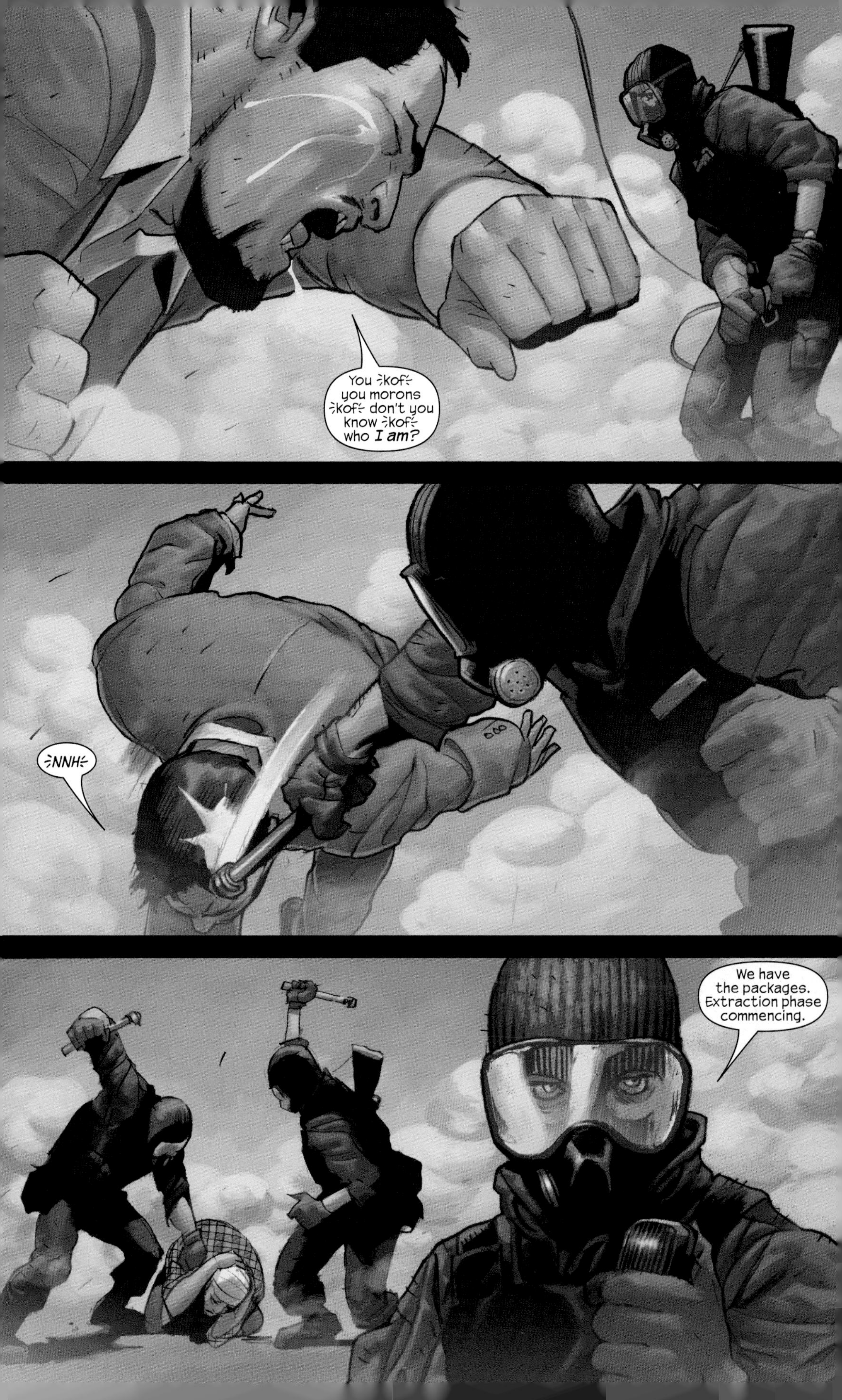
You -kof- you morons -kof- don't you know -kof- who *I am*?
-NNH-
We have the packages. Extraction phase commencing.

3

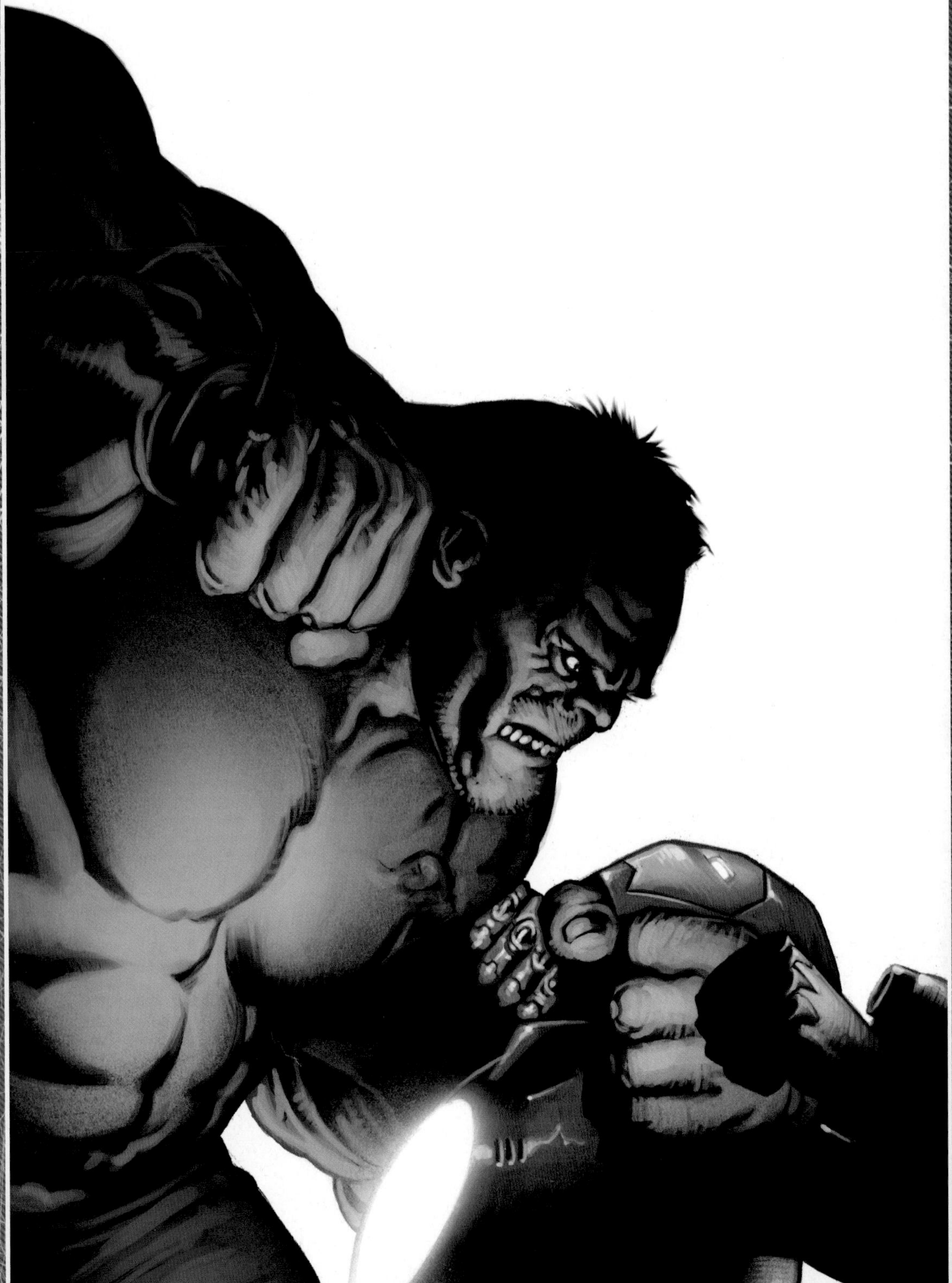

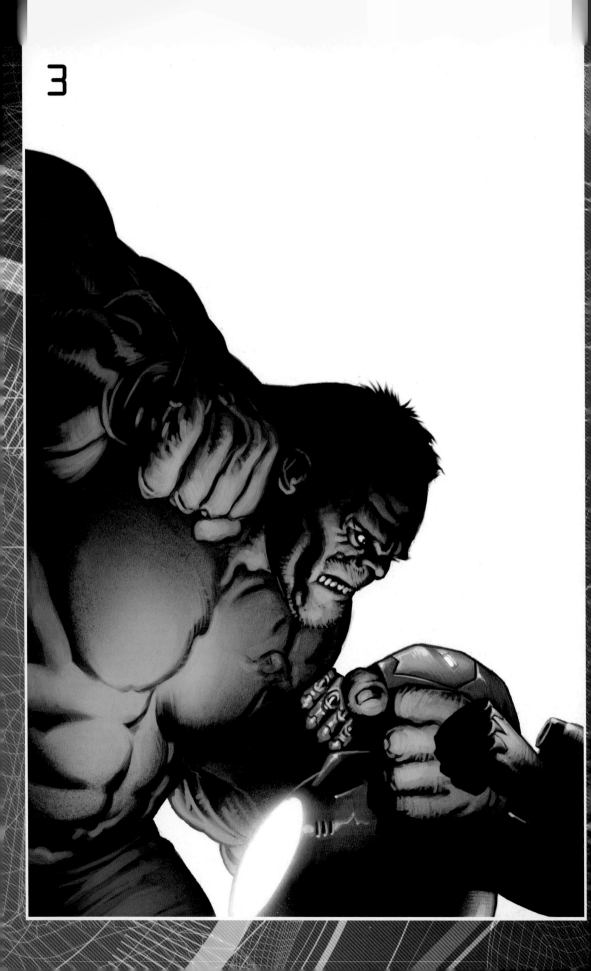

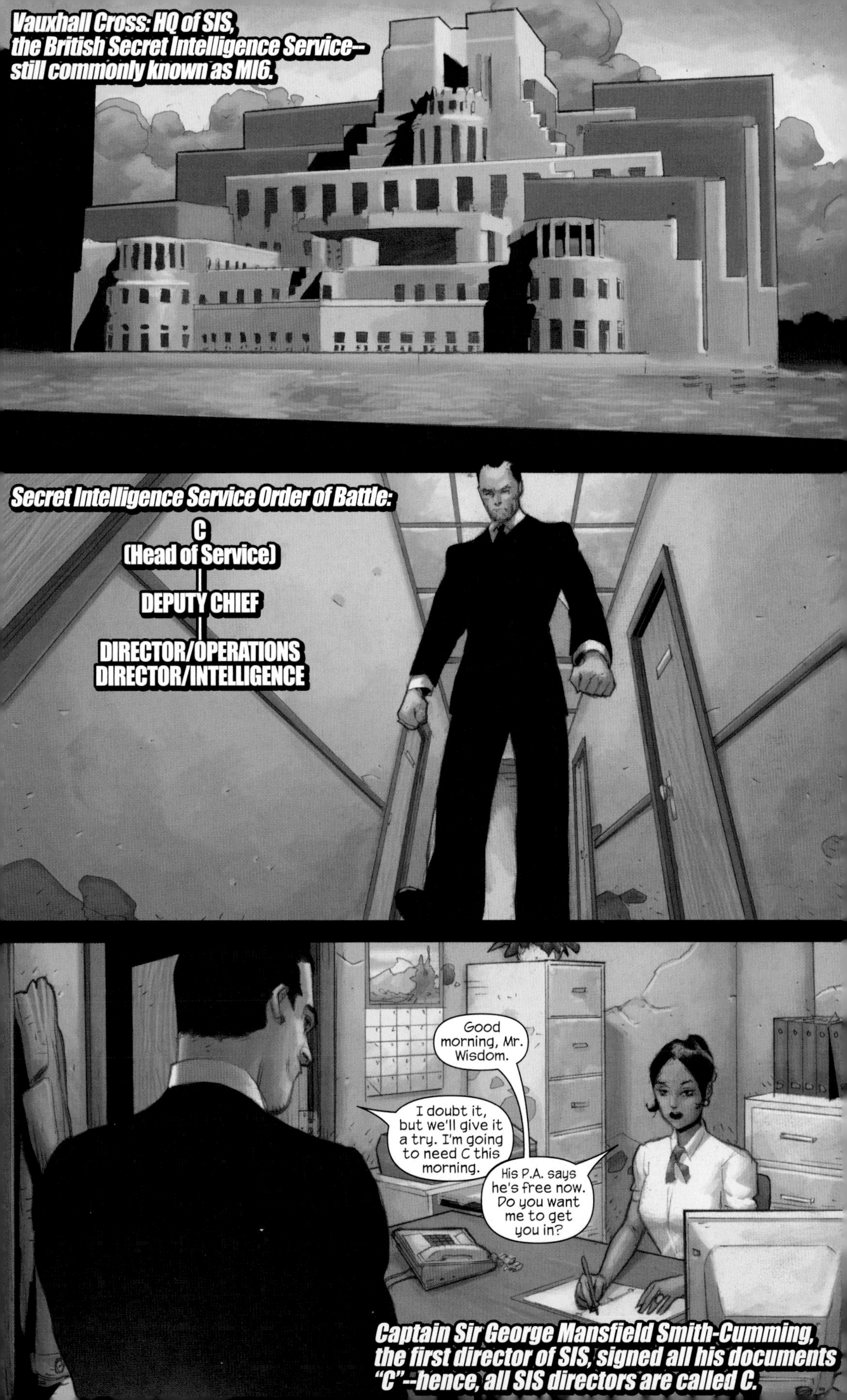
Vauxhall Cross: HQ of SIS, the British Secret Intelligence Service-- still commonly known as MI6.
Secret Intelligence Service Order of Battle:
C (Head of Service)
DEPUTY CHIEF
DIRECTOR/OPERATIONS
DIRECTOR/INTELLIGENCE
Good morning, Mr. Wisdom.
I doubt it, but we'll give it a try. I'm going to need C this morning.
His P.A. says he's free now. Do you want me to get you in?
Captain Sir George Mansfield Smith-Cumming, the first director of SIS, signed all his documents "C"--hence, all SIS directors are called C.

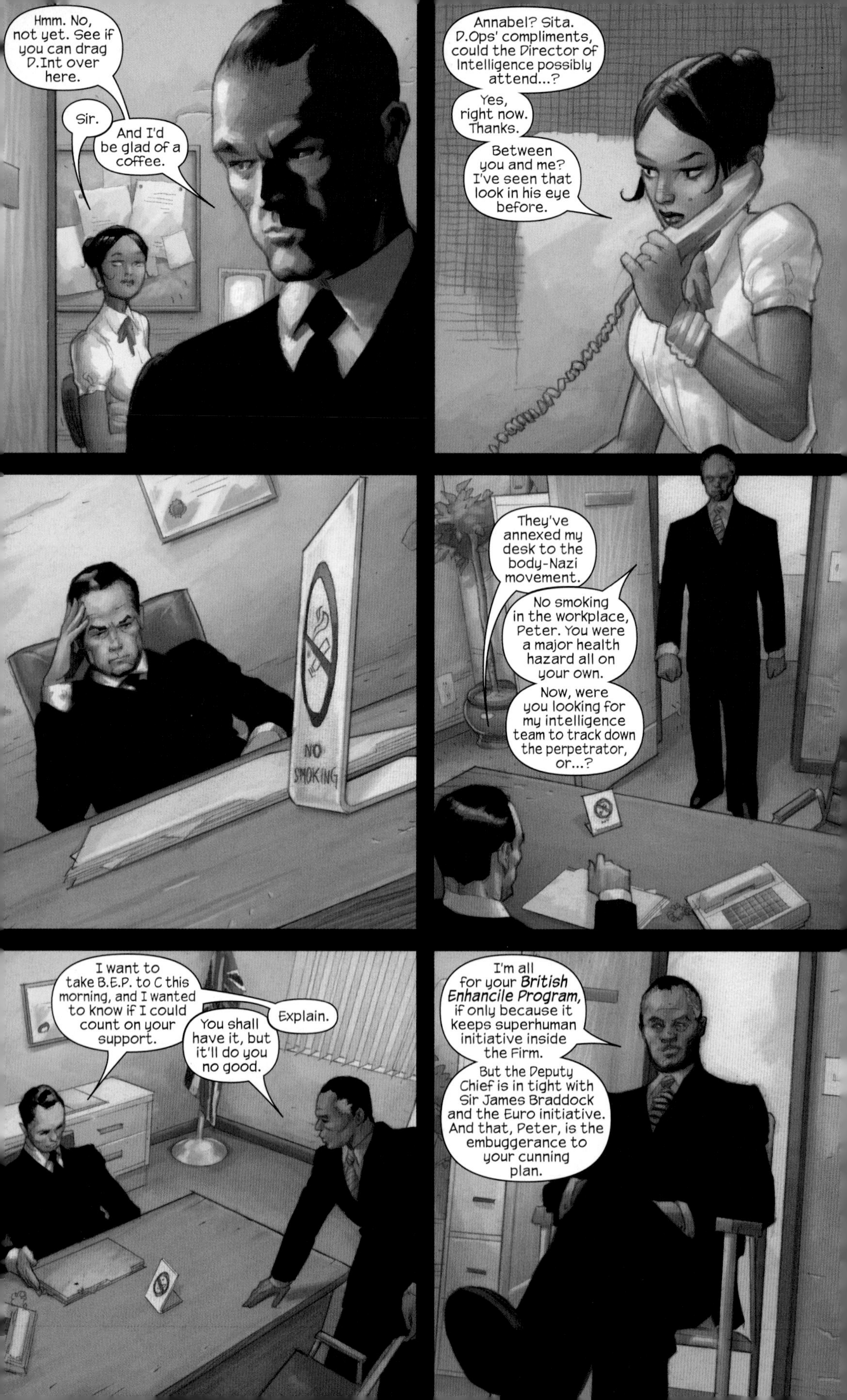

Hmm. No, not yet. See if you can drag D.Int over here.
Sir.
And I'd be glad of a coffee.
Annabel? Sita. D.Ops' compliments, could the Director of Intelligence possibly attend...?
Yes, right now. Thanks.
Between you and me? I've seen that look in his eye before.
NO SMOKING
They've annexed my desk to the body-Nazi movement.
No smoking in the workplace, Peter. You were a major health hazard all on your own.
Now, were you looking for my intelligence team to track down the perpetrator, or...?
I want to take B.E.P. to C this morning, and I wanted to know if I could count on your support.
You shall have it, but it'll do you no good.
Explain.
I'm all for your *British Enhancile Program,* if only because it keeps superhuman initiative inside the Firm.
But the Deputy Chief is in tight with Sir James Braddock and the Euro initiative. And that, Peter, is the embuggerance to your cunning plan.

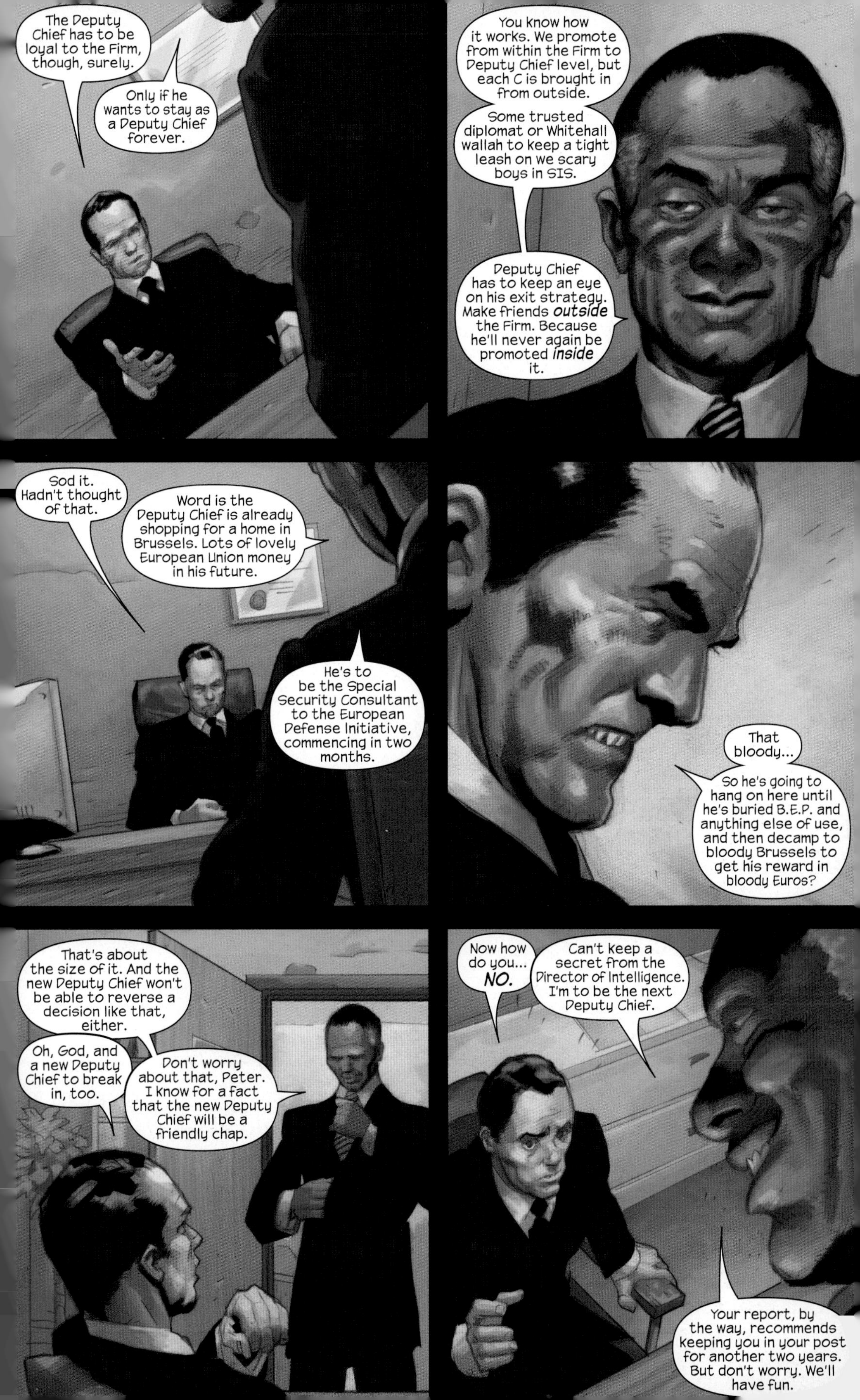
The Deputy Chief has to be loyal to the Firm, though, surely.
Only if he wants to stay as a Deputy Chief forever.
You know how it works. We promote from within the Firm to Deputy Chief level, but each C is brought in from outside.
Some trusted diplomat or Whitehall wallah to keep a tight leash on we scary boys in SIS.
Deputy Chief has to keep an eye on his exit strategy. Make friends *outside* the Firm. Because he'll never again be promoted *inside* it.
Sod it. Hadn't thought of that.
Word is the Deputy Chief is already shopping for a home in Brussels. Lots of lovely European Union money in his future.
He's to be the Special Security Consultant to the European Defense Initiative, commencing in two months.
That bloody...
So he's going to hang on here until he's buried B.E.P. and anything else of use, and then decamp to bloody Brussels to get his reward in bloody Euros?
That's about the size of it. And the new Deputy Chief won't be able to reverse a decision like that, either.
Oh, God, and a new Deputy Chief to break in, too.
Don't worry about that, Peter. I know for a fact that the new Deputy Chief will be a friendly chap.
Now how do you... ***NO.***
Can't keep a secret from the Director of Intelligence. I'm to be the next Deputy Chief.
Your report, by the way, recommends keeping you in your post for another two years. But don't worry. We'll have fun.

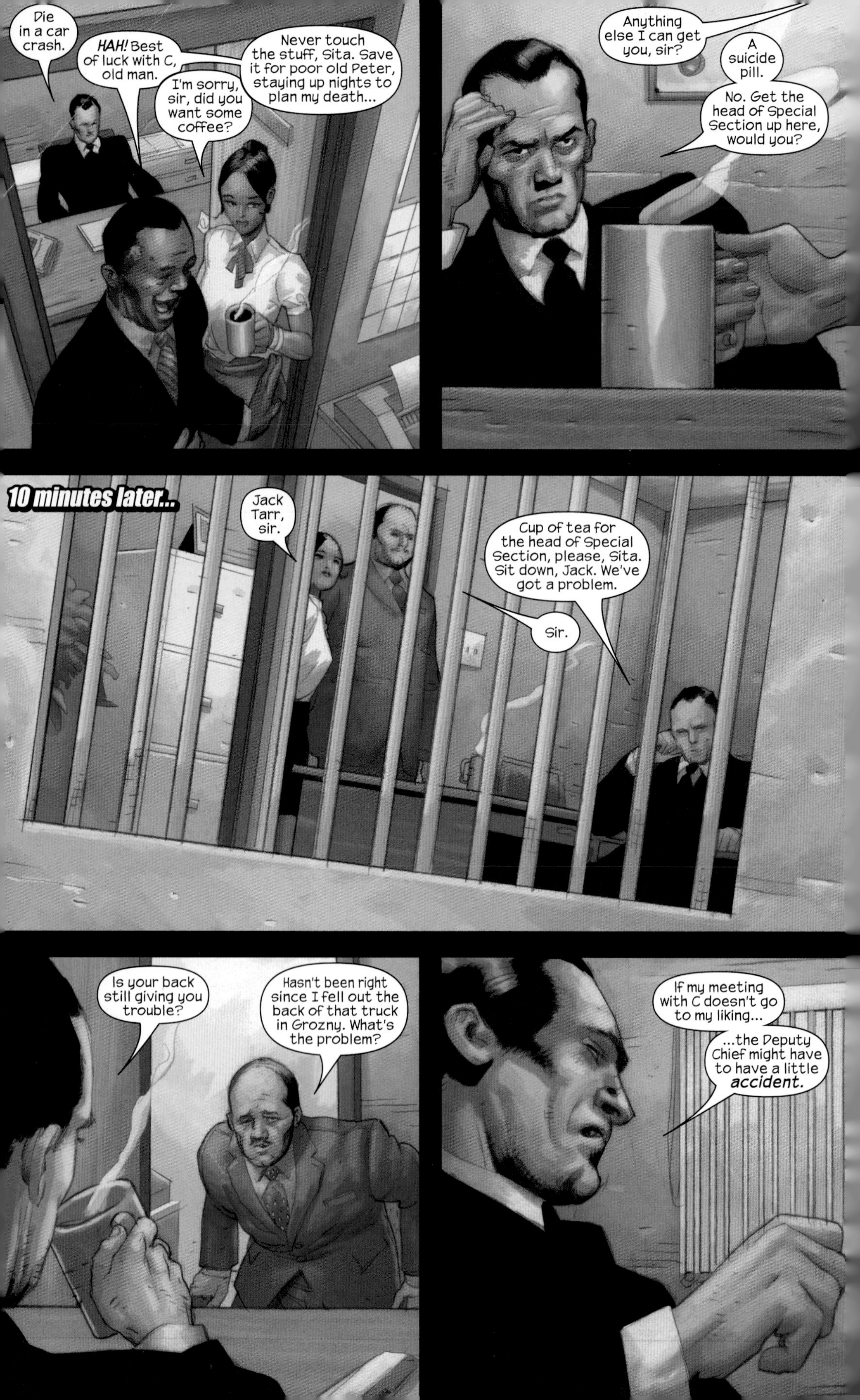
Die in a car crash.
HAH! Best of luck with C, old man.
Never touch the stuff, Sita. Save it for poor old Peter, staying up nights to plan my death...
I'm sorry, sir, did you want some coffee?
Anything else I can get you, sir?
A suicide pill.
No. Get the head of Special Section up here, would you?
10 minutes later...
Jack Tarr, sir.
Cup of tea for the head of Special Section, please, Sita. Sit down, Jack. We've got a problem.
Sir.
Is your back still giving you trouble?
Hasn't been right since I fell out the back of that truck in Grozny. What's the problem?
If my meeting with C doesn't go to my liking...
...the Deputy Chief might have to have a little accident.

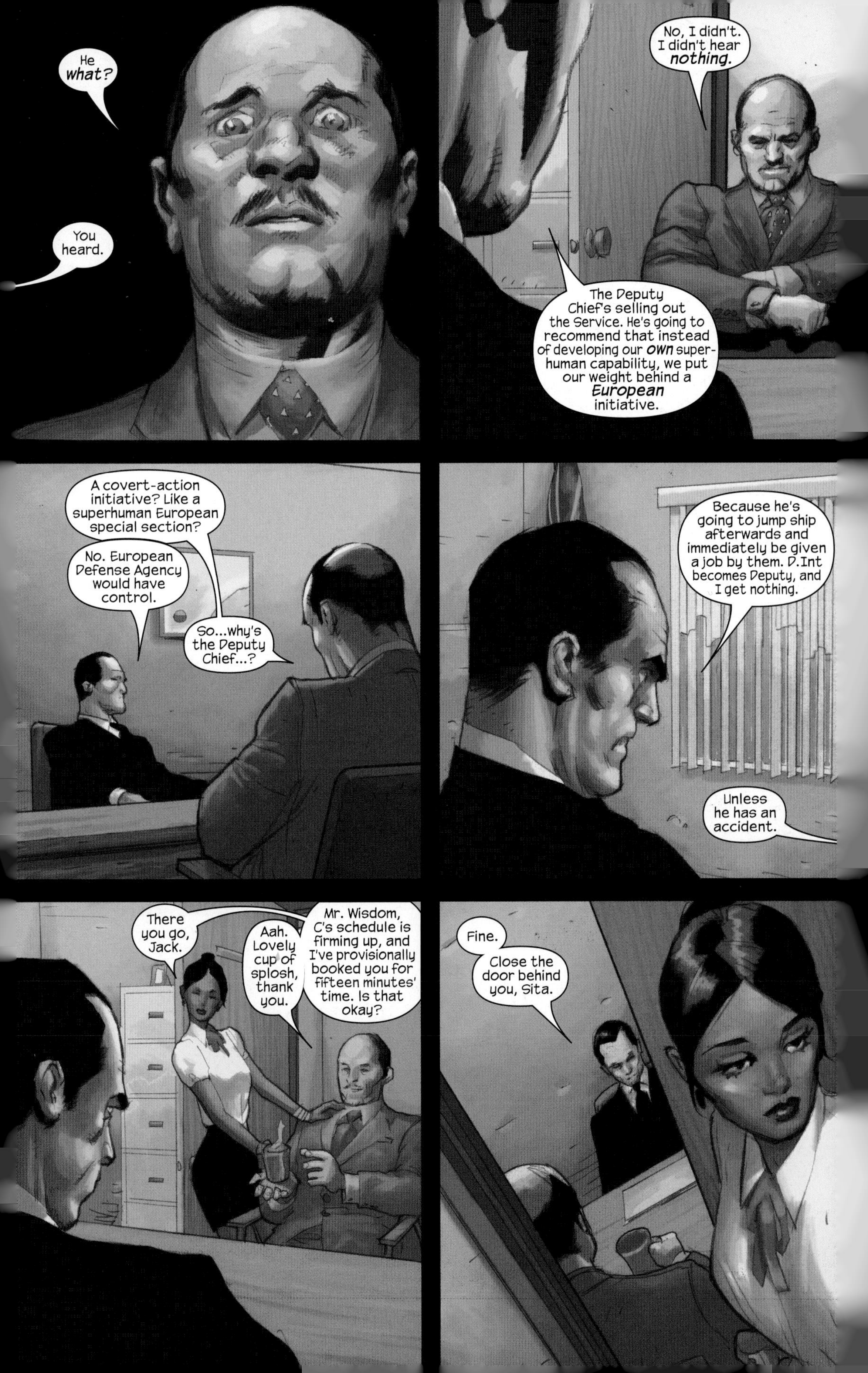

He *what?*
You heard.
No, I didn't. I didn't hear ***nothing.***
The Deputy Chief's selling out the Service. He's going to recommend that instead of developing our ***OWN*** superhuman capability, we put our weight behind a ***European*** initiative.
A covert-action initiative? Like a superhuman European special section?
No. European Defense Agency would have control.
So...why's the Deputy Chief...?
Because he's going to jump ship afterwards and immediately be given a job by them. D.Int becomes Deputy, and I get nothing.
Unless he has an accident.
There you go, Jack.
Aah. Lovely cup of splosh, thank you.
Mr. Wisdom, C's schedule is firming up, and I've provisionally booked you for fifteen minutes' time. Is that okay?
Fine.
Close the door behind you, Sita.

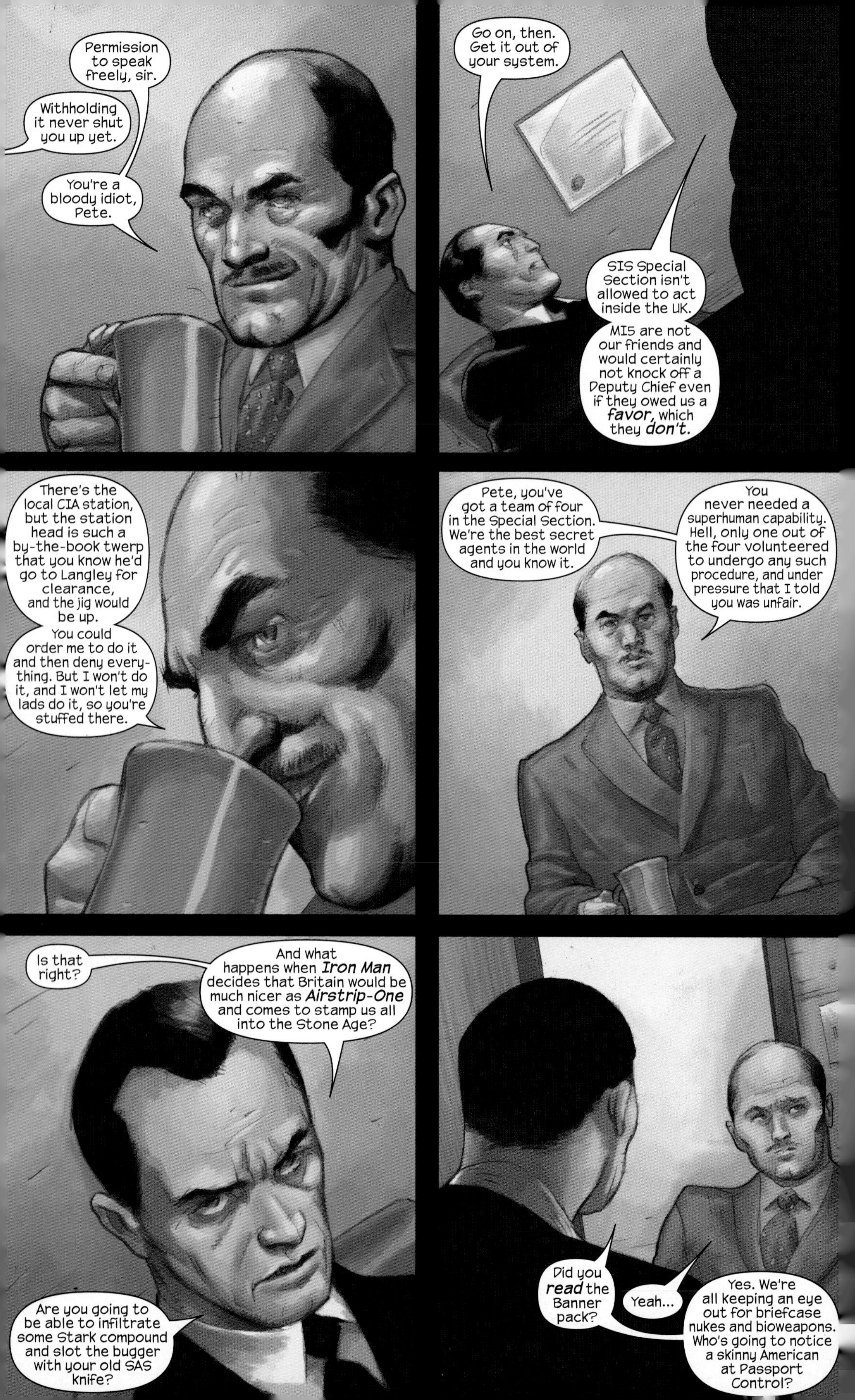

Permission to speak freely, sir.
Withholding it never shut you up yet.
You're a bloody idiot, Pete.
Go on, then. Get it out of your system.
SIS Special Section isn't allowed to act inside the UK.
MI5 are not our friends and would certainly not knock off a Deputy Chief even if they owed us a *favor,* which they *don't.*
There's the local CIA station, but the station head is such a by-the-book twerp that you know he'd go to Langley for clearance, and the jig would be up.
You could order me to do it and then deny everything. But I won't do it, and I won't let my lads do it, so you're stuffed there.
Pete, you've got a team of four in the Special Section. We're the best secret agents in the world and you know it.
You never needed a superhuman capability. Hell, only one out of the four volunteered to undergo any such procedure, and under pressure that I told you was unfair.
Is that right?
And what happens when *Iron Man* decides that Britain would be much nicer as *Airstrip-One* and comes to stamp us all into the Stone Age?
Are you going to be able to infiltrate some Stark compound and slot the bugger with your old SAS knife?
Did you *read* the Banner pack?
Yeah...
Yes. We're all keeping an eye out for briefcase nukes and bioweapons. Who's going to notice a skinny American at Passport Control?

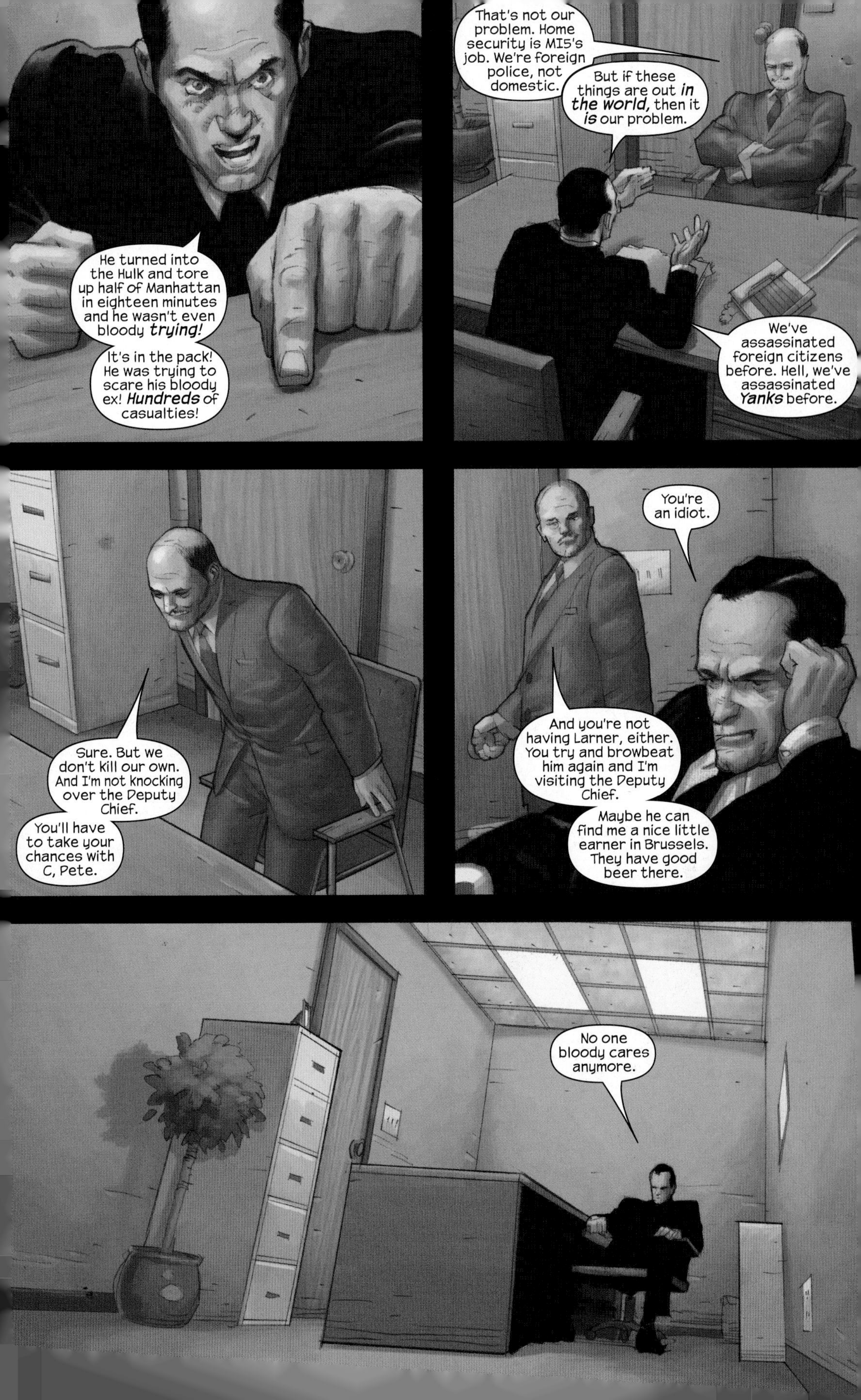
He turned into the Hulk and tore up half of Manhattan in eighteen minutes and he wasn't even bloody trying!
It's in the pack! He was trying to scare his bloody ex! Hundreds of casualties!
That's not our problem. Home security is MI5's job. We're foreign police, not domestic.
But if these things are out in the world, then it is our problem.
We've assassinated foreign citizens before. Hell, we've assassinated Yanks before.
Sure. But we don't kill our own. And I'm not knocking over the Deputy Chief.
You'll have to take your chances with C, Pete.
You're an idiot.
And you're not having Larner, either. You try and browbeat him again and I'm visiting the Deputy Chief.
Maybe he can find me a nice little earner in Brussels. They have good beer there.
No one bloody cares anymore.

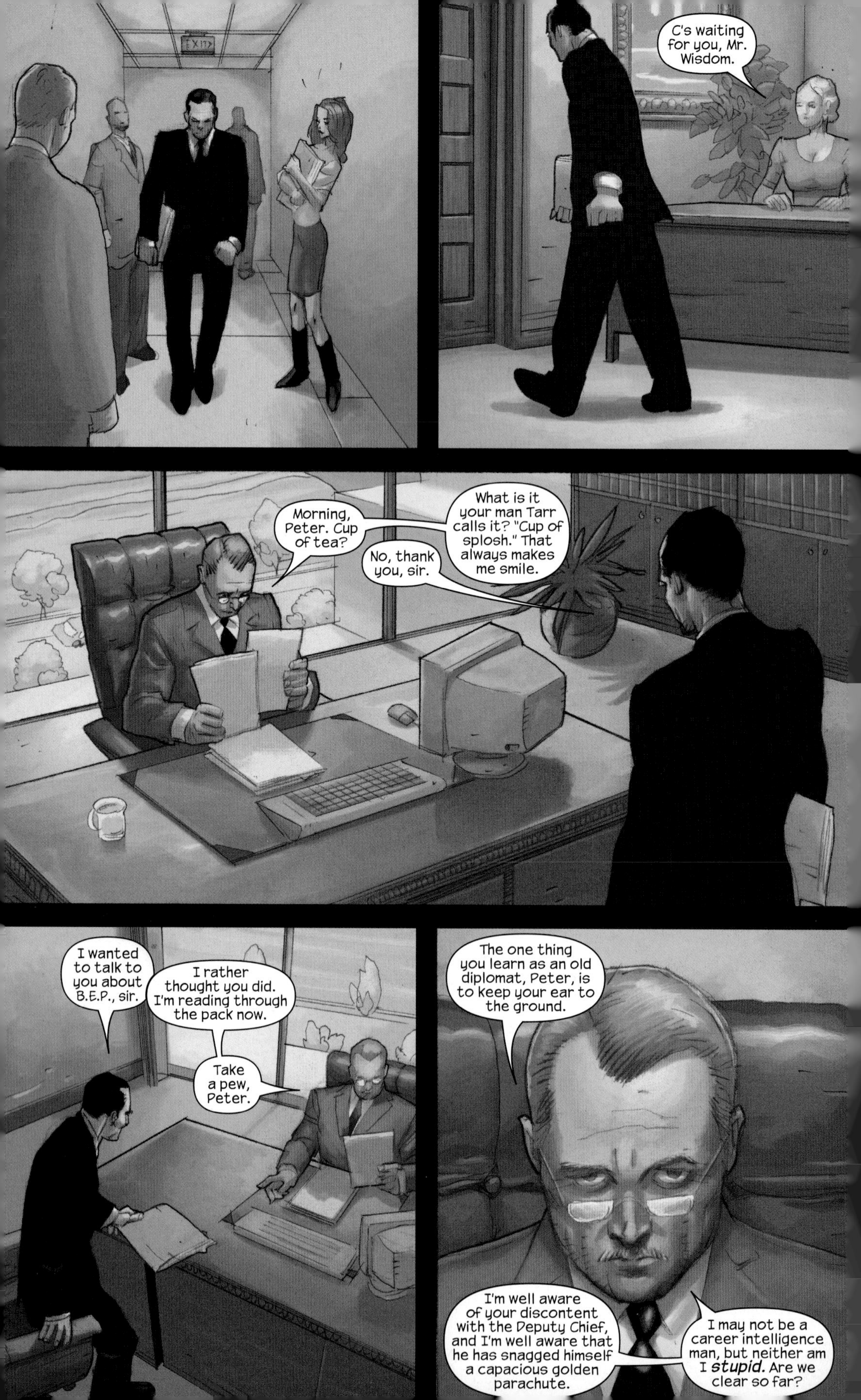

C's waiting for you, Mr. Wisdom.
Morning, Peter. Cup of tea?
What is it your man Tarr calls it? "Cup of splosh." That always makes me smile.
No, thank you, sir.
I wanted to talk to you about B.E.P., sir.
I rather thought you did. I'm reading through the pack now.
Take a pew, Peter.
The one thing you learn as an old diplomat, Peter, is to keep your ear to the ground.
I'm well aware of your discontent with the Deputy Chief, and I'm well aware that he has snagged himself a capacious golden parachute.
I may not be a career intelligence man, but neither am I *stupid.* Are we clear so far?

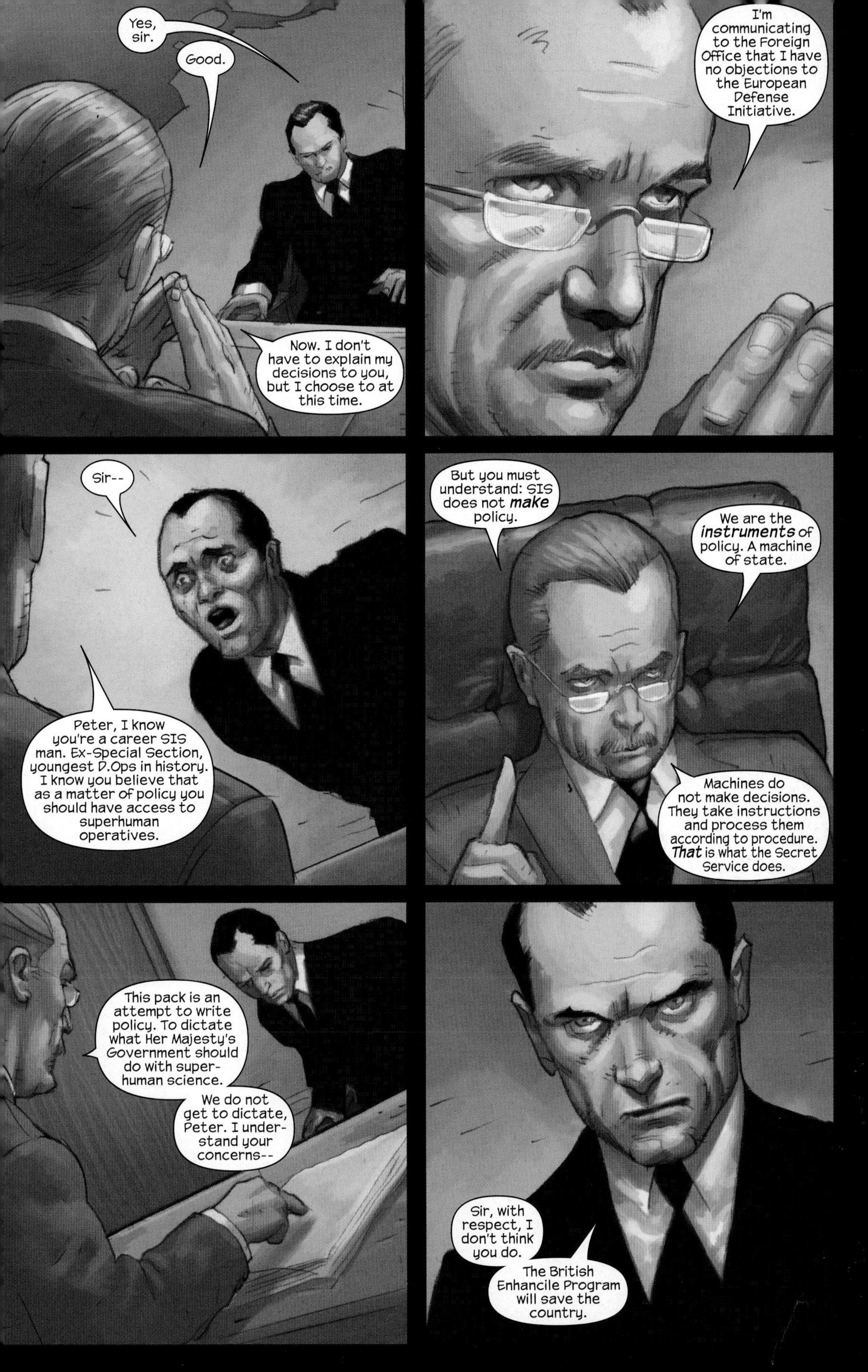
Yes, sir.
Good.
Now. I don't have to explain my decisions to you, but I choose to at this time.
I'm communicating to the Foreign Office that I have no objections to the European Defense Initiative.
Sir--
Peter, I know you're a career SIS man. Ex-Special Section, youngest D.Ops in history. I know you believe that as a matter of policy you should have access to superhuman operatives.
But you must understand: SIS does not *make* policy.
We are the *instruments* of policy. A machine of state.
Machines do not make decisions. They take instructions and process them according to procedure. *That* is what the Secret Service does.
This pack is an attempt to write policy. To dictate what Her Majesty's Government should do with super-human science.
We do not get to dictate, Peter. I under-stand your concerns--
Sir, with respect, I don't think you do.
The British Enhancile Program will save the country.

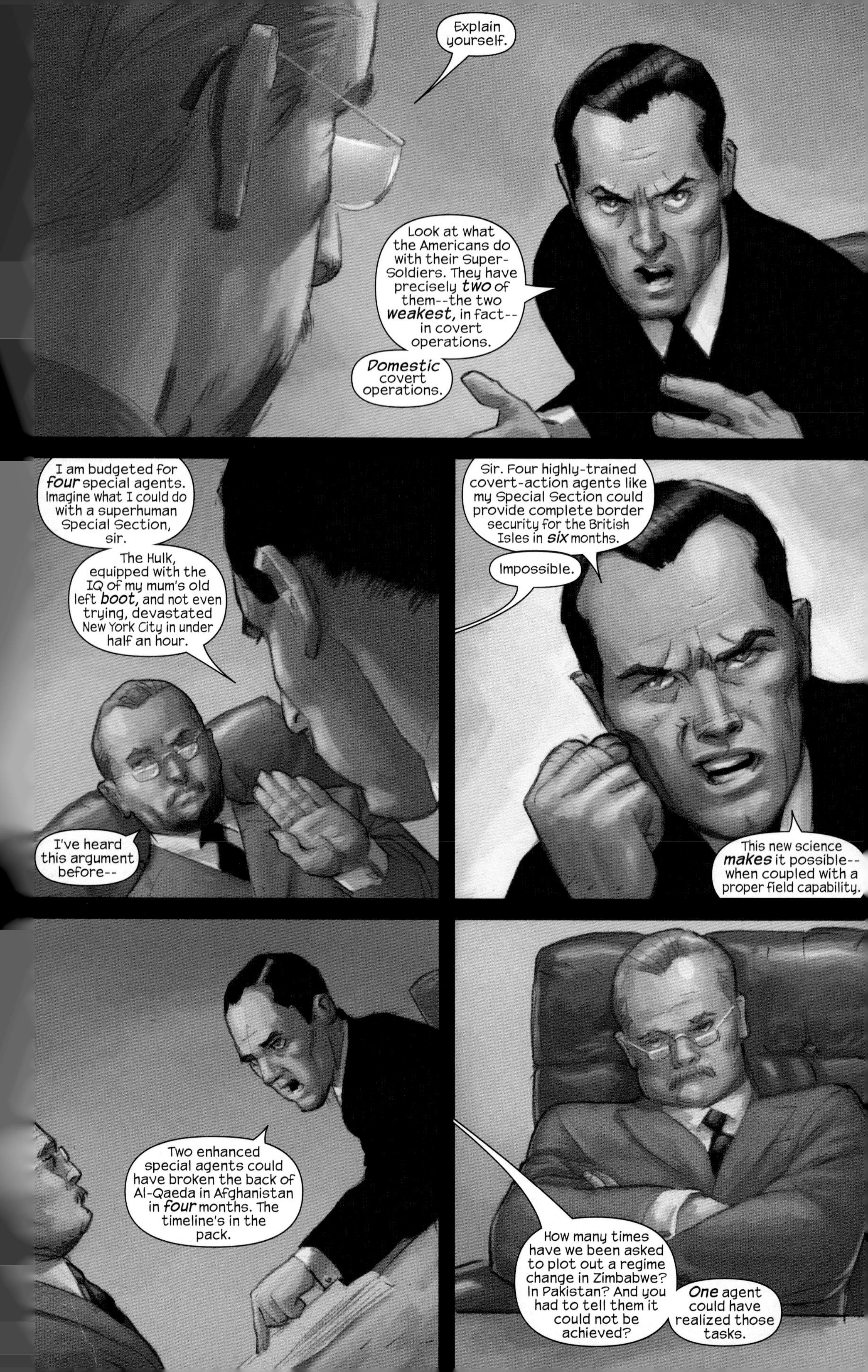
Explain yourself.
Look at what the Americans do with their Super-Soldiers. They have precisely two of them--the two weakest, in fact--in covert operations.
Domestic covert operations.
I am budgeted for four special agents. Imagine what I could do with a superhuman Special Section, sir.
The Hulk, equipped with the IQ of my mum's old left boot, and not even trying, devastated New York City in under half an hour.
I've heard this argument before--
Sir. Four highly-trained covert-action agents like my Special Section could provide complete border security for the British Isles in six months.
Impossible.
This new science makes it possible--when coupled with a proper field capability.
Two enhanced special agents could have broken the back of Al-Qaeda in Afghanistan in four months. The timeline's in the pack.
How many times have we been asked to plot out a regime change in Zimbabwe? In Pakistan? And you had to tell them it could not be achieved?
One agent could have realized those tasks.

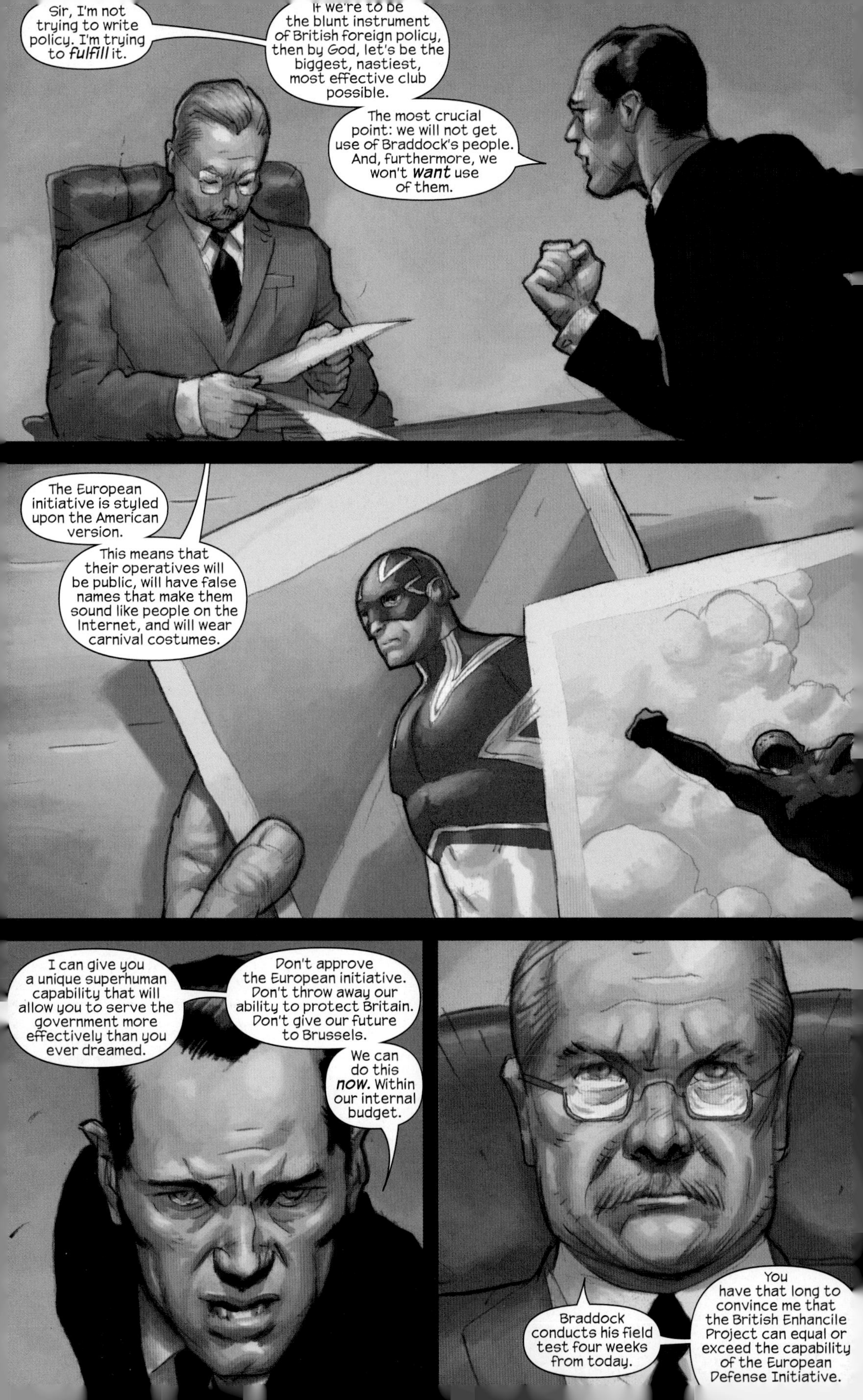
Sir, I'm not trying to write policy. I'm trying to fulfill it.
If we're to be the blunt instrument of British foreign policy, then by God, let's be the biggest, nastiest, most effective club possible.
The most crucial point: we will not get use of Braddock's people. And, furthermore, we won't want use of them.
The European initiative is styled upon the American version.
This means that their operatives will be public, will have false names that make them sound like people on the Internet, and will wear carnival costumes.
I can give you a unique superhuman capability that will allow you to serve the government more effectively than you ever dreamed.
Don't approve the European initiative. Don't throw away our ability to protect Britain. Don't give our future to Brussels.
We can do this now. Within our internal budget.
Braddock conducts his field test four weeks from today.
You have that long to convince me that the British Enhancile Project can equal or exceed the capability of the European Defense Initiative.

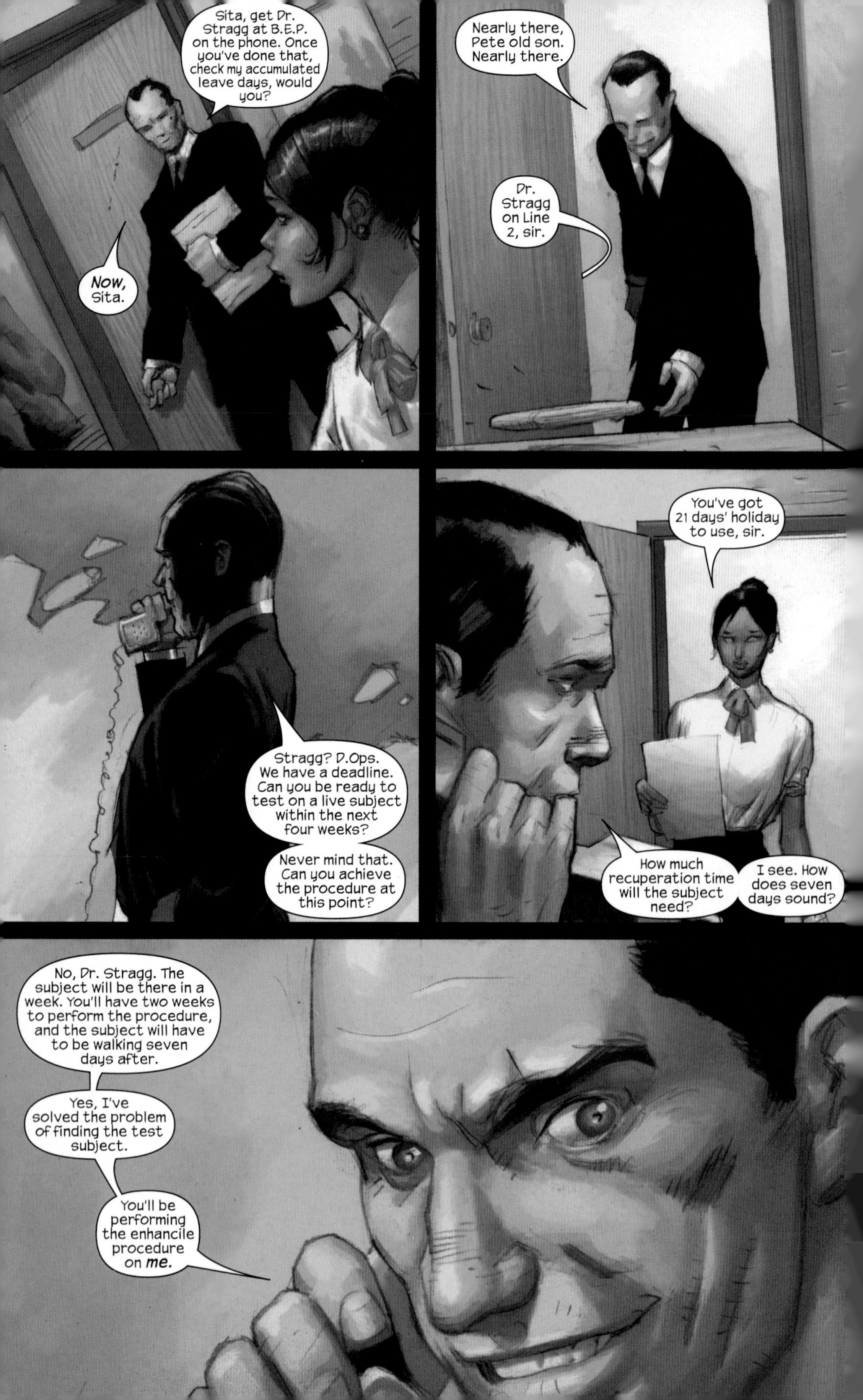

Sita, get Dr. Stragg at B.E.P. on the phone. Once you've done that, check my accumulated leave days, would you?
Now, Sita.
Nearly there, Pete old son. Nearly there.
Dr. Stragg on Line 2, sir.
Stragg? D.Ops. We have a deadline. Can you be ready to test on a live subject within the next four weeks?
Never mind that. Can you achieve the procedure at this point?
You've got 21 days' holiday to use, sir.
How much recuperation time will the subject need?
I see. How does seven days sound?
No, Dr. Stragg. The subject will be there in a week. You'll have two weeks to perform the procedure, and the subject will have to be walking seven days after.
Yes, I've solved the problem of finding the test subject.
You'll be performing the enhancile procedure on *me.*

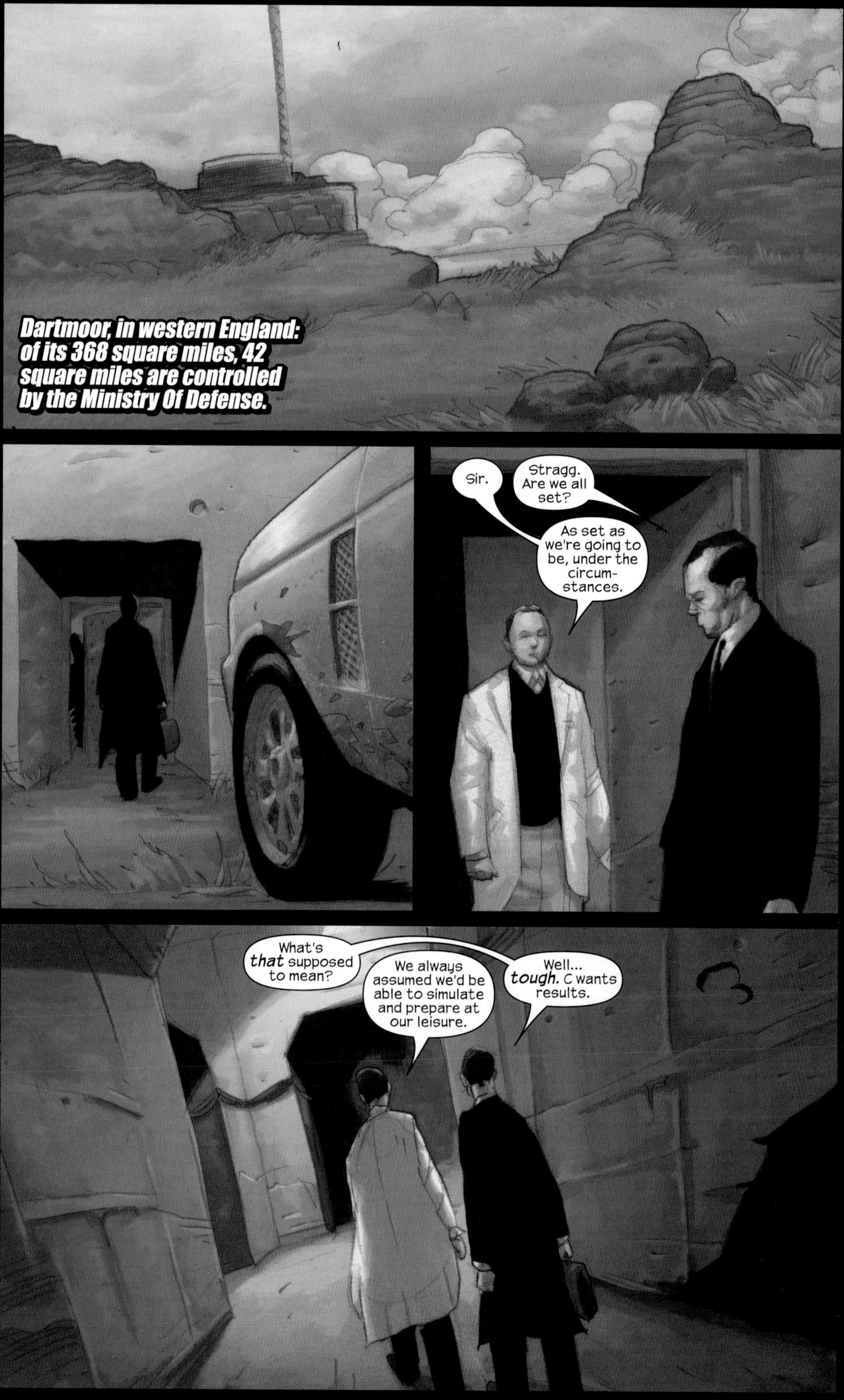
Dartmoor, in western England: of its 368 square miles, 42 square miles are controlled by the Ministry Of Defense.
Sir.
Stragg. Are we all set?
As set as we're going to be, under the circum-stances.
What's *that* supposed to mean?
We always assumed we'd be able to simulate and prepare at our leisure.
Well... *tough.* C wants results.

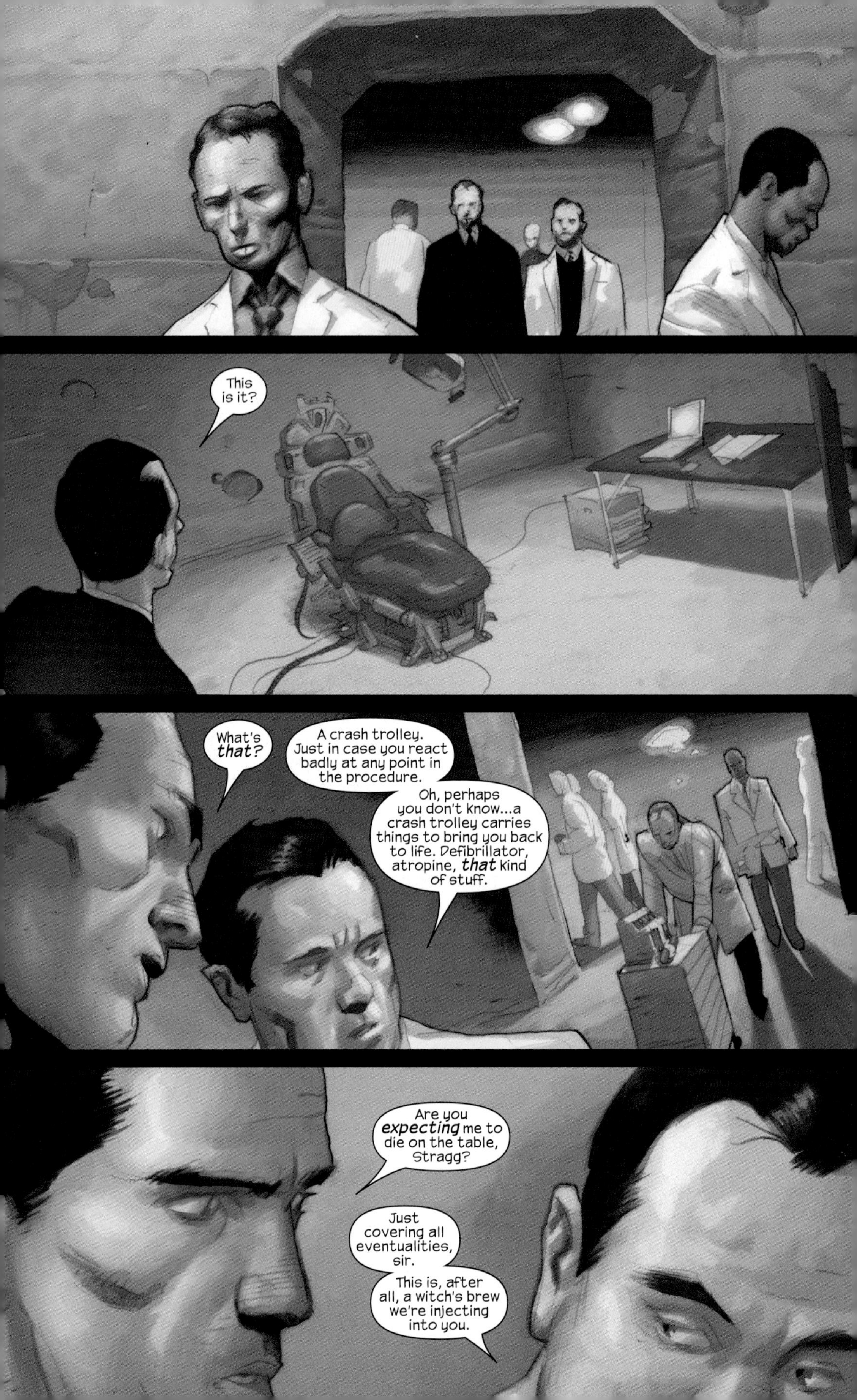

This is it?
What's *that?*
A crash trolley. Just in case you react badly at any point in the procedure.
Oh, perhaps you don't know...a crash trolley carries things to bring you back to life. Defibrillator, atropine, *that* kind of stuff.
Are you *expecting* me to die on the table, Stragg?
Just covering all eventualities, sir.
This is, after all, a witch's brew we're injecting into you.

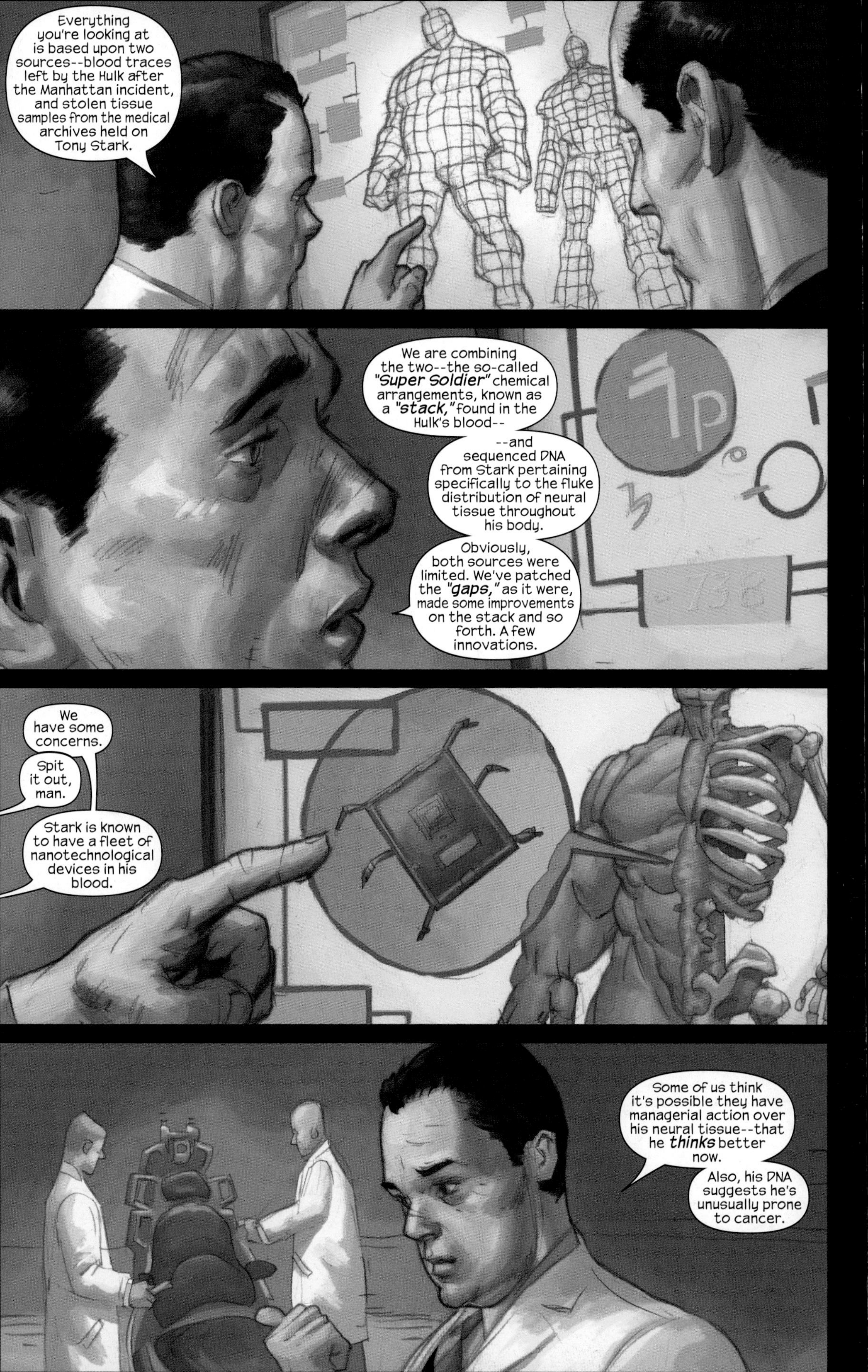
Everything you're looking at is based upon two sources--blood traces left by the Hulk after the Manhattan incident, and stolen tissue samples from the medical archives held on Tony Stark.
We are combining the two--the so-called "Super Soldier" chemical arrangements, known as a "stack," found in the Hulk's blood--
--and sequenced DNA from Stark pertaining specifically to the fluke distribution of neural tissue throughout his body.
Obviously, both sources were limited. We've patched the "gaps," as it were, made some improvements on the stack and so forth. A few innovations.
We have some concerns.
Spit it out, man.
Stark is known to have a fleet of nanotechnological devices in his blood.
Some of us think it's possible they have managerial action over his neural tissue--that he thinks better now.
Also, his DNA suggests he's unusually prone to cancer.

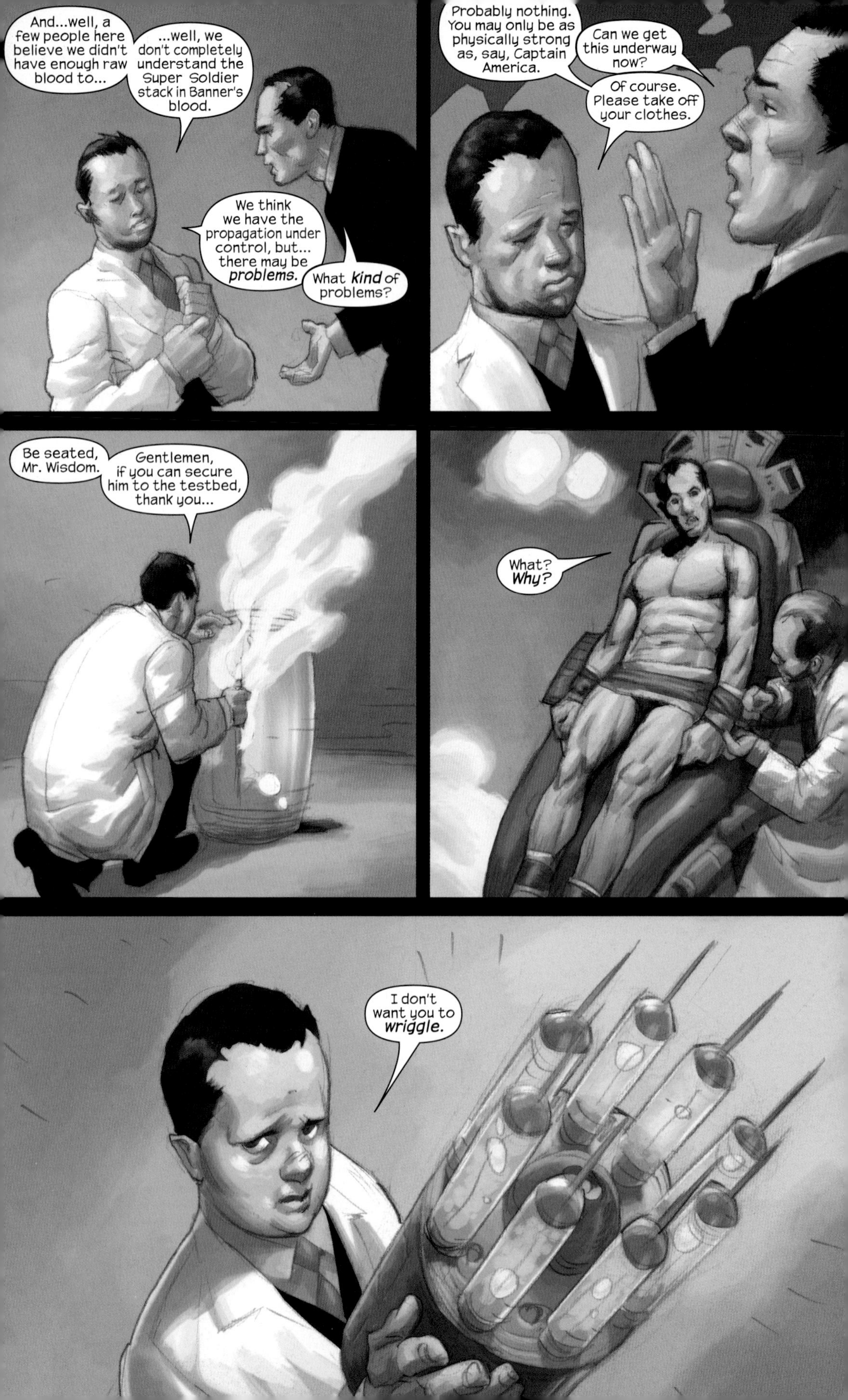
And...well, a few people here believe we didn't have enough raw blood to...
...well, we don't completely understand the Super Soldier stack in Banner's blood.
We think we have the propagation under control, but... there may be *problems.*
What *kind* of problems?
Probably nothing. You may only be as physically strong as, say, Captain America.
Can we get this underway now?
Of course. Please take off your clothes.
Be seated, Mr. Wisdom.
Gentlemen, if you can secure him to the testbed, thank you...
What? *Why?*
I don't want you to *wriggle.*

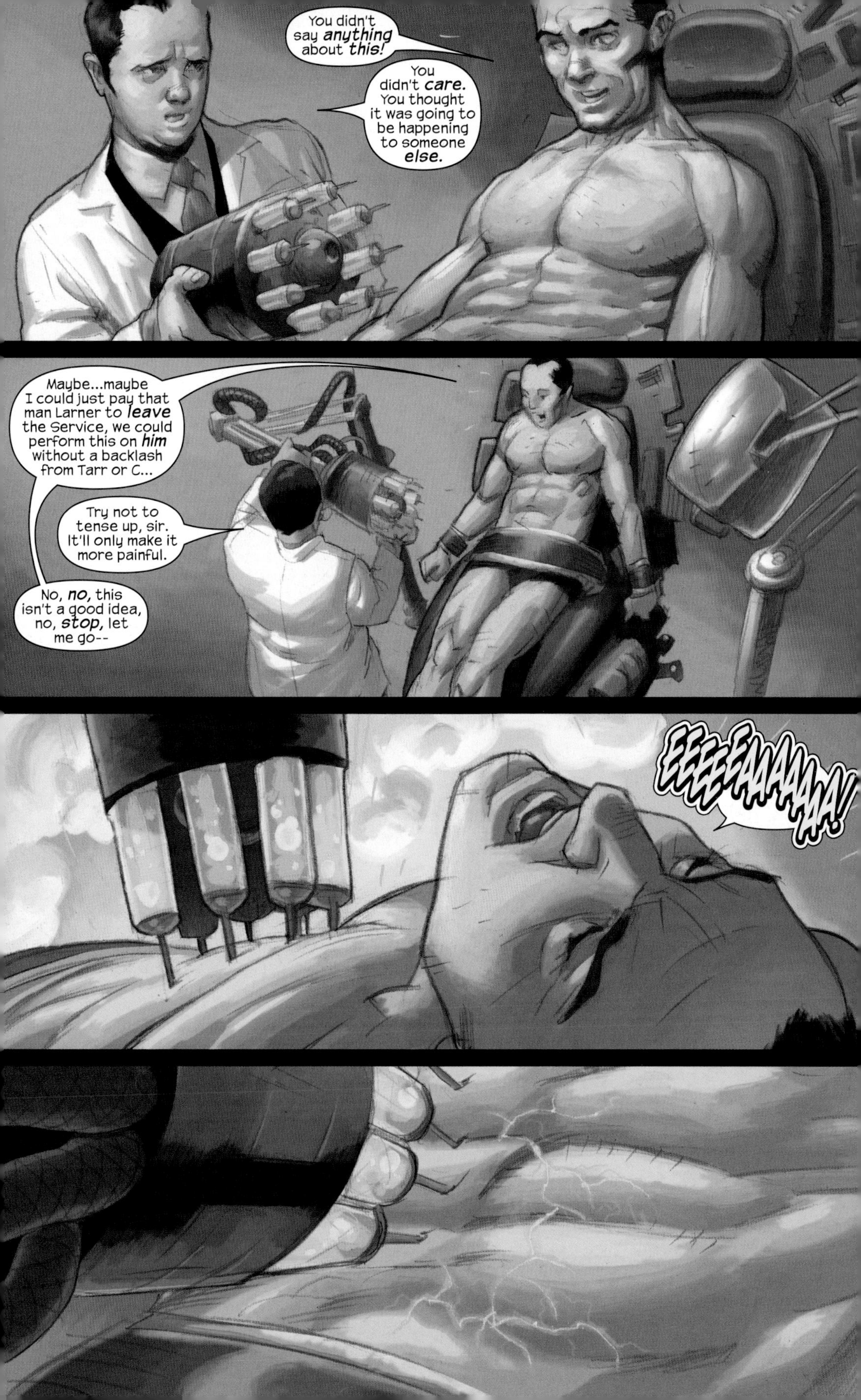
You didn't say *anything* about *this!*
You didn't *care.* You thought it was going to be happening to someone *else.*
Maybe...maybe I could just pay that man Larner to *leave* the Service, we could perform this on *him* without a backlash from Tarr or C...
Try not to tense up, sir. It'll only make it more painful.
No, *no,* this isn't a good idea, no, *stop,* let me go--
EEEEEAAAAAAAA!

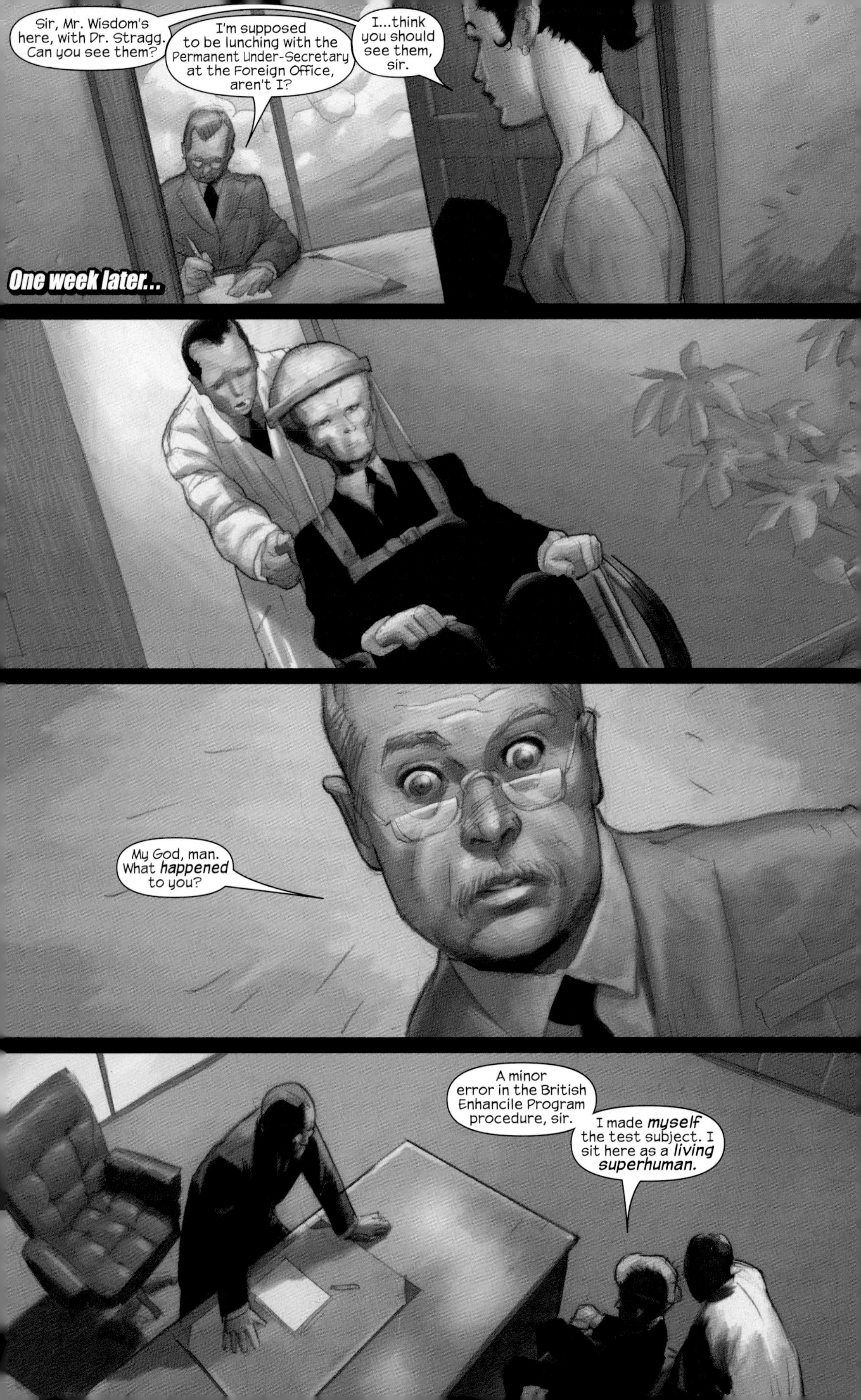
Sir, Mr. Wisdom's here, with Dr. Stragg. Can you see them?
I'm supposed to be lunching with the Permanent Under-Secretary at the Foreign Office, aren't I?
I...think you should see them, sir.
One week later...
My God, man. What *happened* to you?
A minor error in the British Enhancile Program procedure, sir.
I made *myself* the test subject. I sit here as a *living superhuman*.

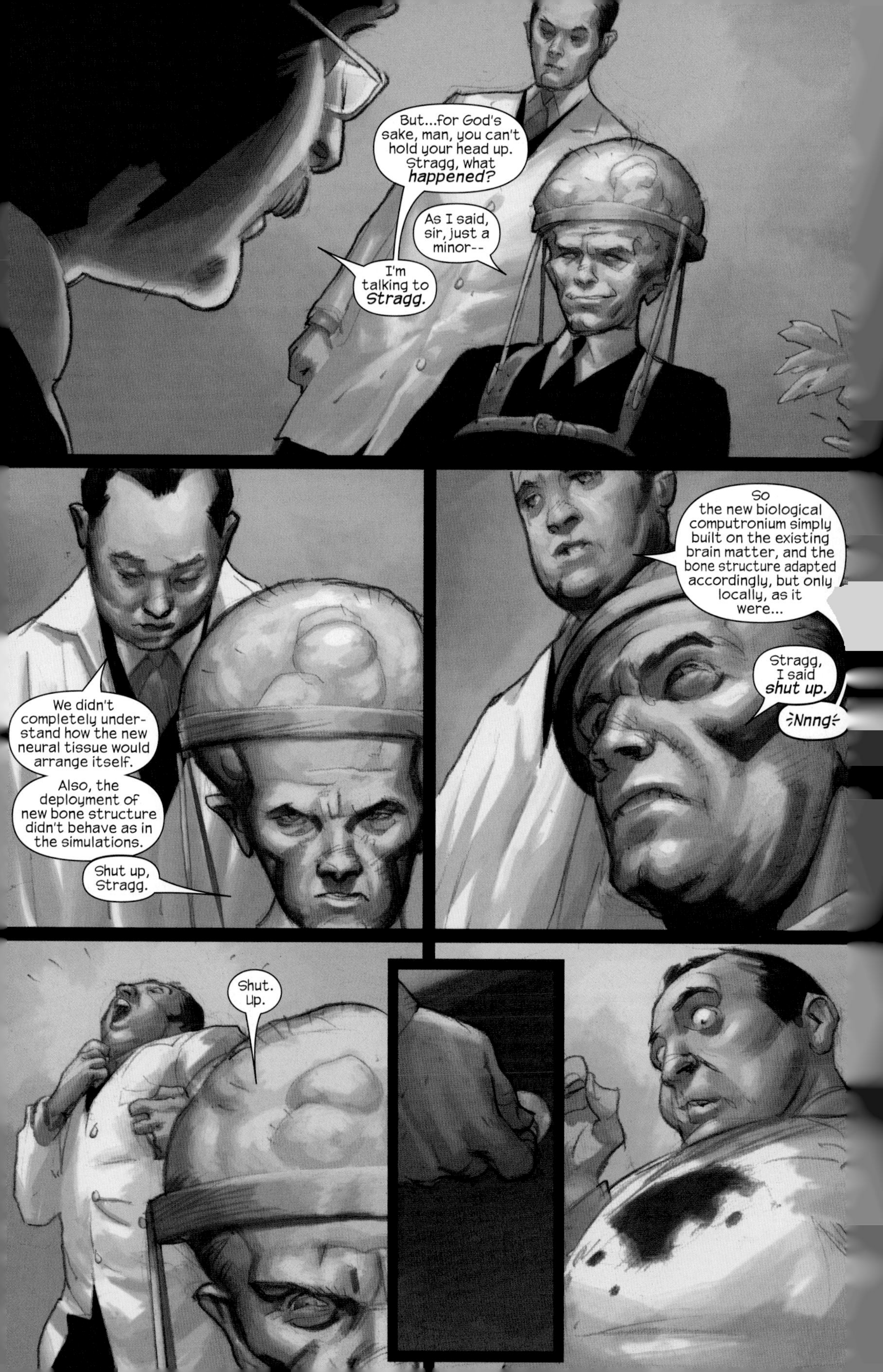
But...for God's sake, man, you can't hold your head up. Stragg, what *happened?*
As I said, sir, just a minor--
I'm talking to *Stragg.*
We didn't completely under-stand how the new neural tissue would arrange itself.
Also, the deployment of new bone structure didn't behave as in the simulations.
Shut up, Stragg.
So the new biological computronium simply built on the existing brain matter, and the bone structure adapted accordingly, but only locally, as it were...
Stragg, I said *shut up.*
Nnng
Shut. Up.

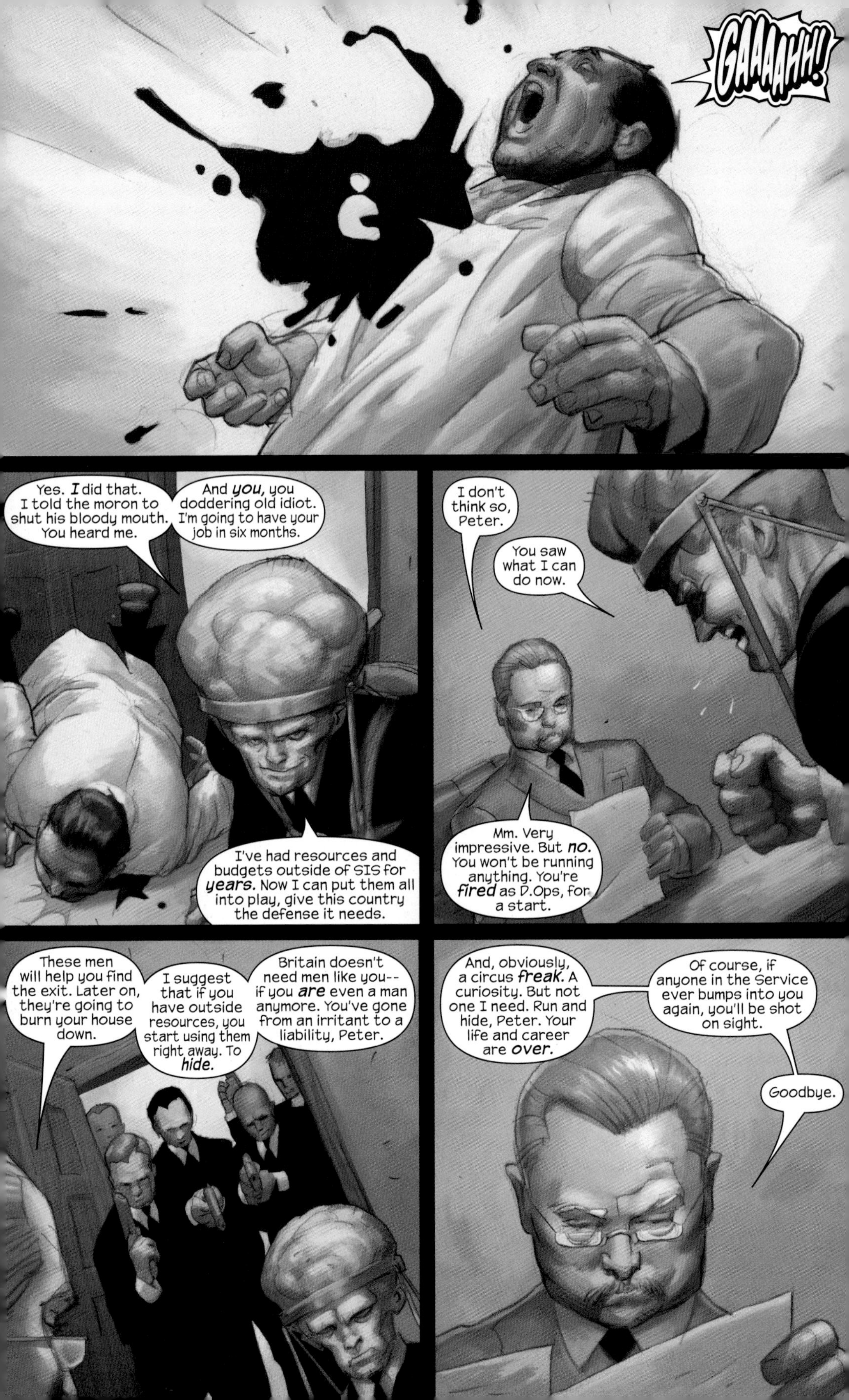
GAAAAHH!
Yes. I did that. I told the moron to shut his bloody mouth. You heard me.
And you, you doddering old idiot. I'm going to have your job in six months.
I've had resources and budgets outside of SIS for years. Now I can put them all into play, give this country the defense it needs.
I don't think so, Peter.
You saw what I can do now.
Mm. Very impressive. But no. You won't be running anything. You're fired as D.Ops, for a start.
These men will help you find the exit. Later on, they're going to burn your house down.
I suggest that if you have outside resources, you start using them right away. To hide.
Britain doesn't need men like you-- if you are even a man anymore. You've gone from an irritant to a liability, Peter.
And, obviously, a circus freak. A curiosity. But not one I need. Run and hide, Peter. Your life and career are over.
Of course, if anyone in the Service ever bumps into you again, you'll be shot on sight.
Goodbye.

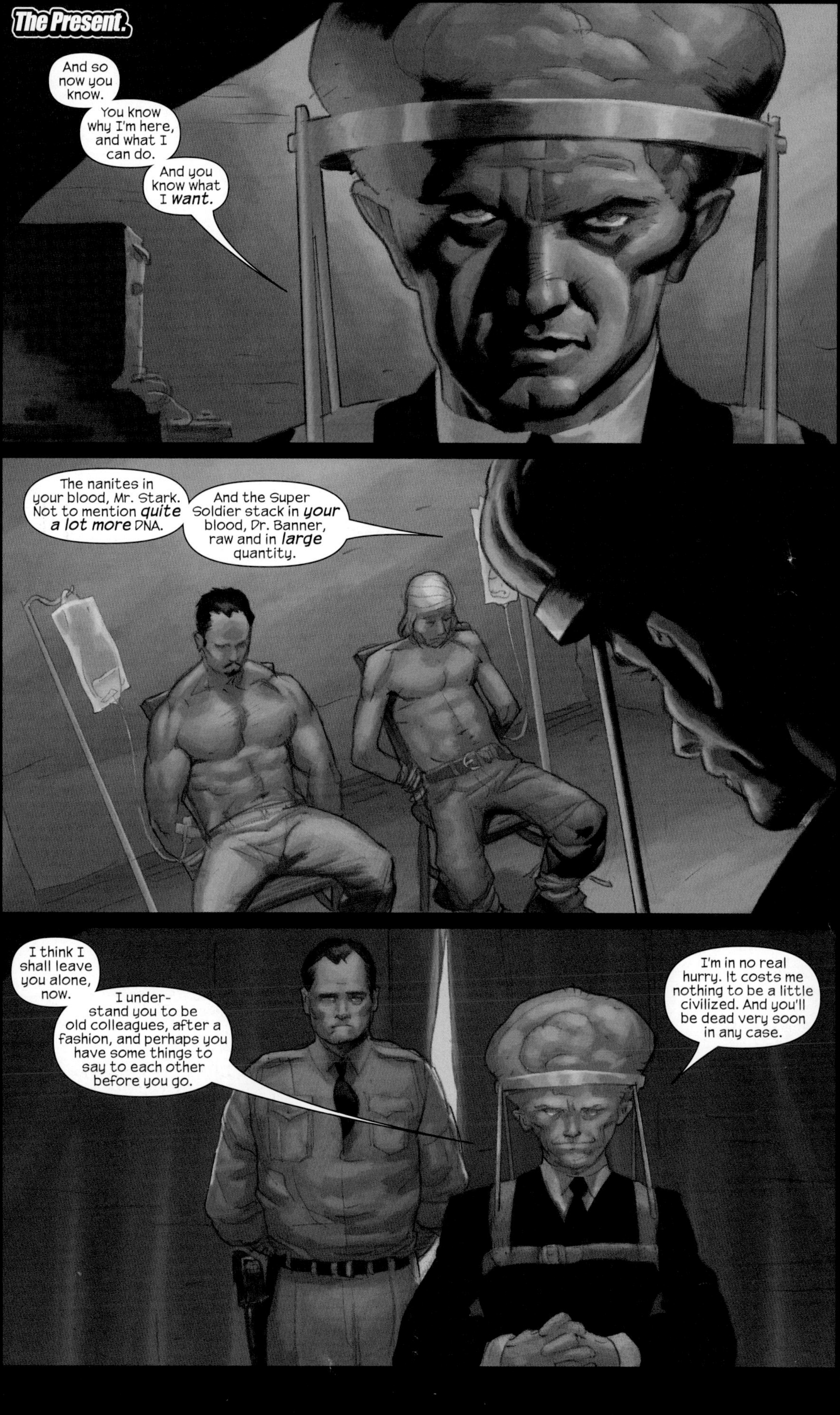
The Present.
And so now you know.
You know why I'm here, and what I can do.
And you know what I *want.*
The nanites in your blood, Mr. Stark. Not to mention *quite a lot more* DNA.
And the Super Soldier stack in *your* blood, Dr. Banner, raw and in *large* quantity.
I think I shall leave you alone, now.
I understand you to be old colleagues, after a fashion, and perhaps you have some things to say to each other before you go.
I'm in no real hurry. It costs me nothing to be a little civilized. And you'll be dead very soon in any case.

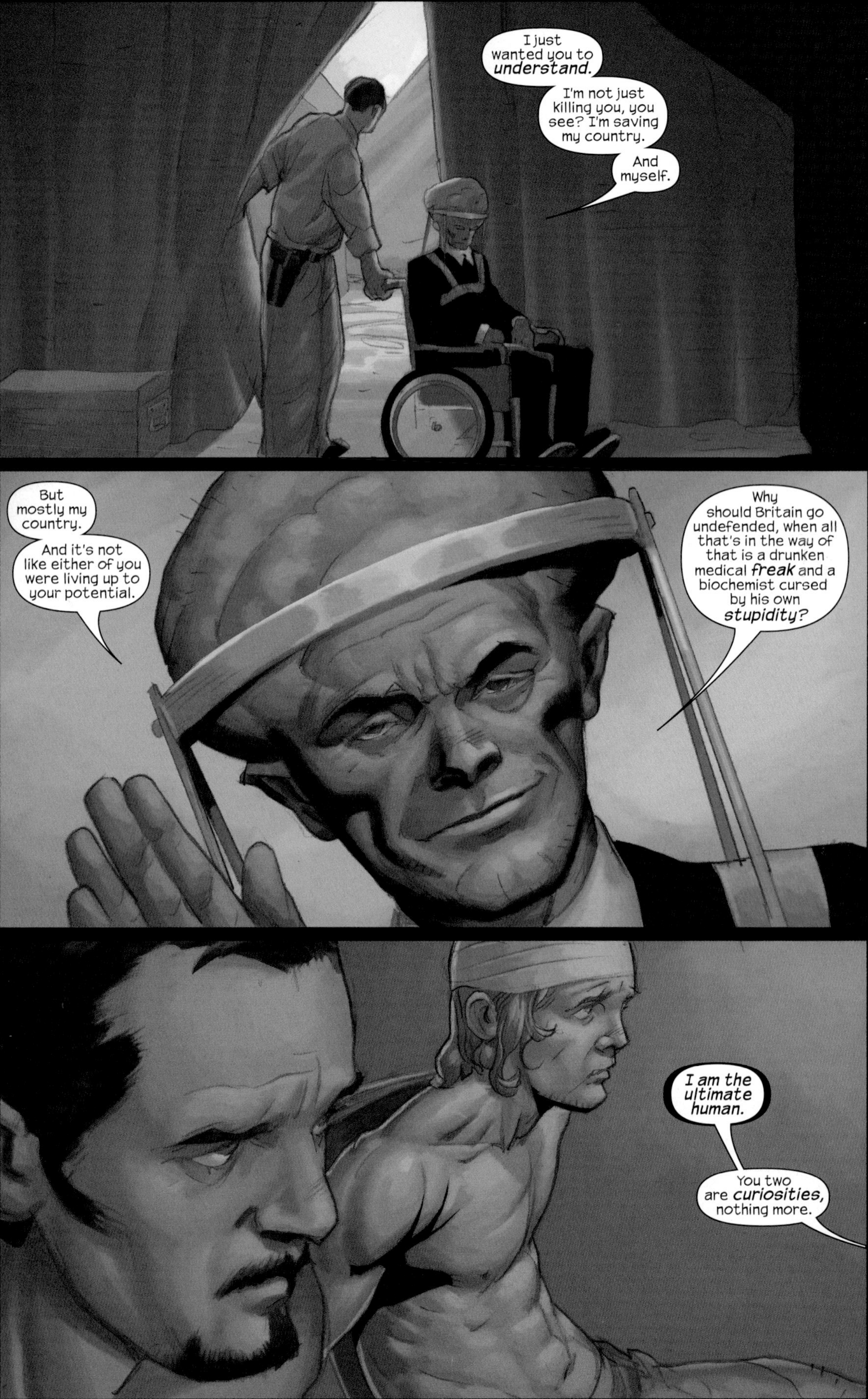
I just wanted you to *understand.*
I'm not just killing you, you see? I'm saving my country.
And myself.
But mostly my country.
And it's not like either of you were living up to your potential.
Why should Britain go undefended, when all that's in the way of that is a drunken medical *freak* and a biochemist cursed by his own *stupidity?*
I am the ultimate human.
You two are *curiosities,* nothing more.

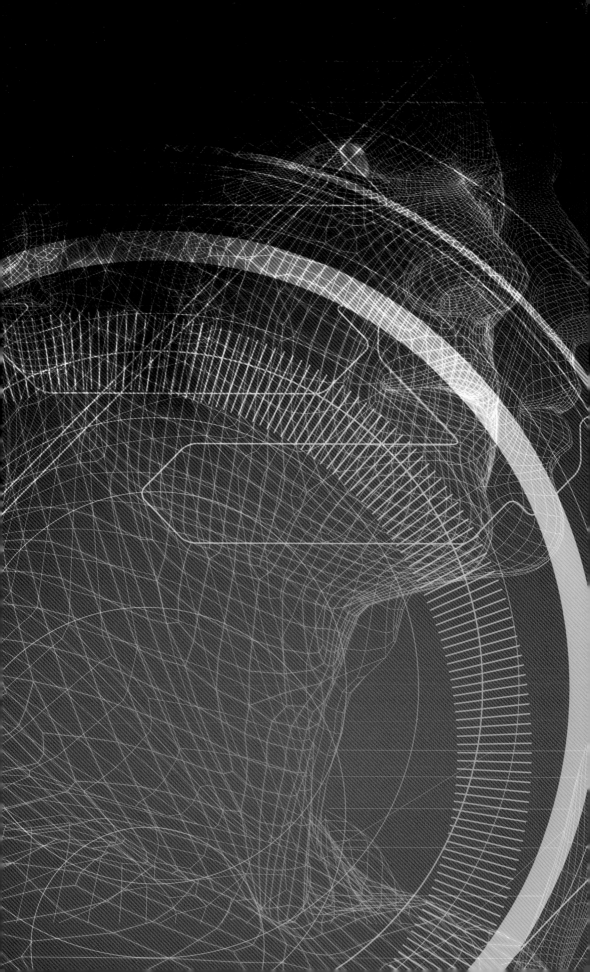

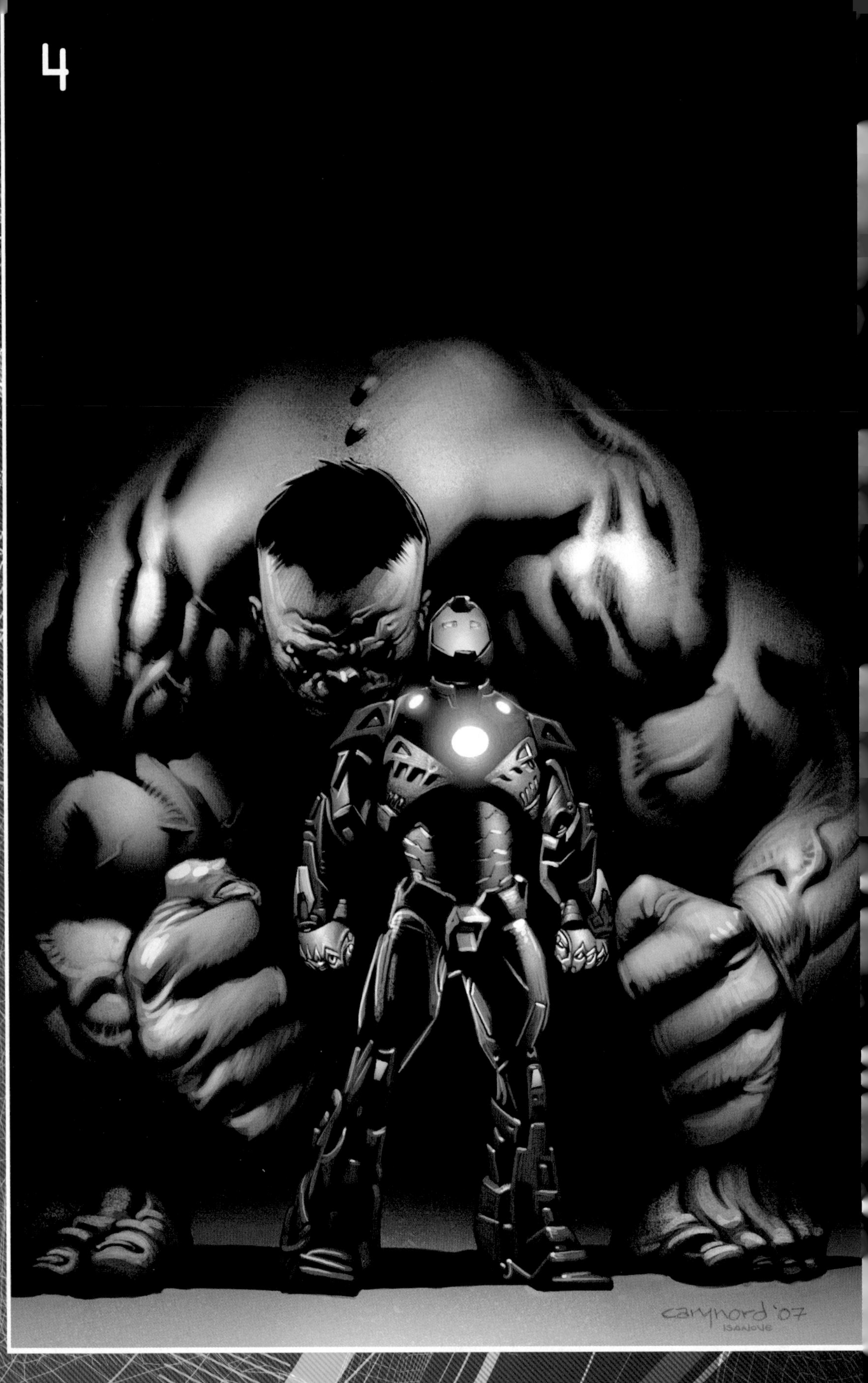

carynord '07
Isanove

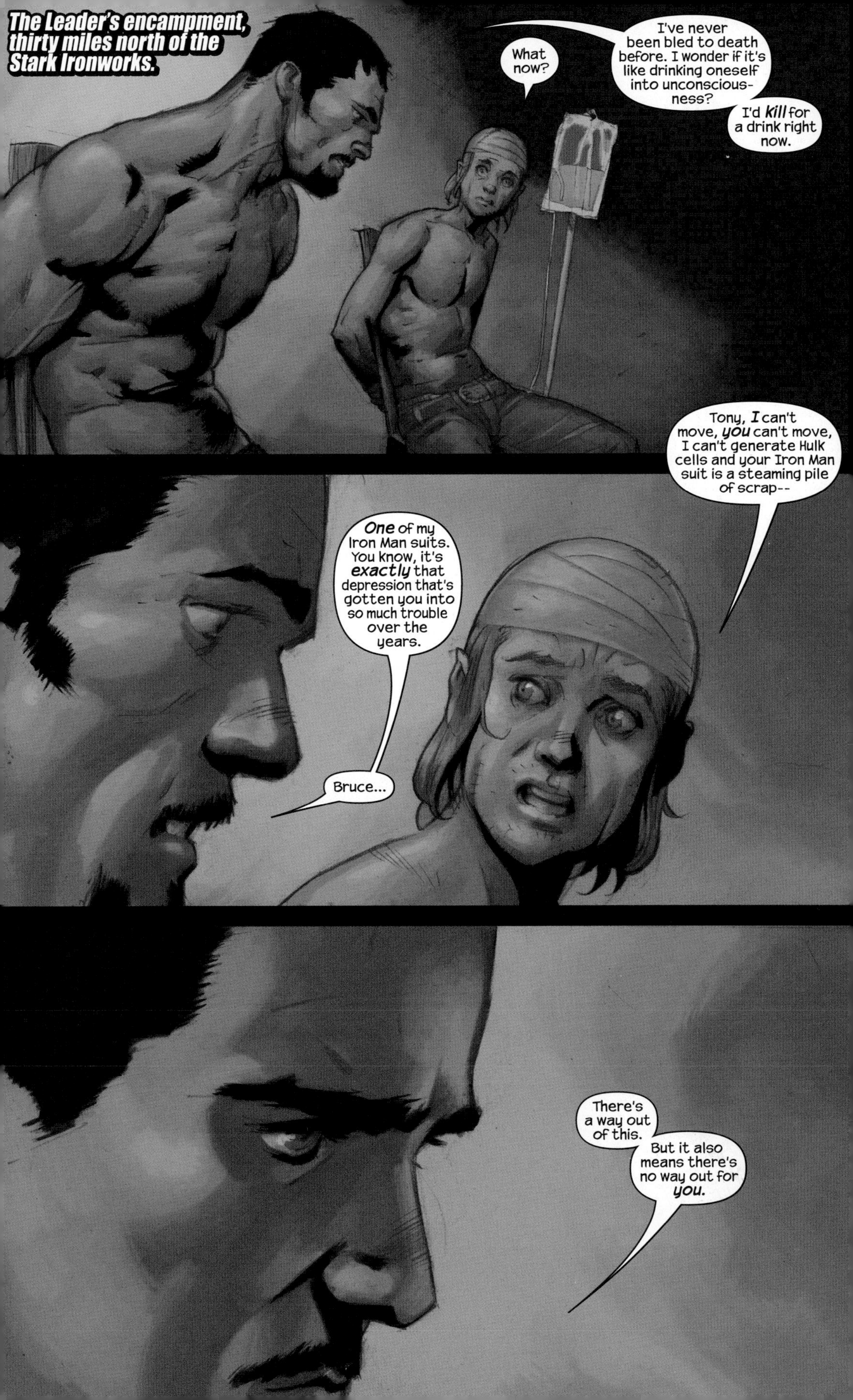
The Leader's encampment, thirty miles north of the Stark Ironworks.
What now?
I've never been bled to death before. I wonder if it's like drinking oneself into unconsciousness?
I'd kill for a drink right now.
Tony, I can't move, you can't move, I can't generate Hulk cells and your Iron Man suit is a steaming pile of scrap--
One of my Iron Man suits. You know, it's exactly that depression that's gotten you into so much trouble over the years.
Bruce...
There's a way out of this.
But it also means there's no way out for you.

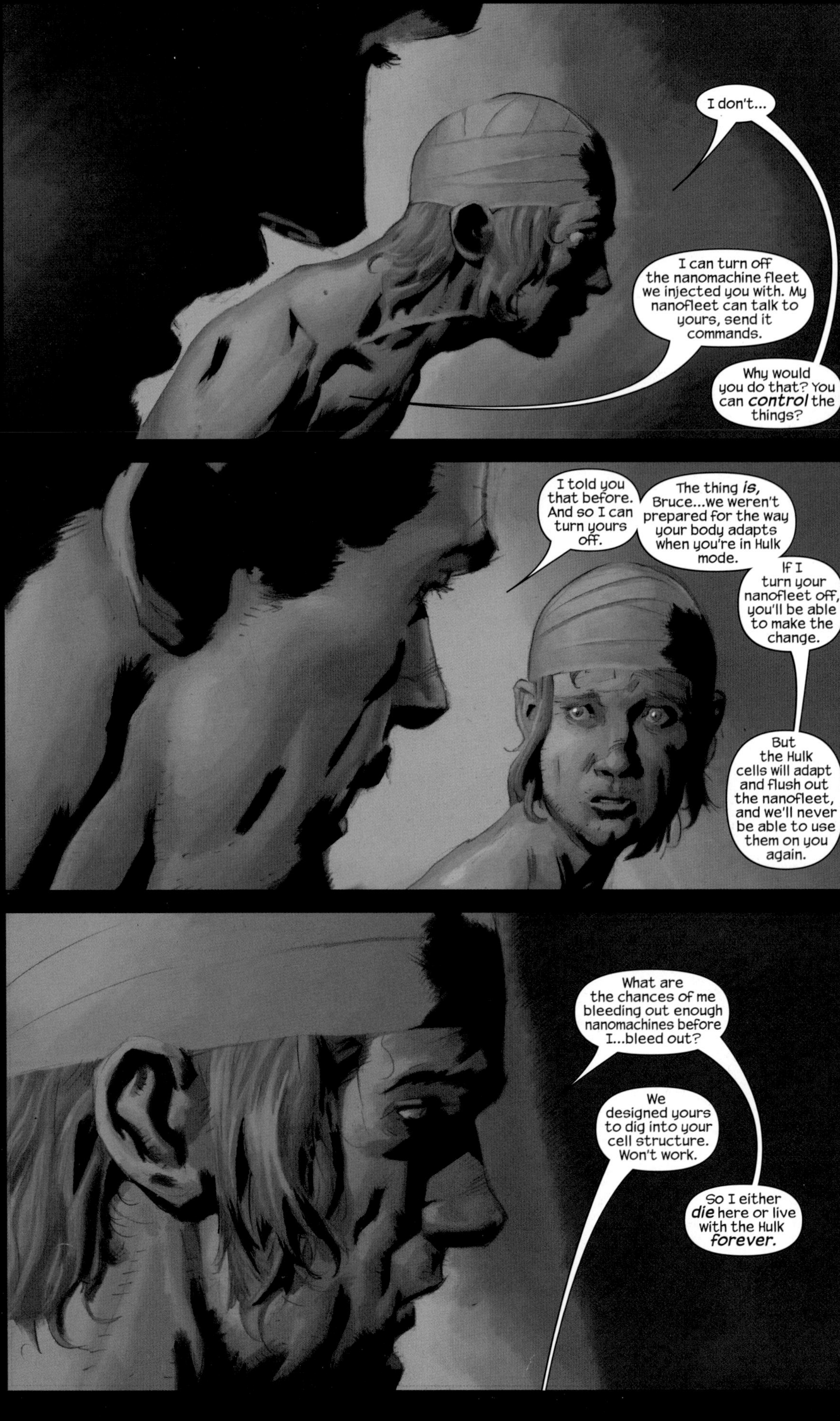

I don't...
I can turn off the nanomachine fleet we injected you with. My nanofleet can talk to yours, send it commands.
Why would you do that? You can *control* the things?
I told you that before. And so I can turn yours off.
The thing *is*, Bruce...we weren't prepared for the way your body adapts when you're in Hulk mode.
If I turn your nanofleet off, you'll be able to make the change.
But the Hulk cells will adapt and flush out the nanofleet, and we'll never be able to use them on you again.
What are the chances of me bleeding out enough nanomachines before I...bleed out?
We designed yours to dig into your cell structure. Won't work.
So I either *die* here or live with the Hulk *forever.*

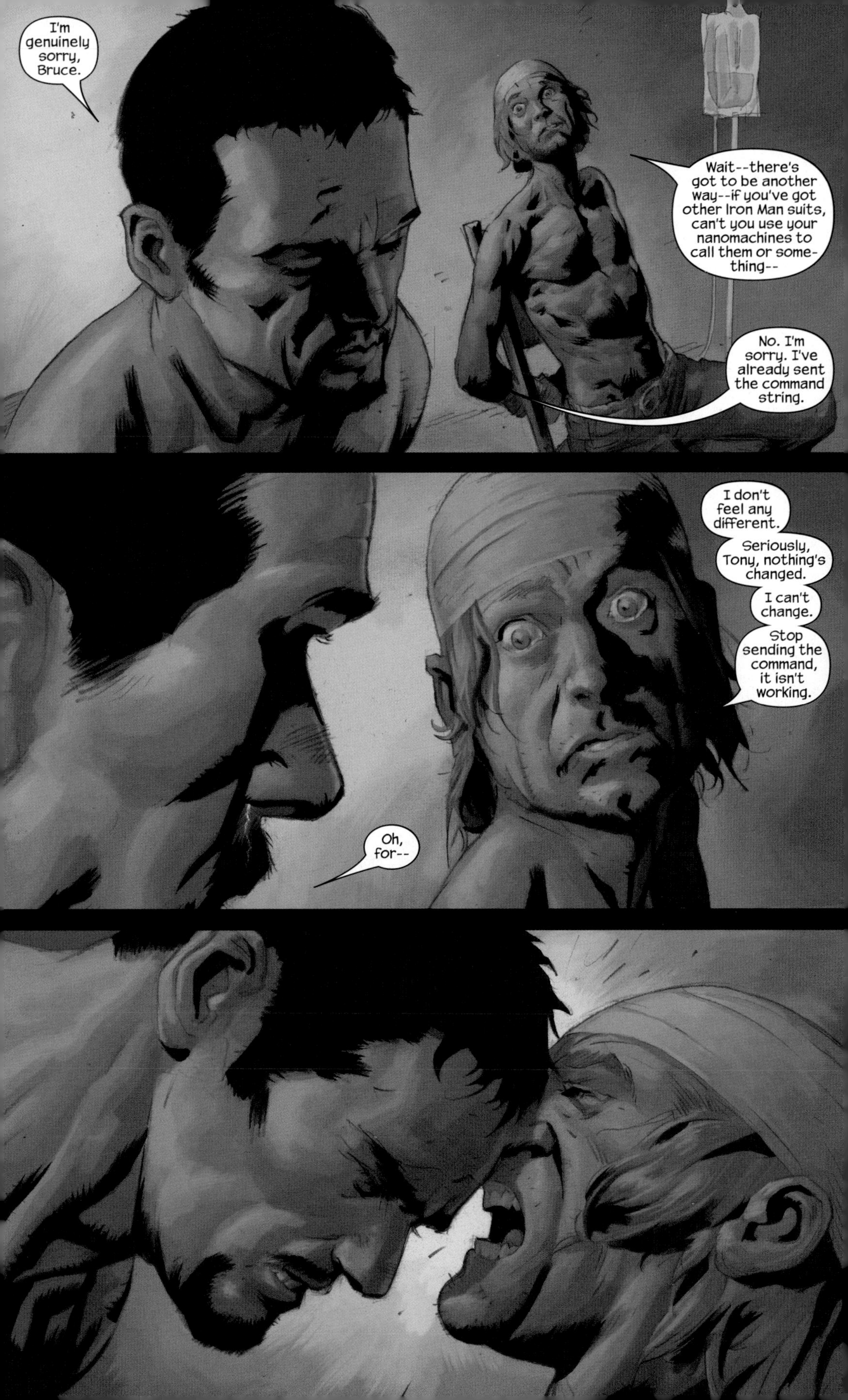
I'm genuinely sorry, Bruce.
Wait--there's got to be another way--if you've got other Iron Man suits, can't you use your nanomachines to call them or some-thing--
No. I'm sorry. I've already sent the command string.
I don't feel any different.
Seriously, Tony, nothing's changed.
I can't change.
Stop sending the command, it isn't working.
Oh, for--

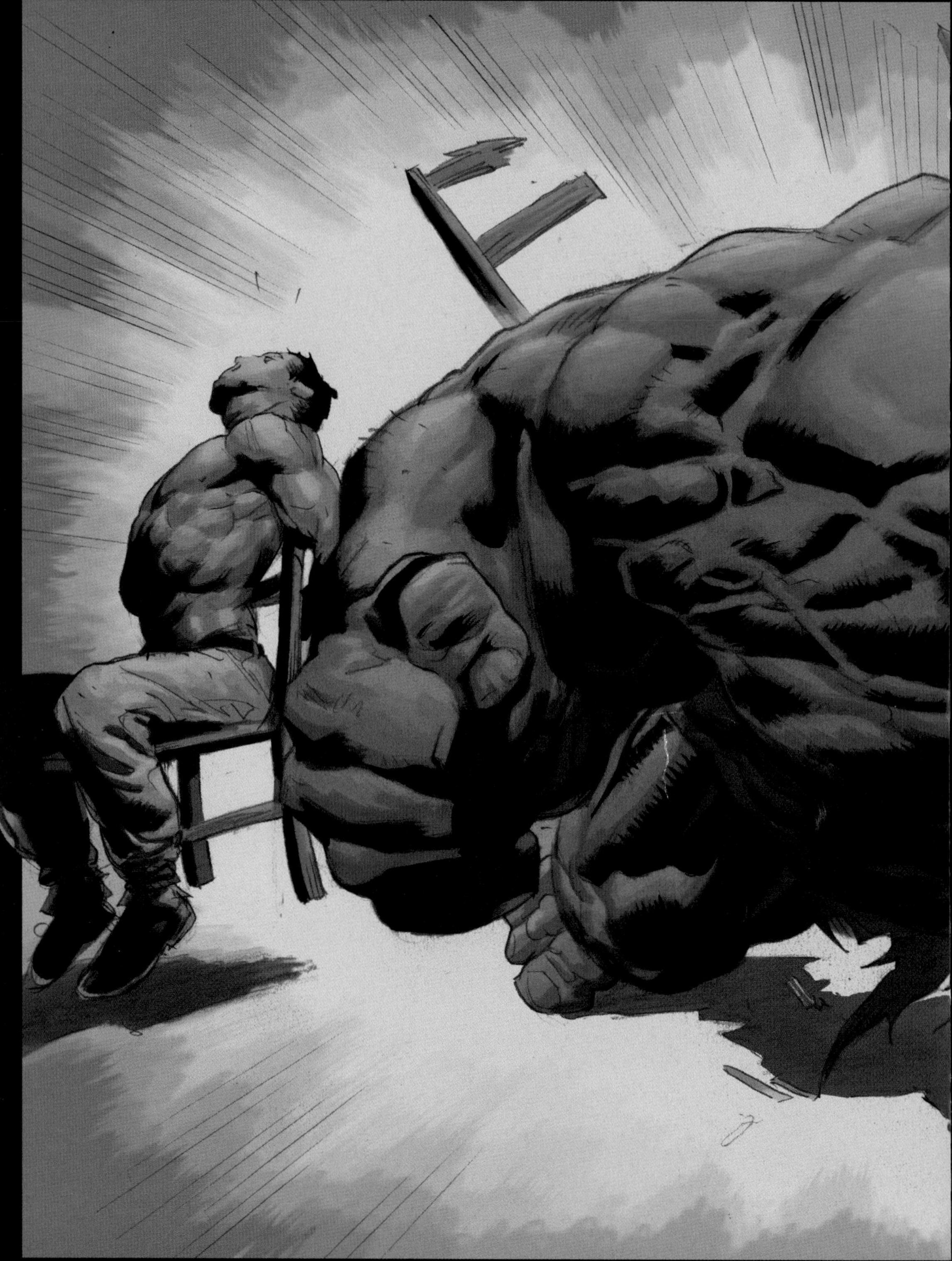

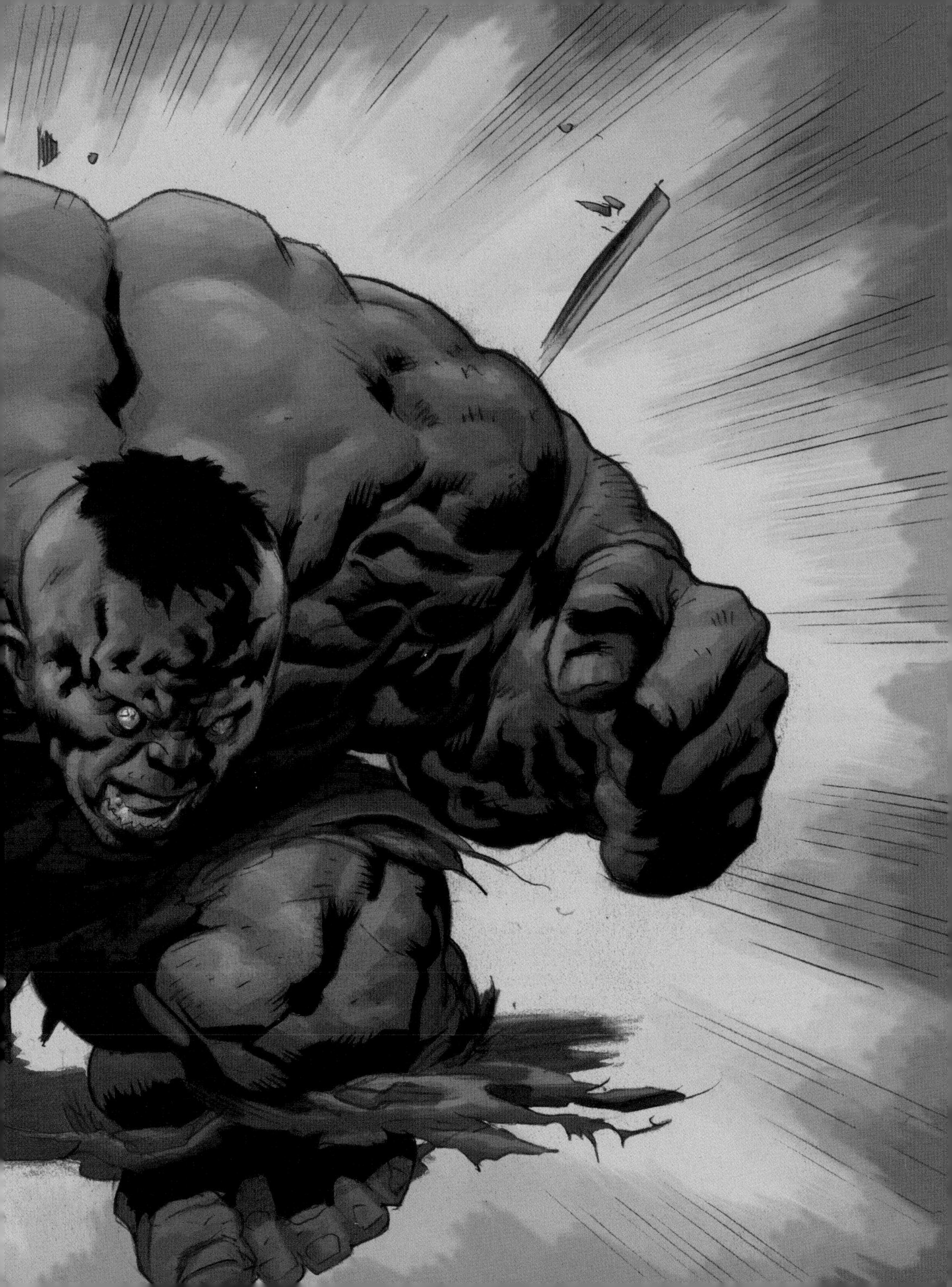

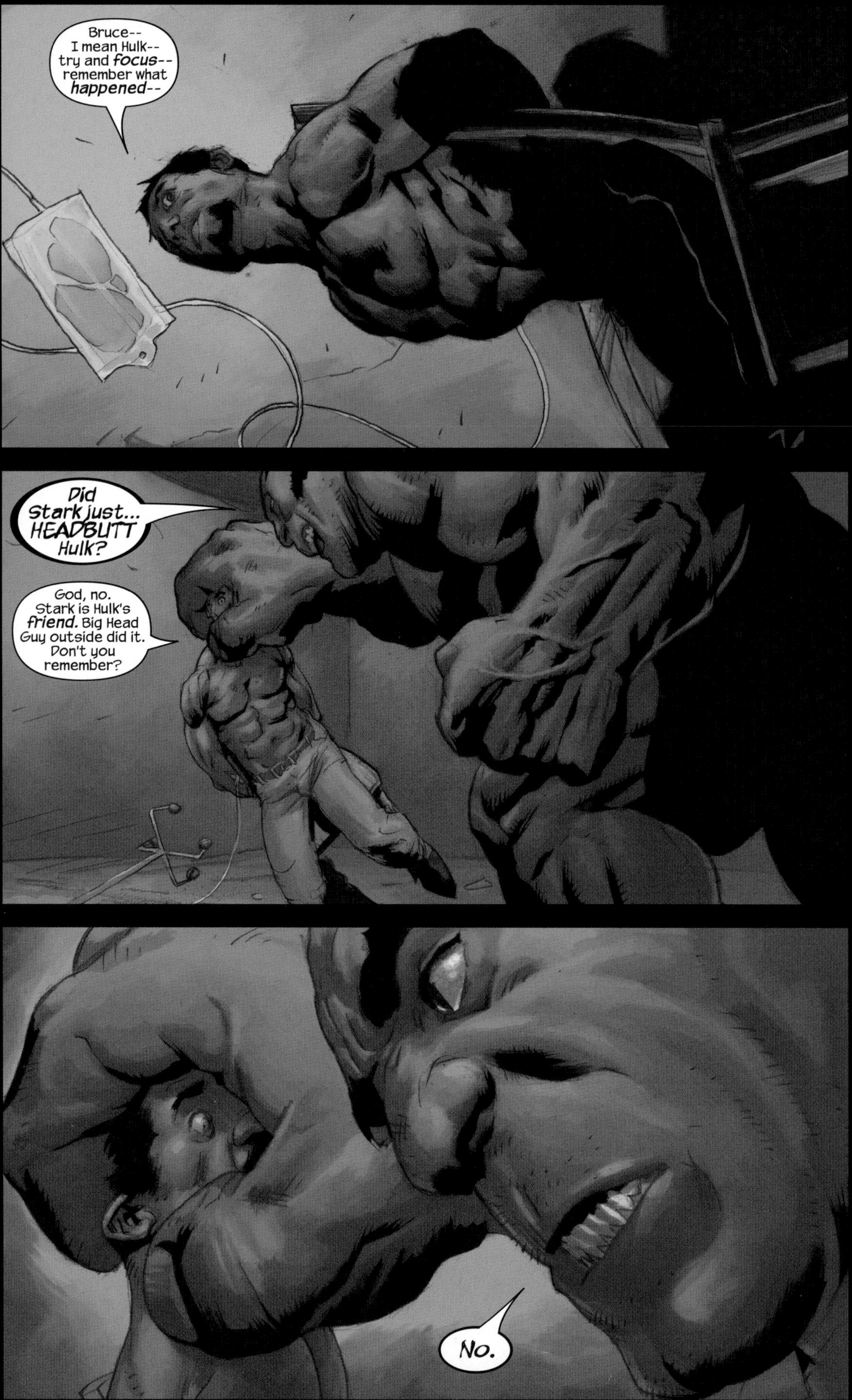

Bruce-- I mean Hulk-- try and focus-- remember what happened--
Did Stark just... HEADBUTT Hulk?
God, no. Stark is Hulk's friend. Big Head Guy outside did it. Don't you remember?
No.

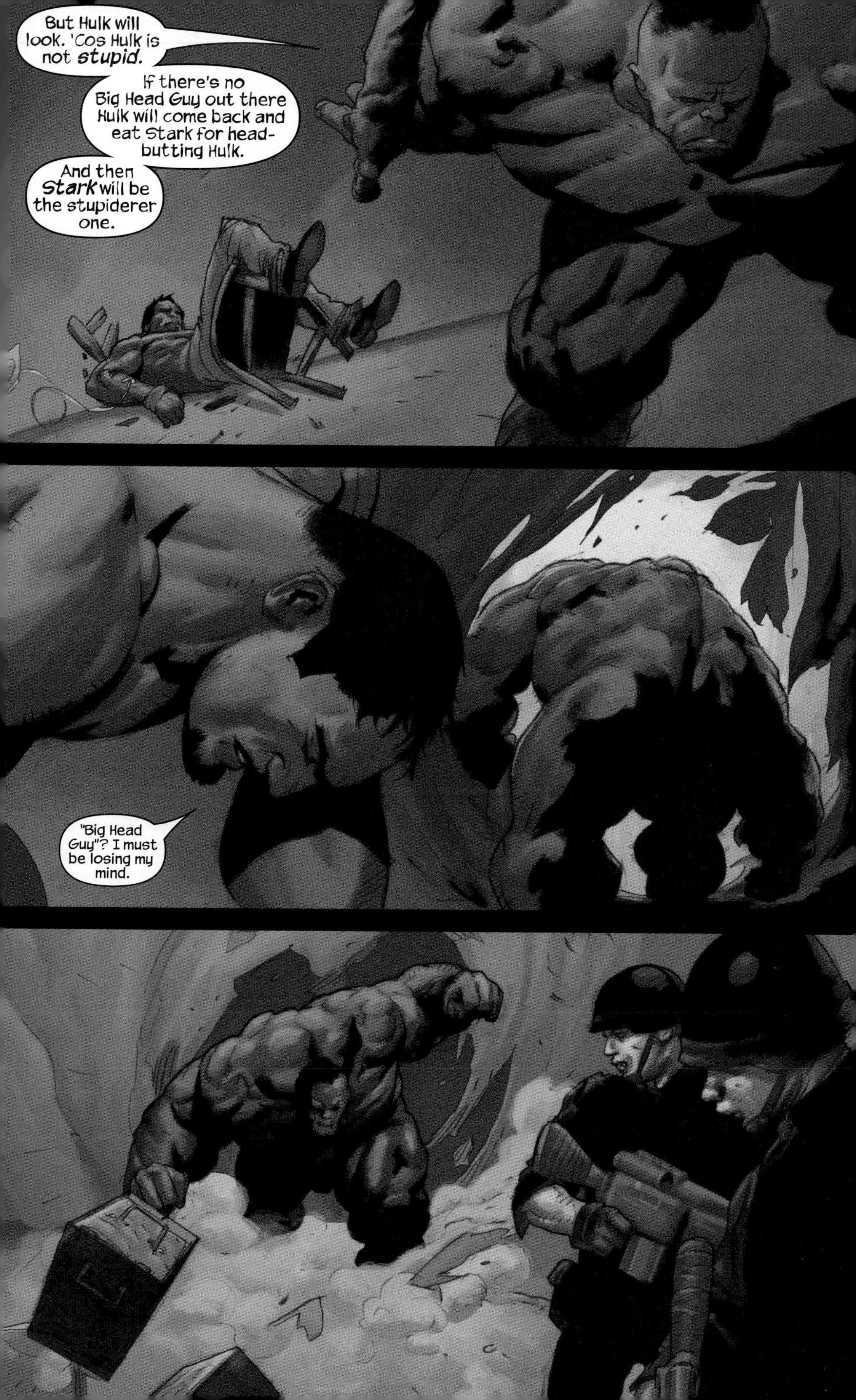
But Hulk will look. 'Cos Hulk is not *stupid.*
If there's no Big Head Guy out there Hulk will come back and eat Stark for head-butting Hulk.
And then *Stark* will be the stupiderer one.
"Big Head Guy"? I must be losing my mind.

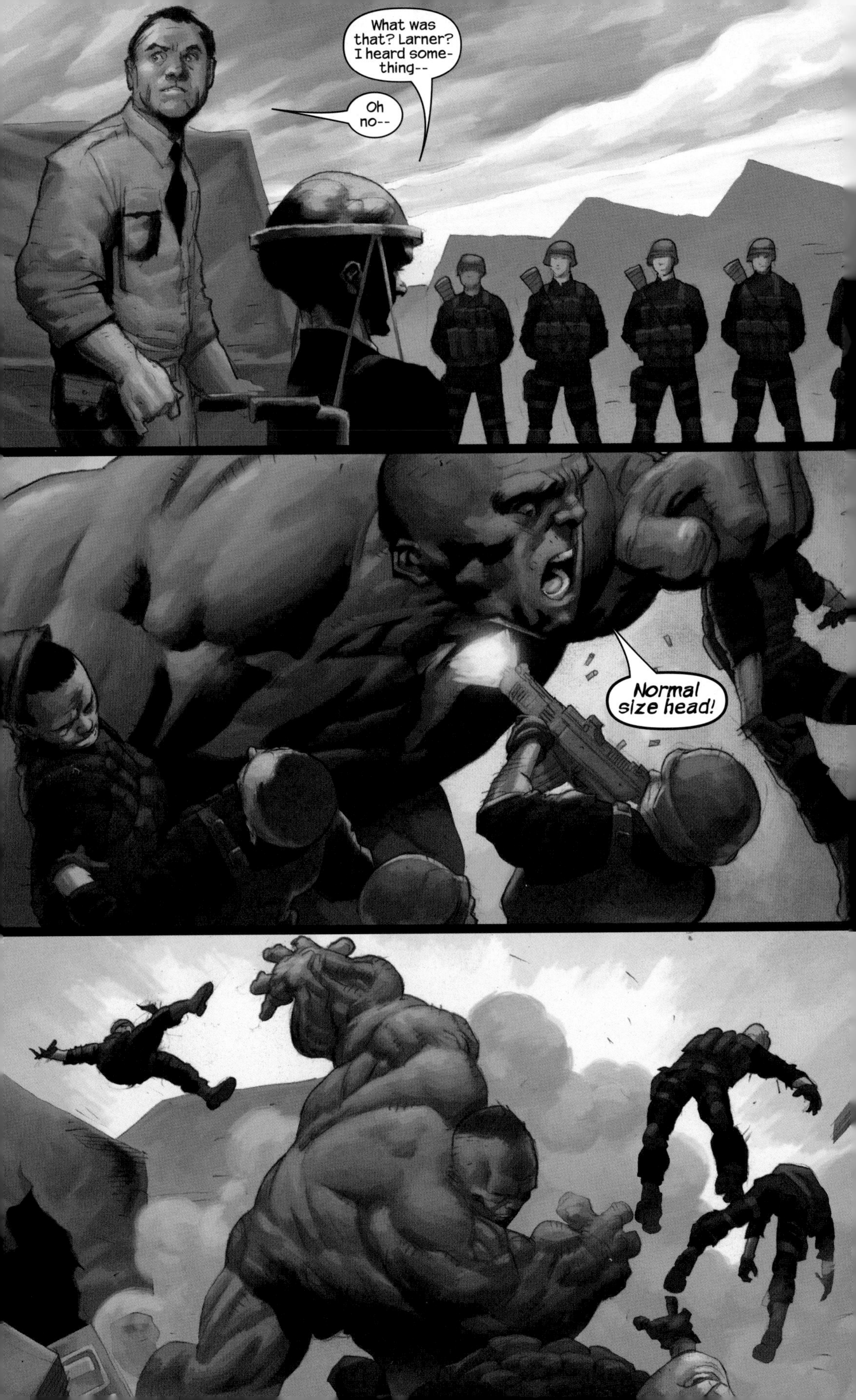
What was that? Larner? I heard something--
Oh no--
Normal size head!

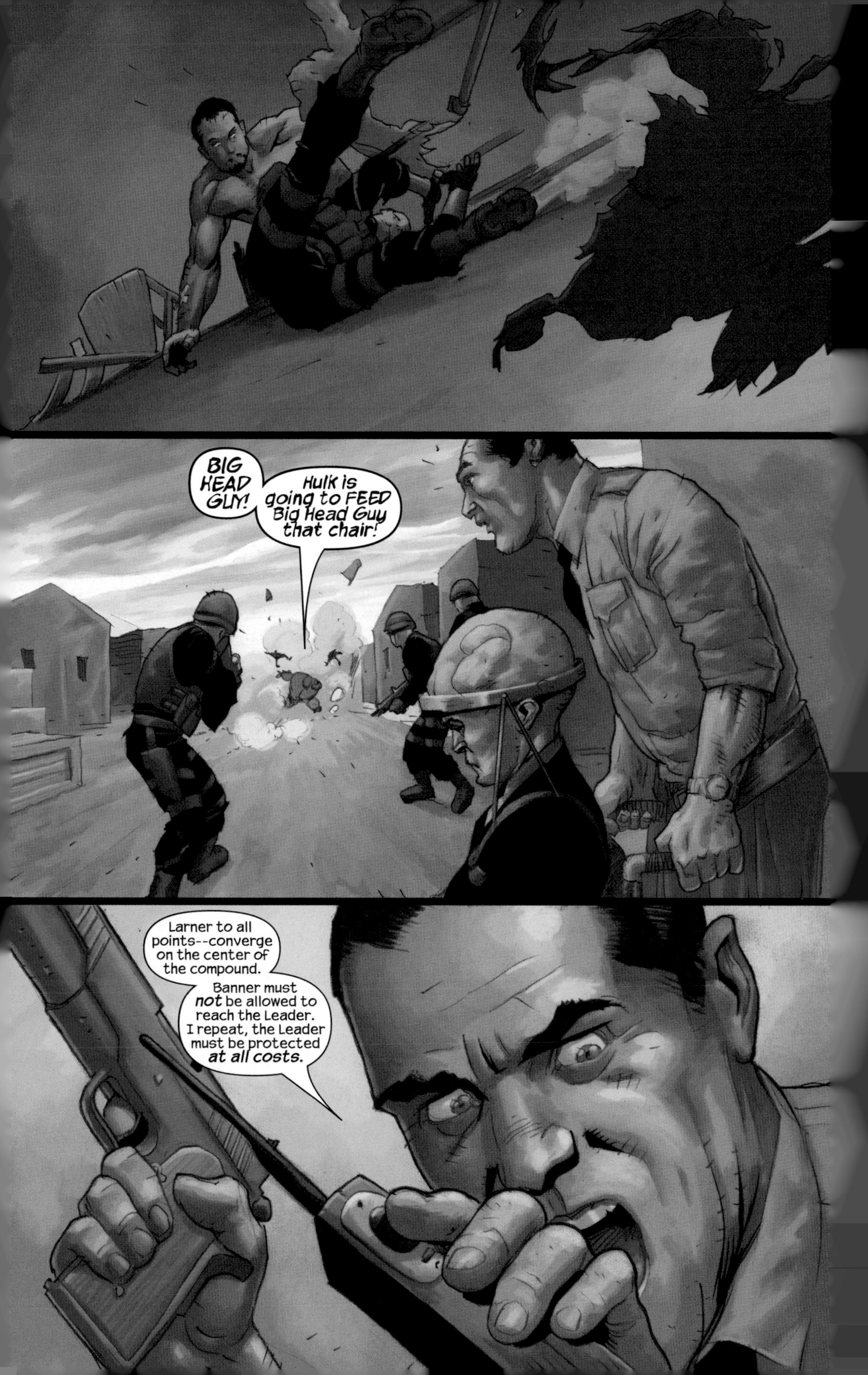
BIG HEAD GUY!
Hulk is going to FEED Big Head Guy that chair!
Larner to all points--converge on the center of the compound.
Banner must **not** be allowed to reach the Leader. I repeat, the Leader must be protected **at all costs**.

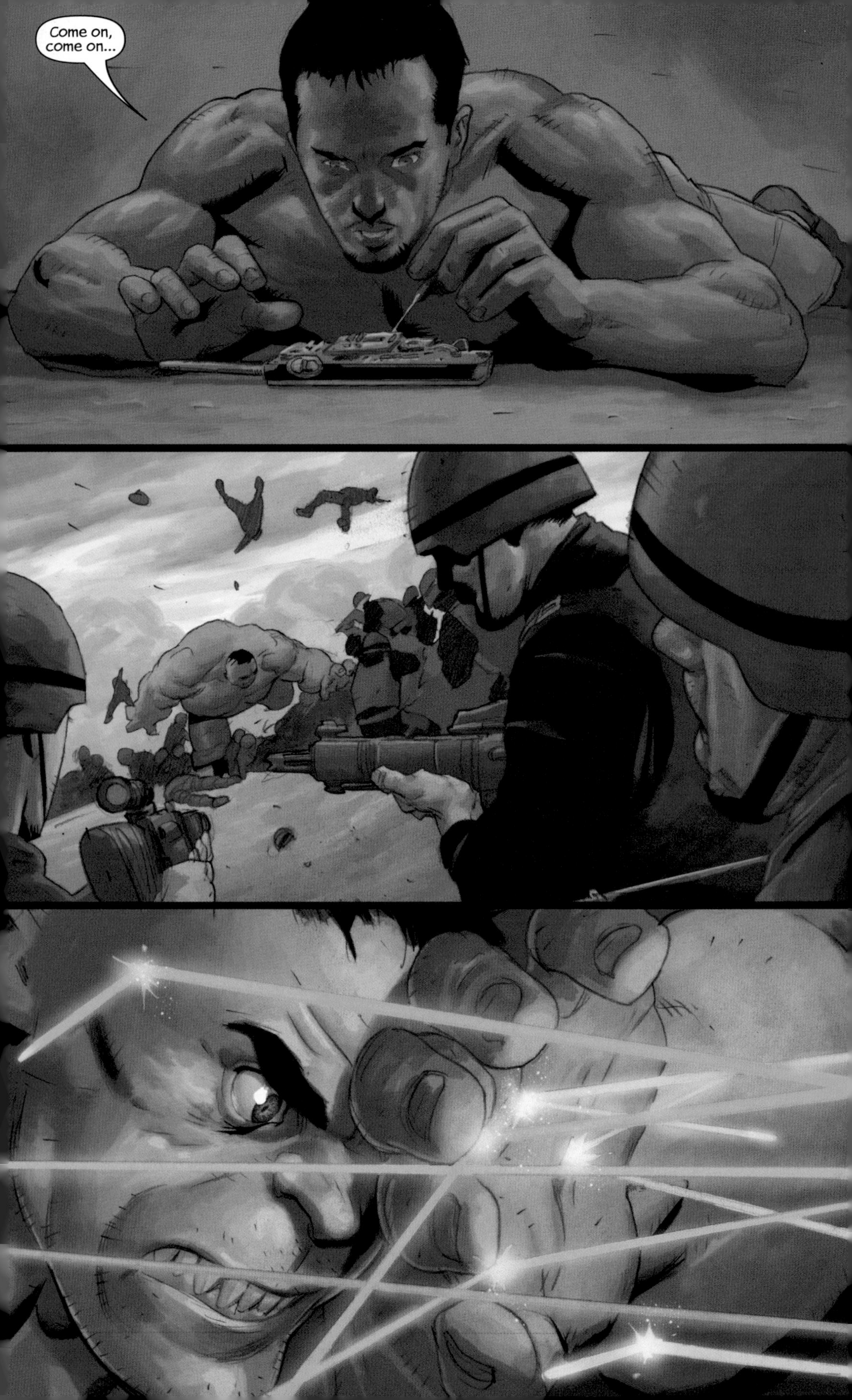
Come on, come on...

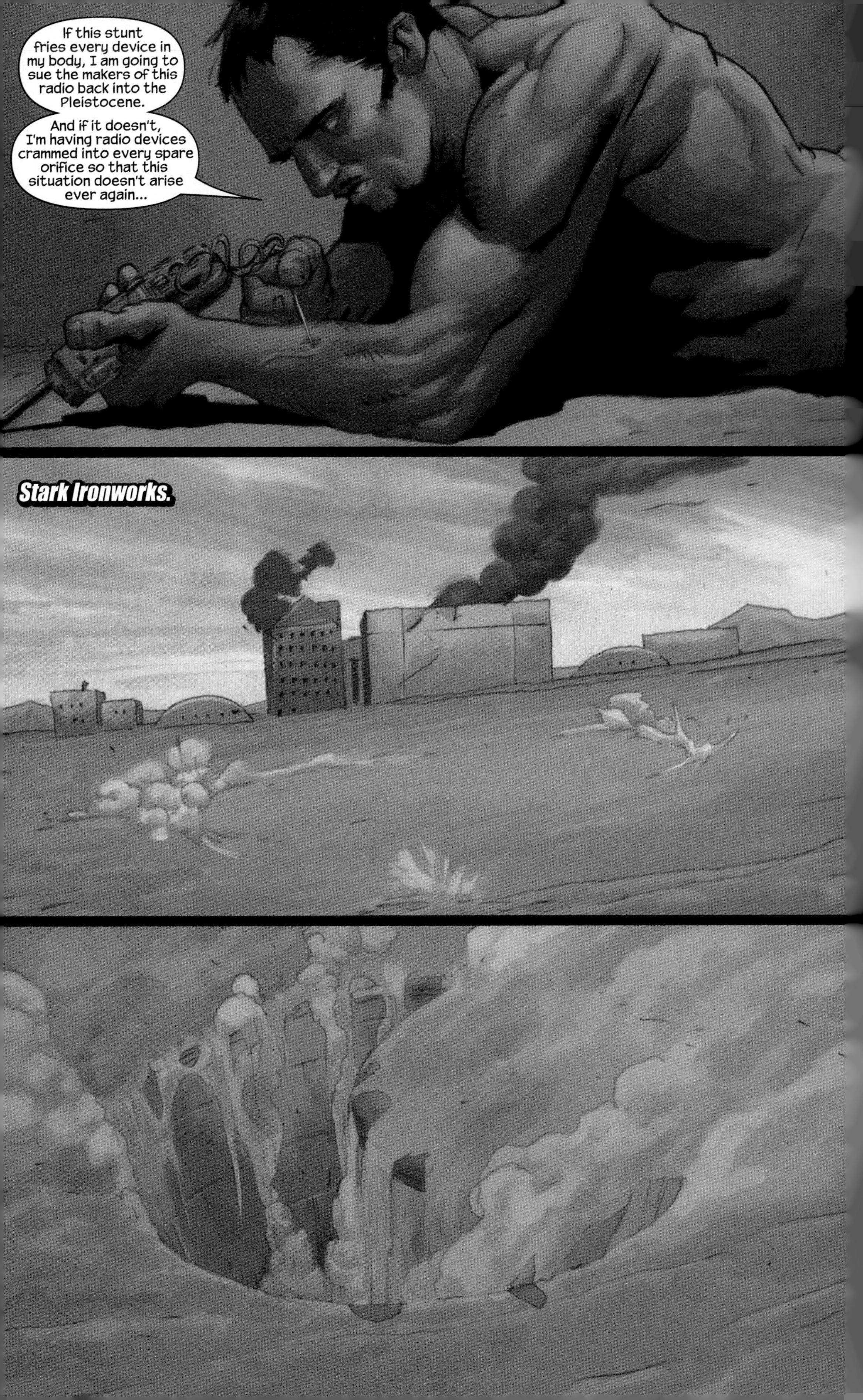
If this stunt fries every device in my body, I am going to sue the makers of this radio back into the Pleistocene.
And if it doesn't, I'm having radio devices crammed into every spare orifice so that this situation doesn't arise ever again...
Stark Ironworks.

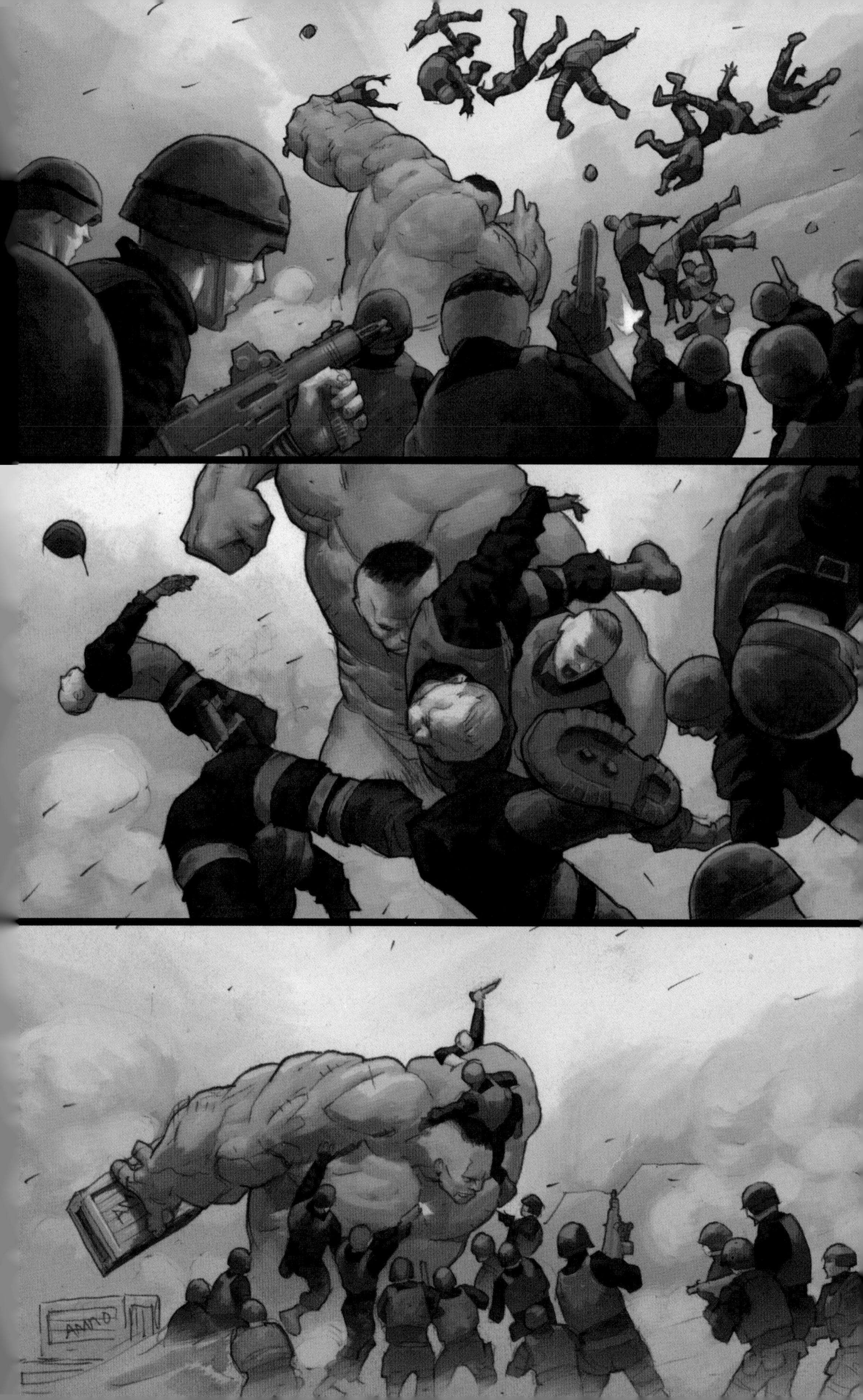
AMMO

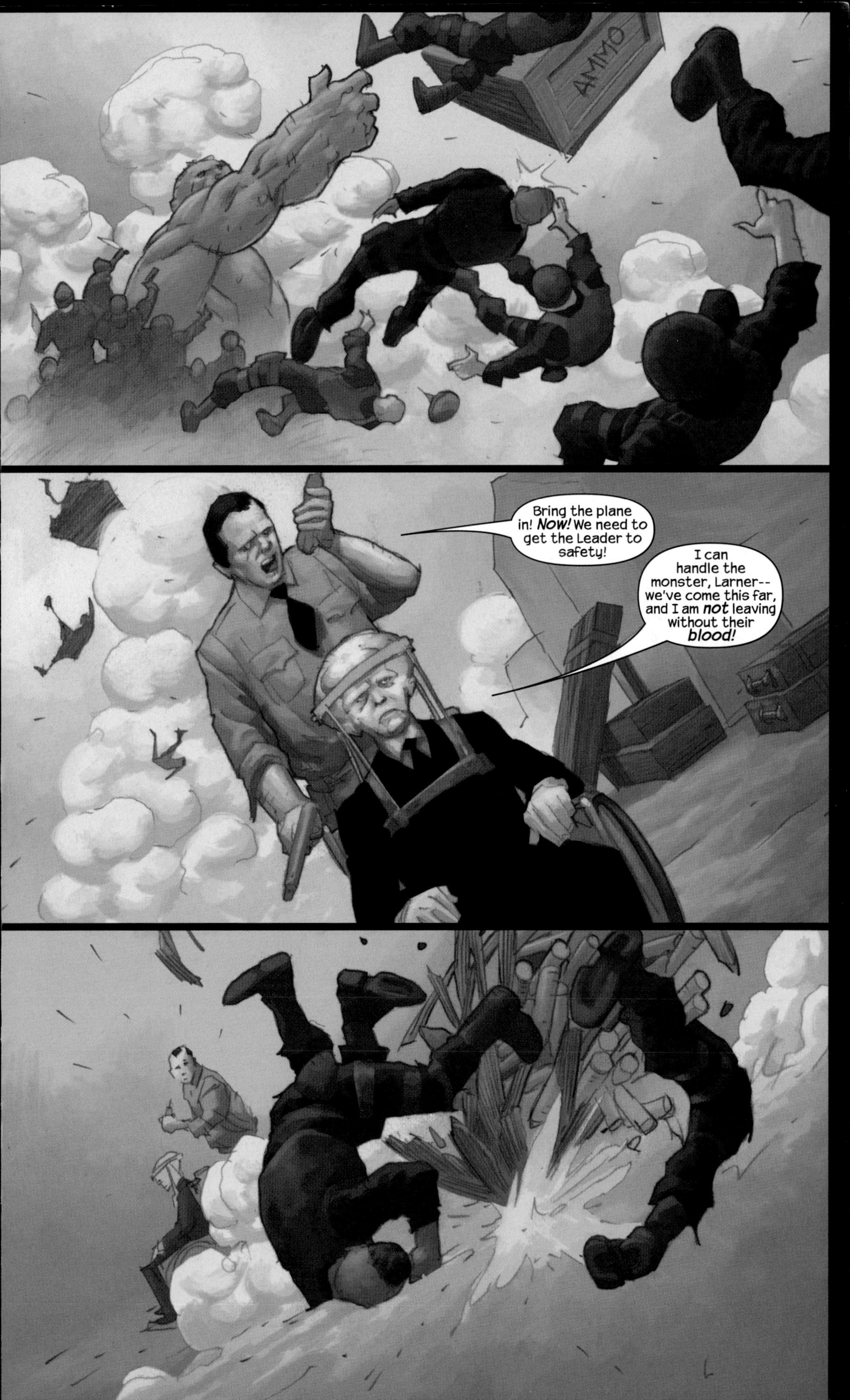
AMMO
Bring the plane in! *NOW!* We need to get the Leader to safety!
I can handle the monster, Larner-- we've come this far, and I am *not* leaving without their *blood!*

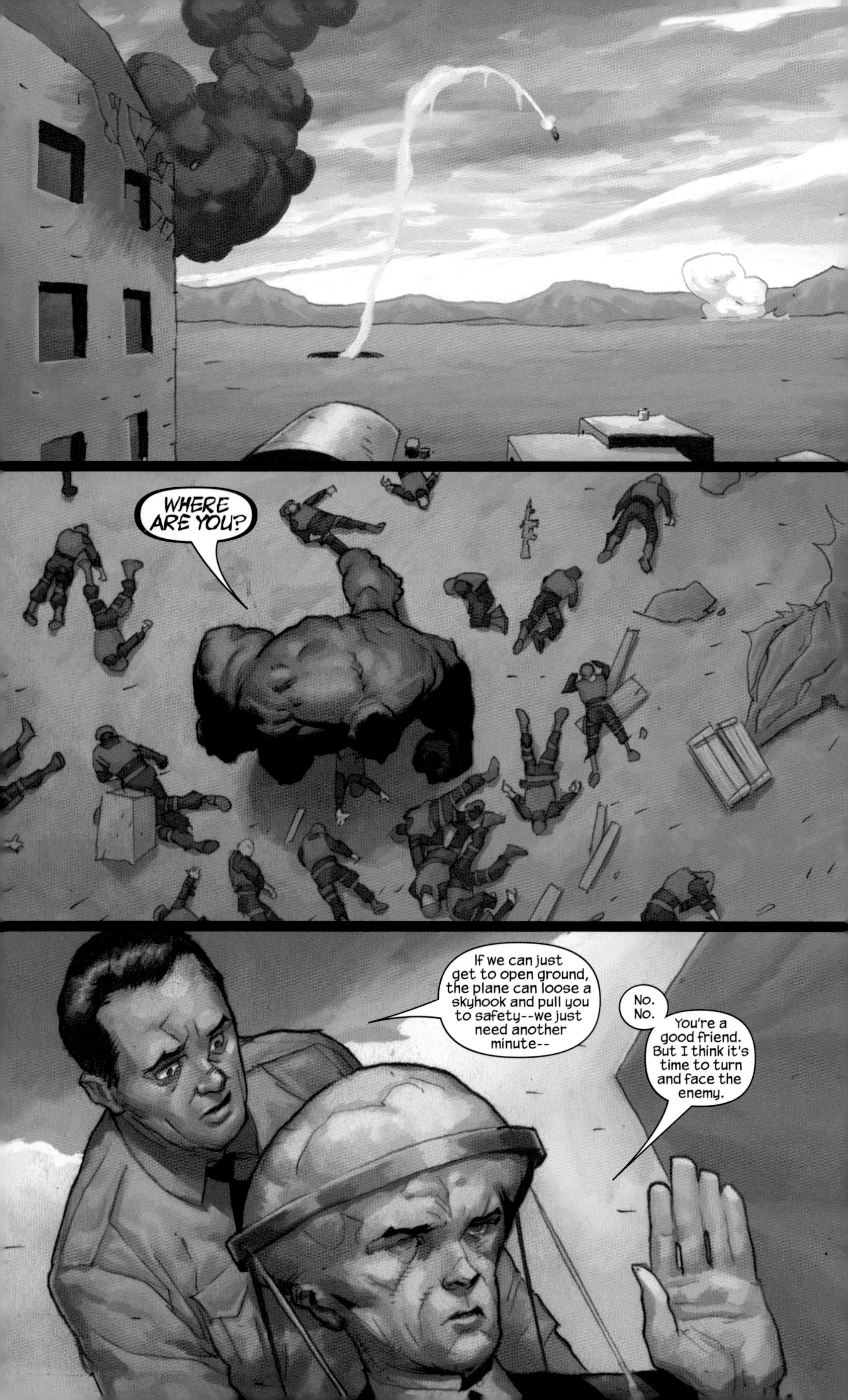
WHERE ARE YOU?
If we can just get to open ground, the plane can loose a skyhook and pull you to safety--we just need another minute--
No. No.
You're a good friend. But I think it's time to turn and face the enemy.

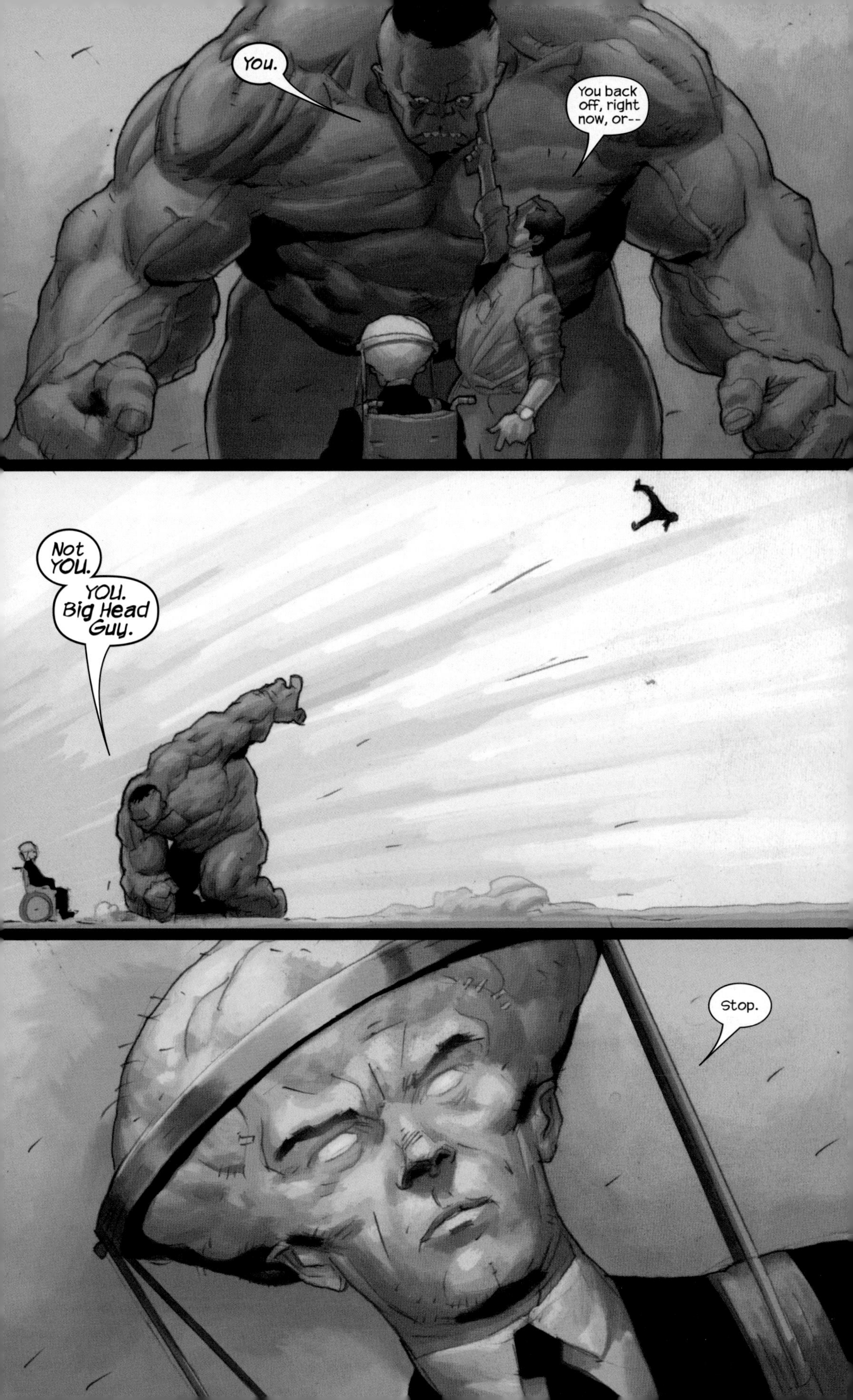
You.
You back off, right now, or--
Not YOU.
YOU. Big Head Guy.
Stop.

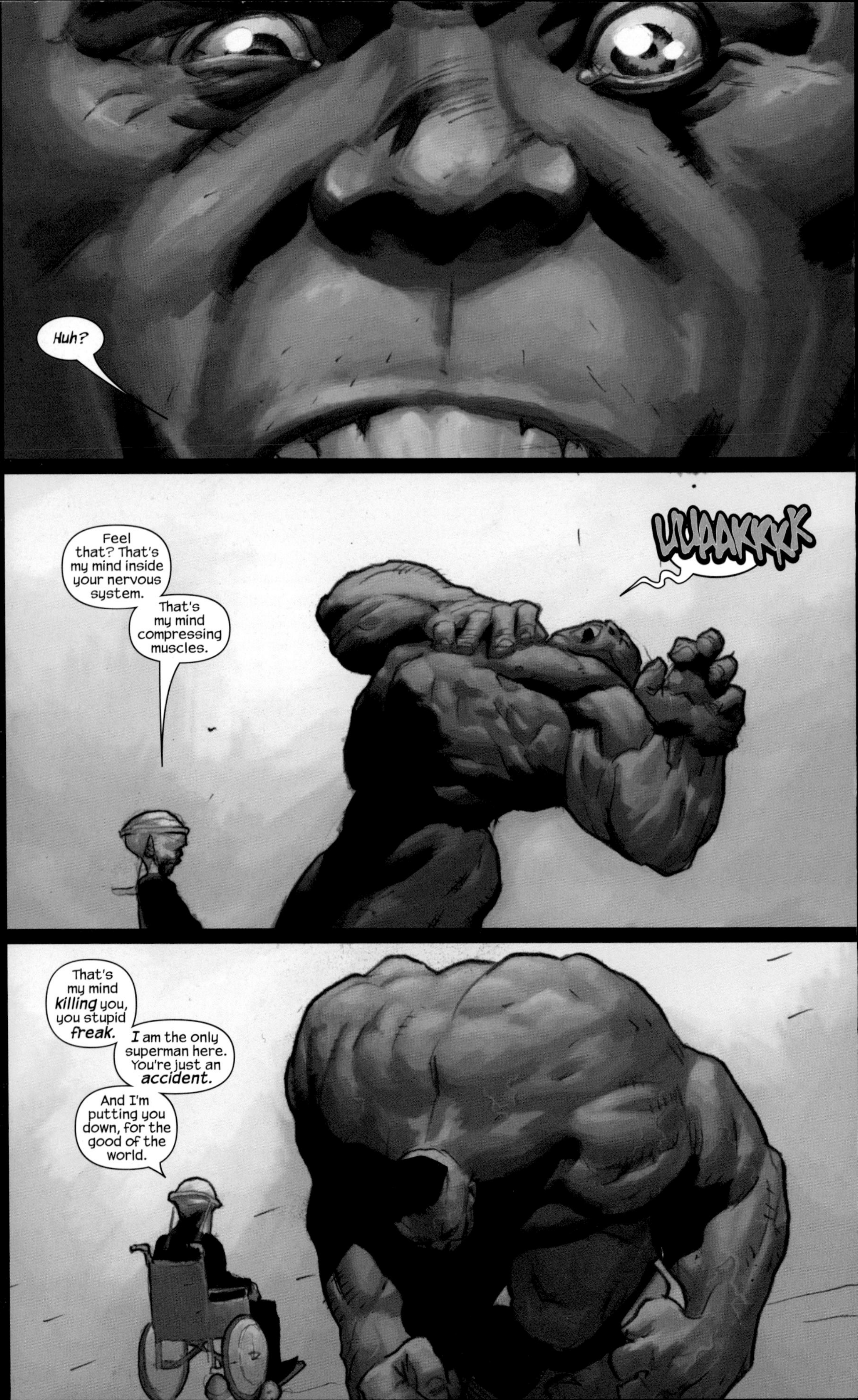

Huh?
Feel that? That's my mind inside your nervous system.
That's my mind compressing muscles.
UUAAKKKK
That's my mind *killing* you, you stupid *freak.*
I am the only superman here. You're just an *accident.*
And I'm putting you down, for the good of the world.

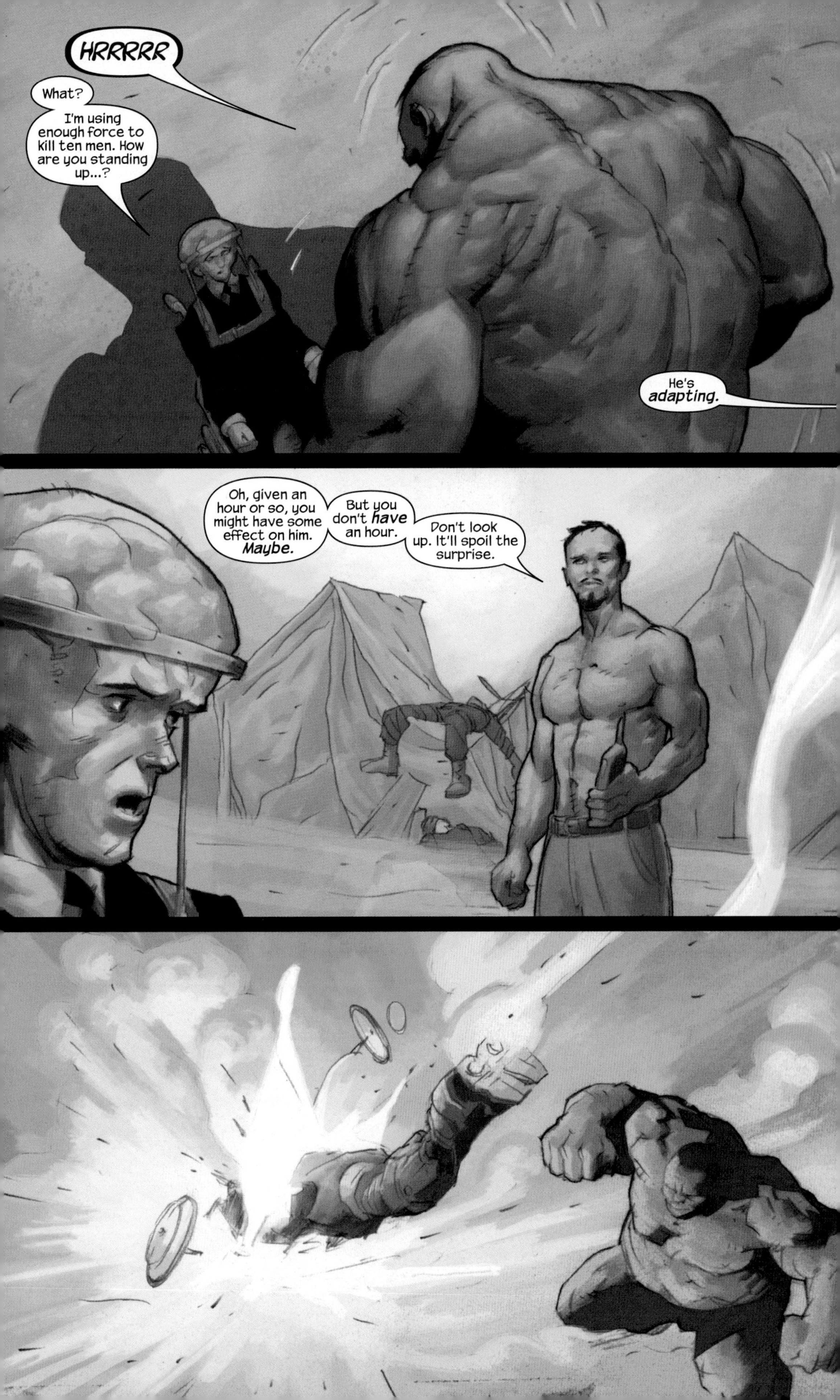
HRRRRR
What?
I'm using enough force to kill ten men. How are you standing up...?
He's adapting.
Oh, given an hour or so, you might have some effect on him. Maybe.
But you don't have an hour.
Don't look up. It'll spoil the surprise.

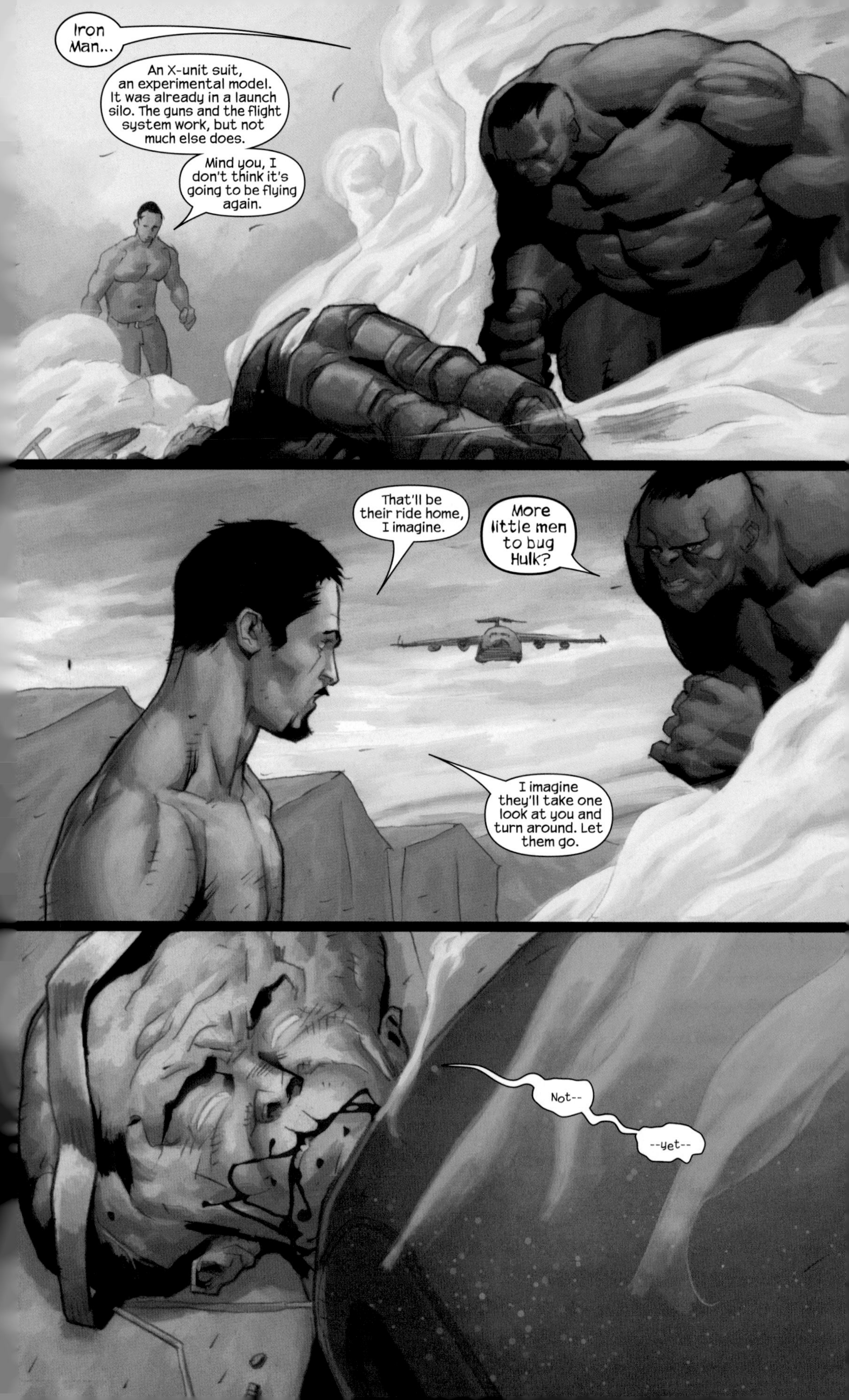

Iron Man...
An X-unit suit, an experimental model. It was already in a launch silo. The guns and the flight system work, but not much else does.
Mind you, I don't think it's going to be flying again.
That'll be their ride home, I imagine.
More little men to bug Hulk?
I imagine they'll take one look at you and turn around. Let them go.
Not--
--yet--

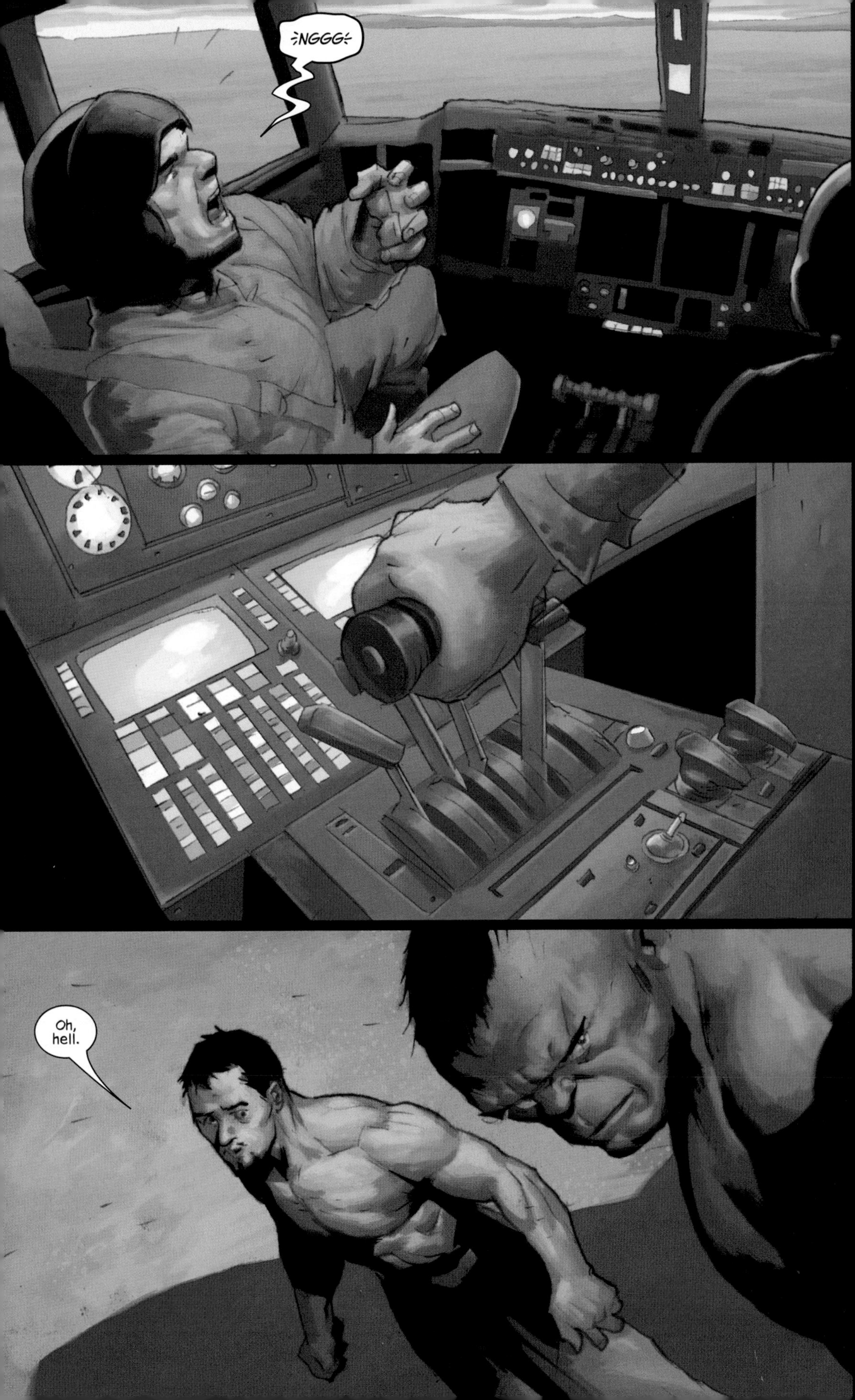
NGGG
Oh, hell.

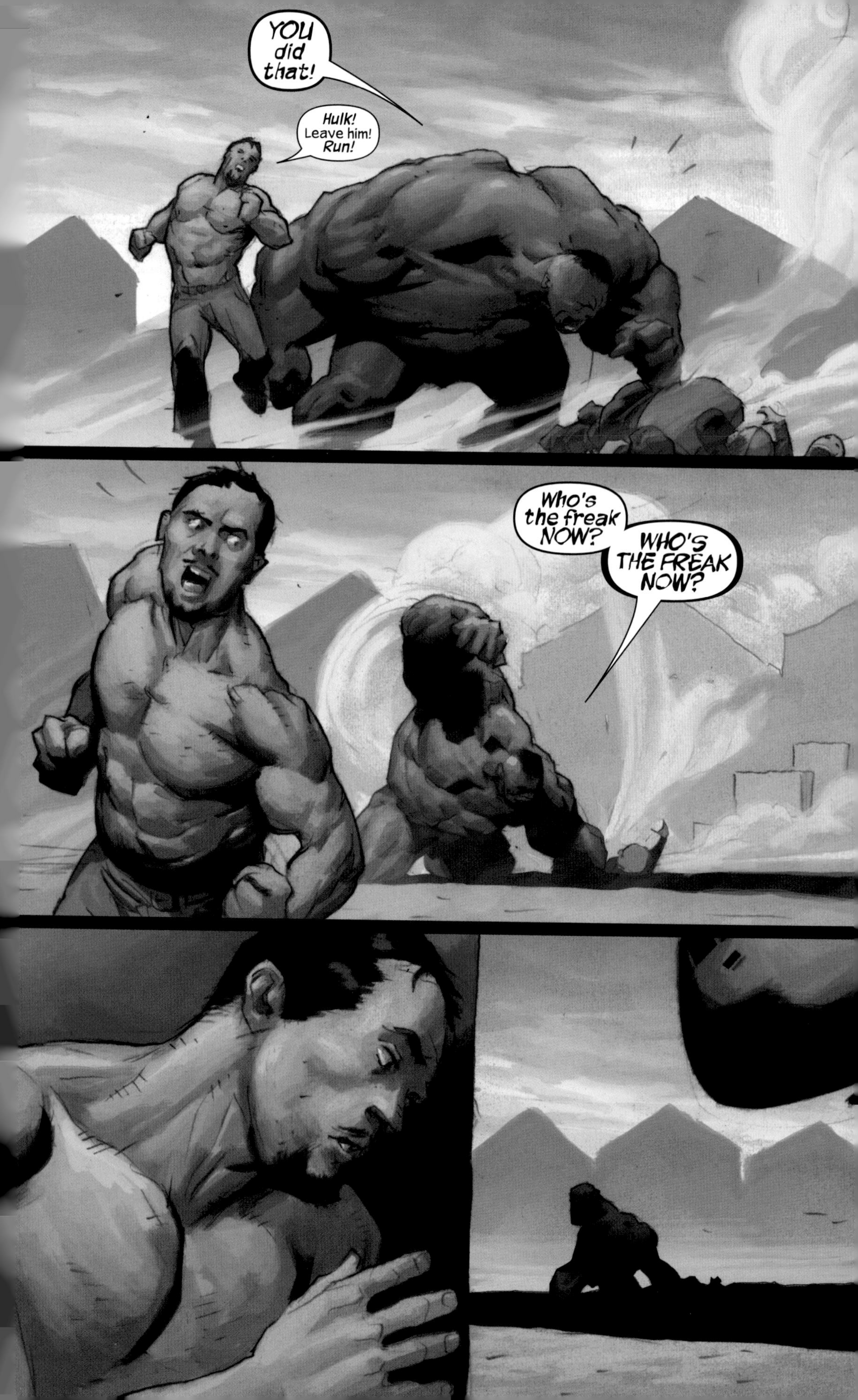
YOU did that!
Hulk! Leave him! Run!
Who's the freak NOW?
WHO'S THE FREAK NOW?

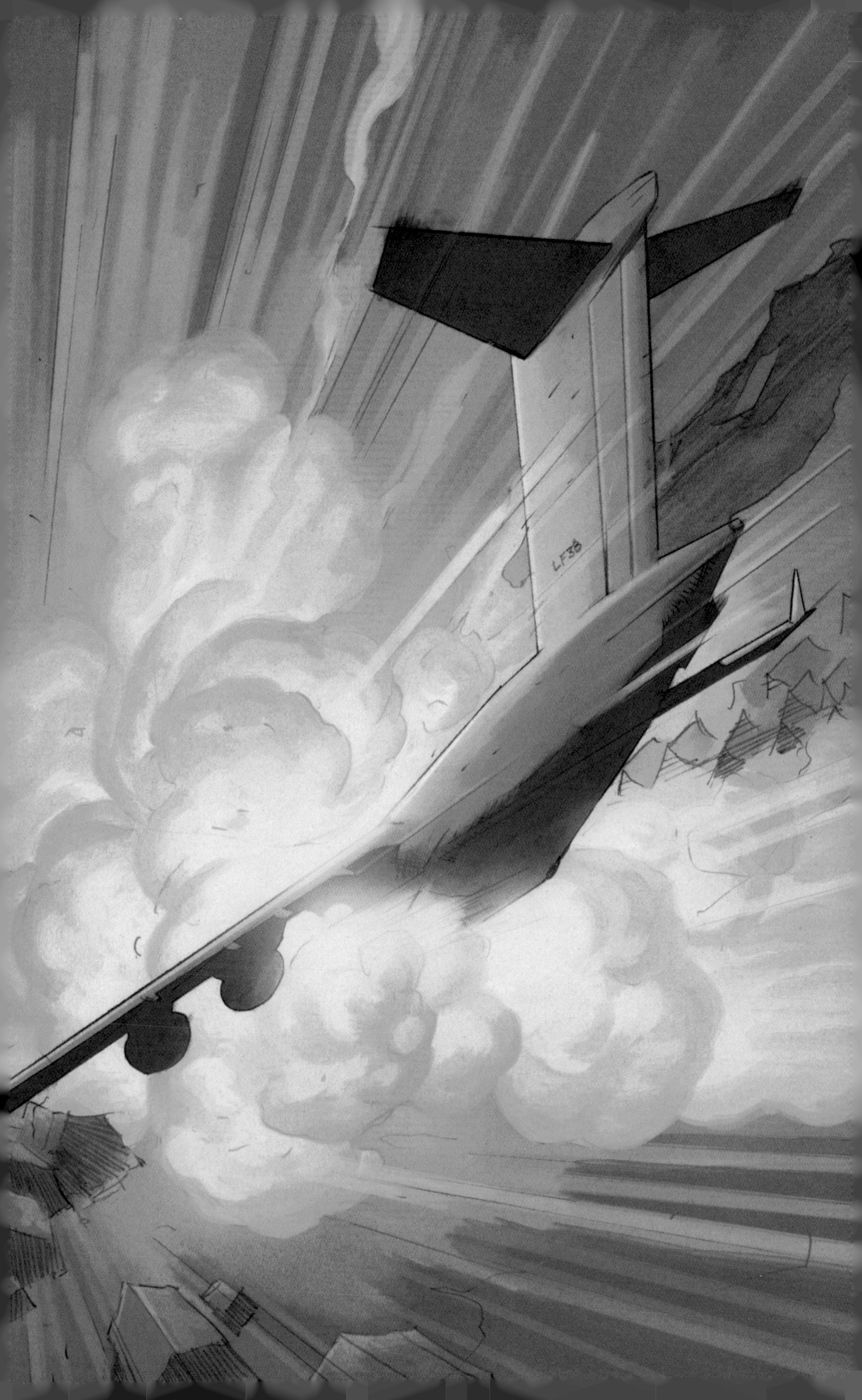
LF38

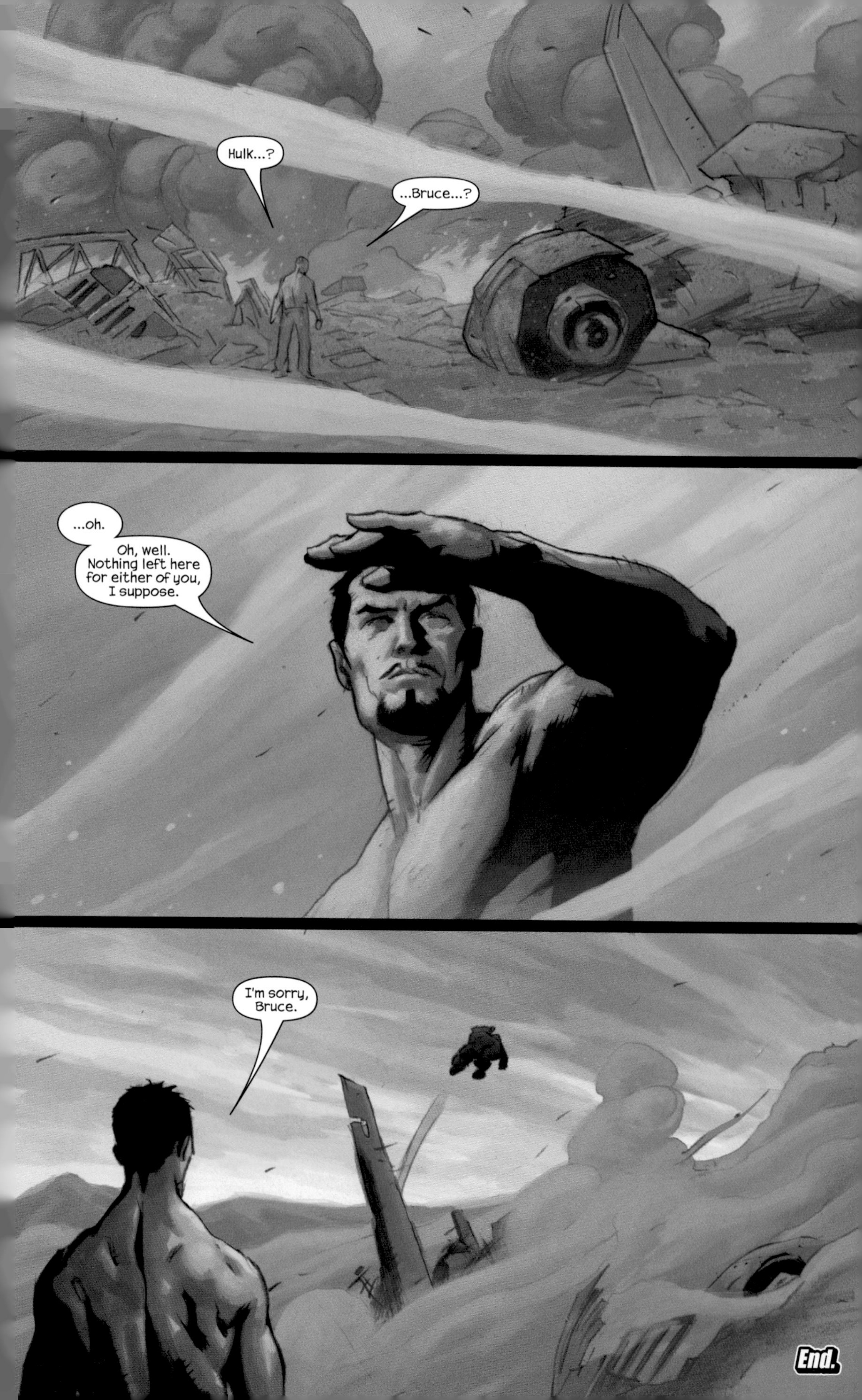
Hulk...?
...Bruce...?
...oh.
Oh, well.
Nothing left here
for either of you,
I suppose.
I'm sorry,
Bruce.
End.

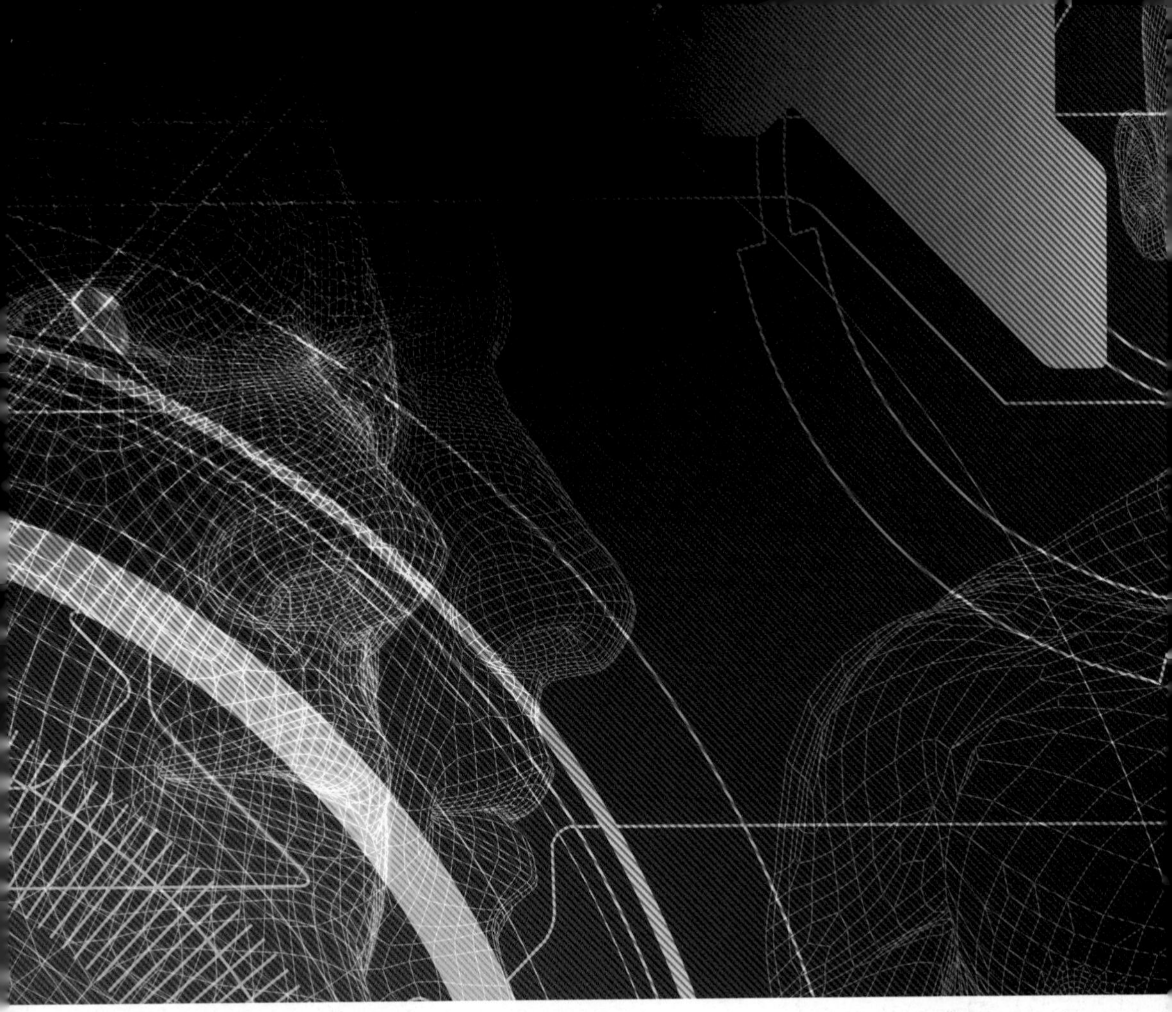

COVER SKETCHES
BY CARY NORD

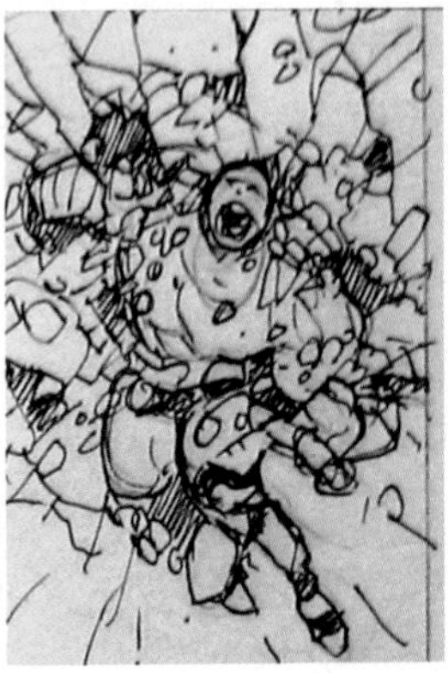

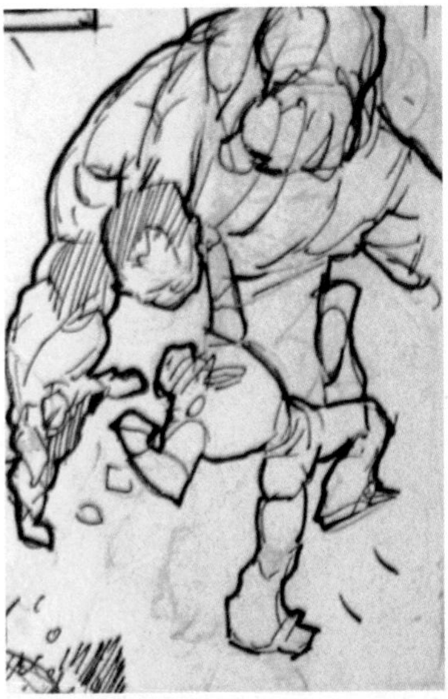

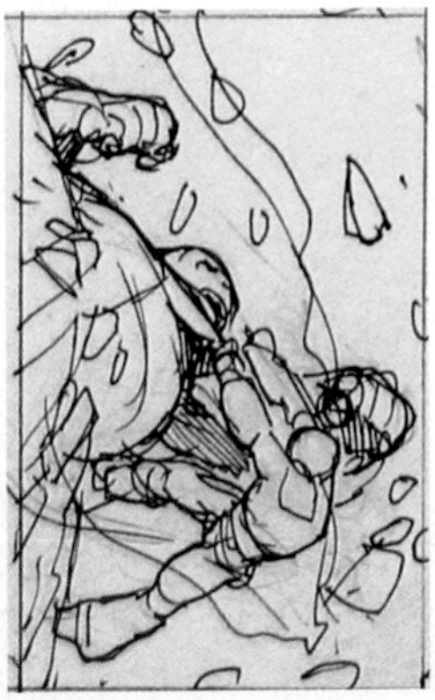

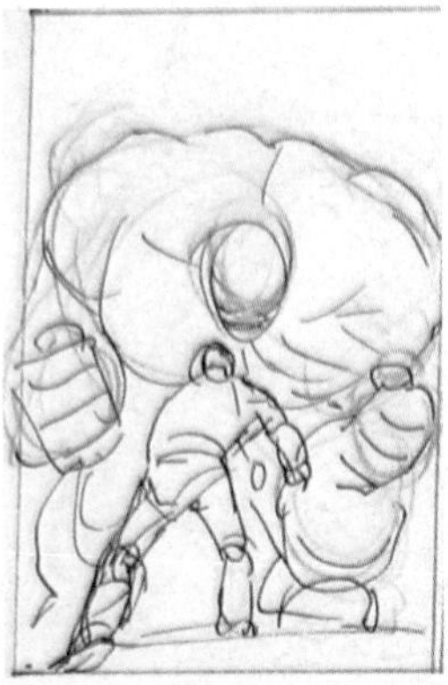

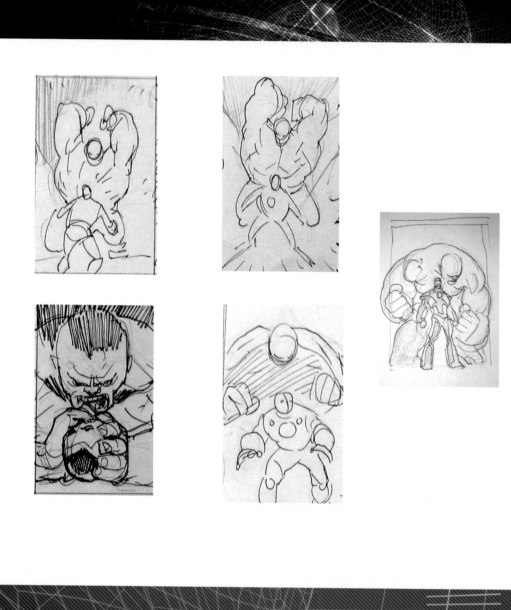

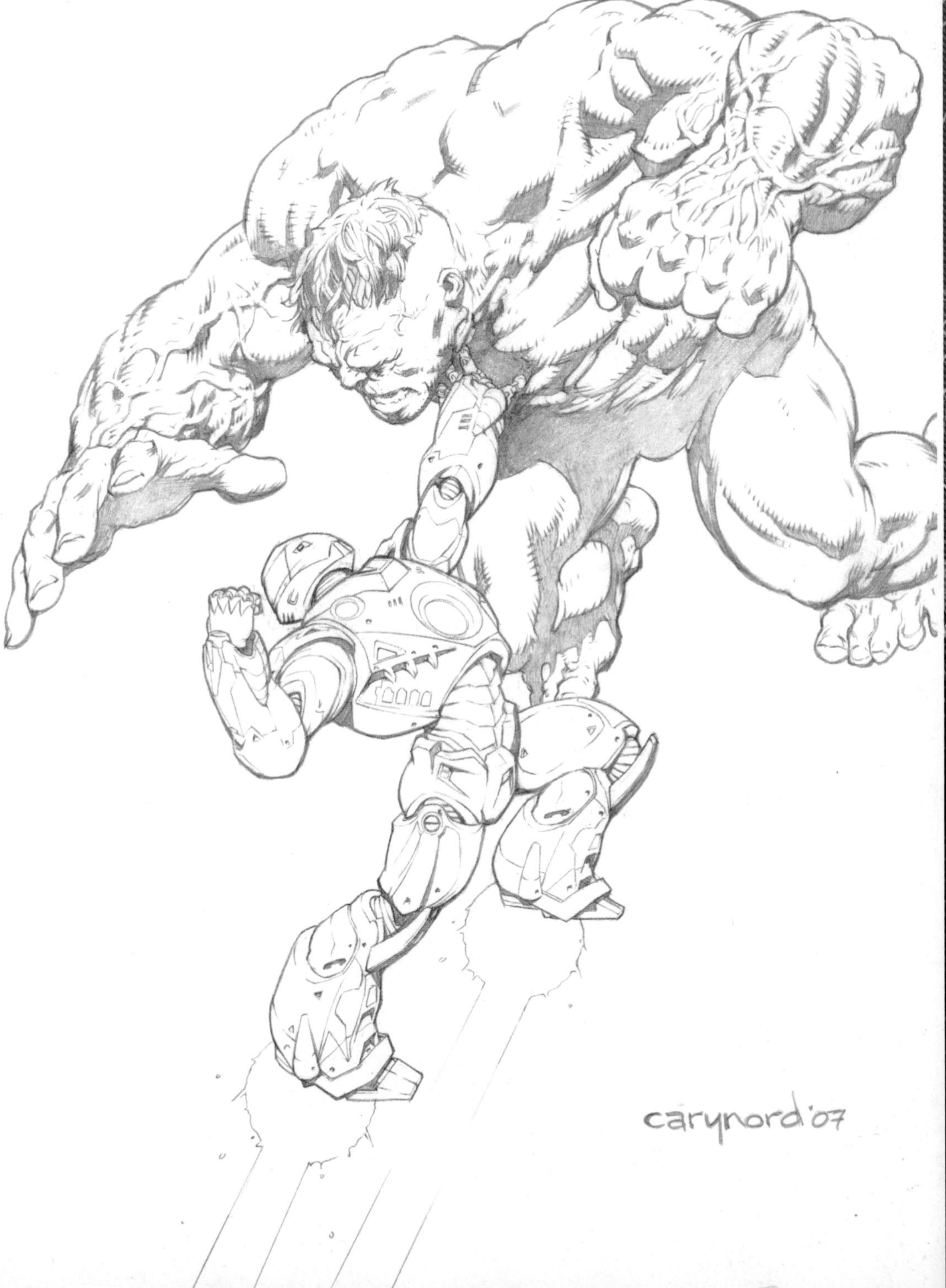
carynord '07

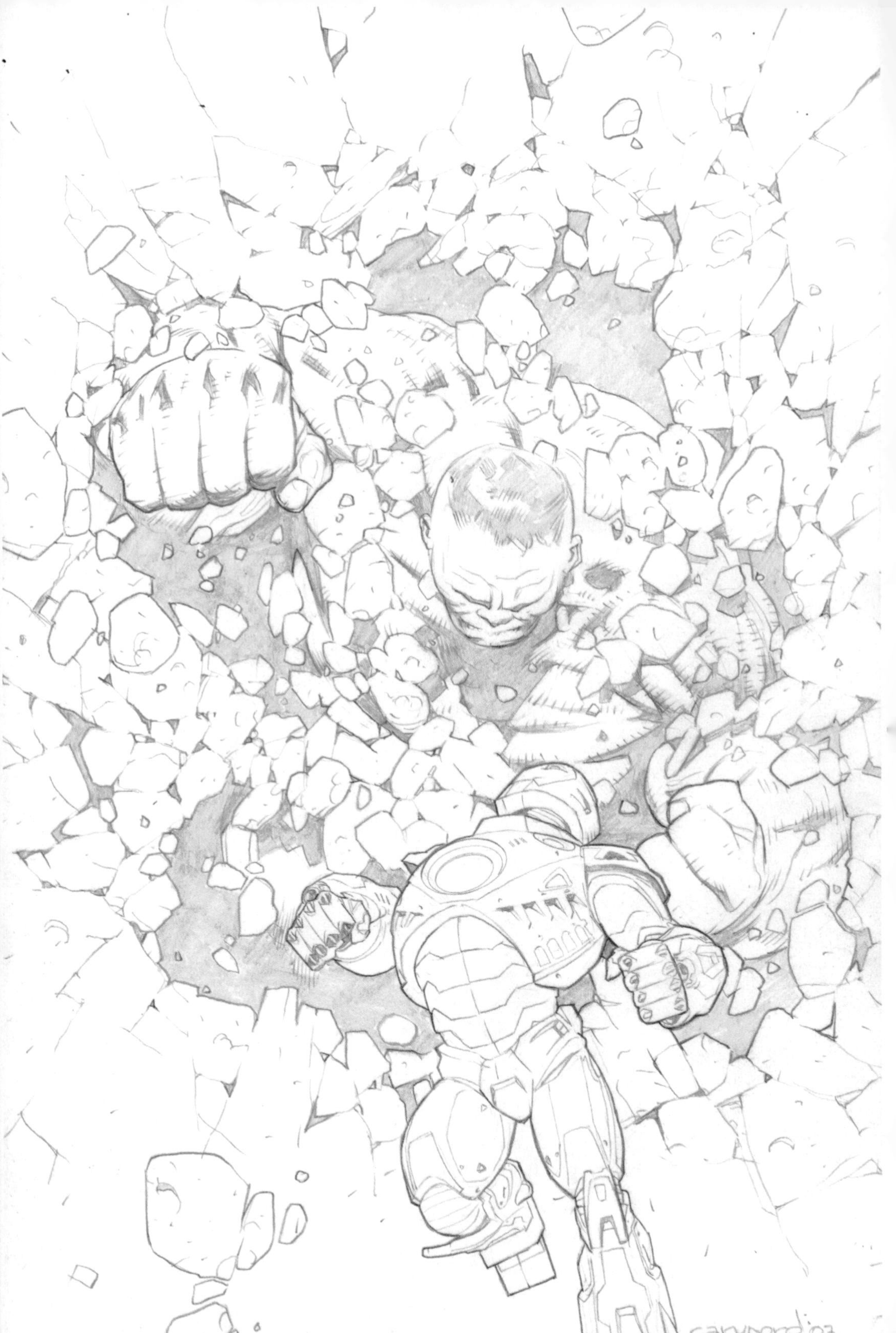
carynord '07

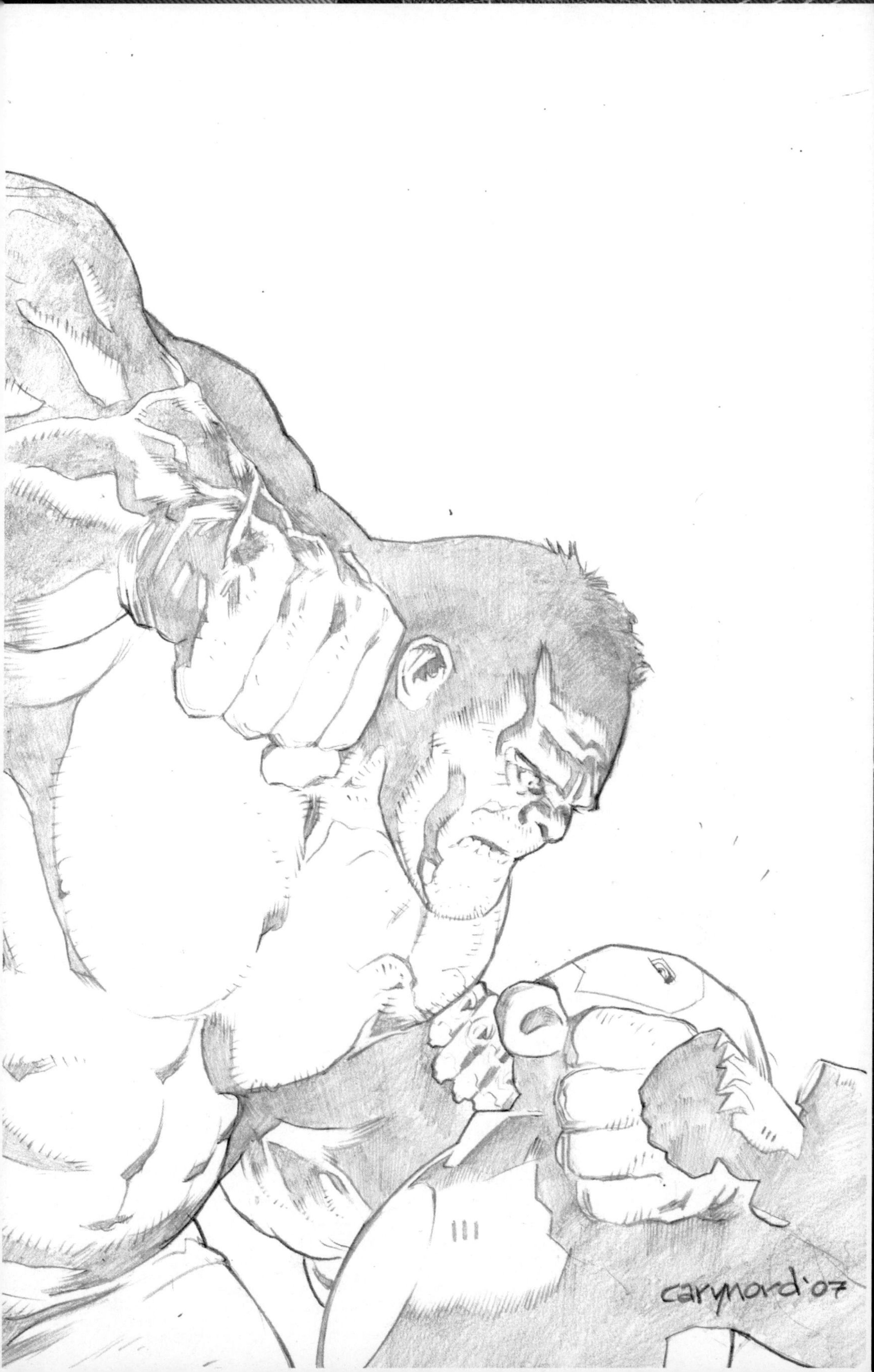
carynord'07

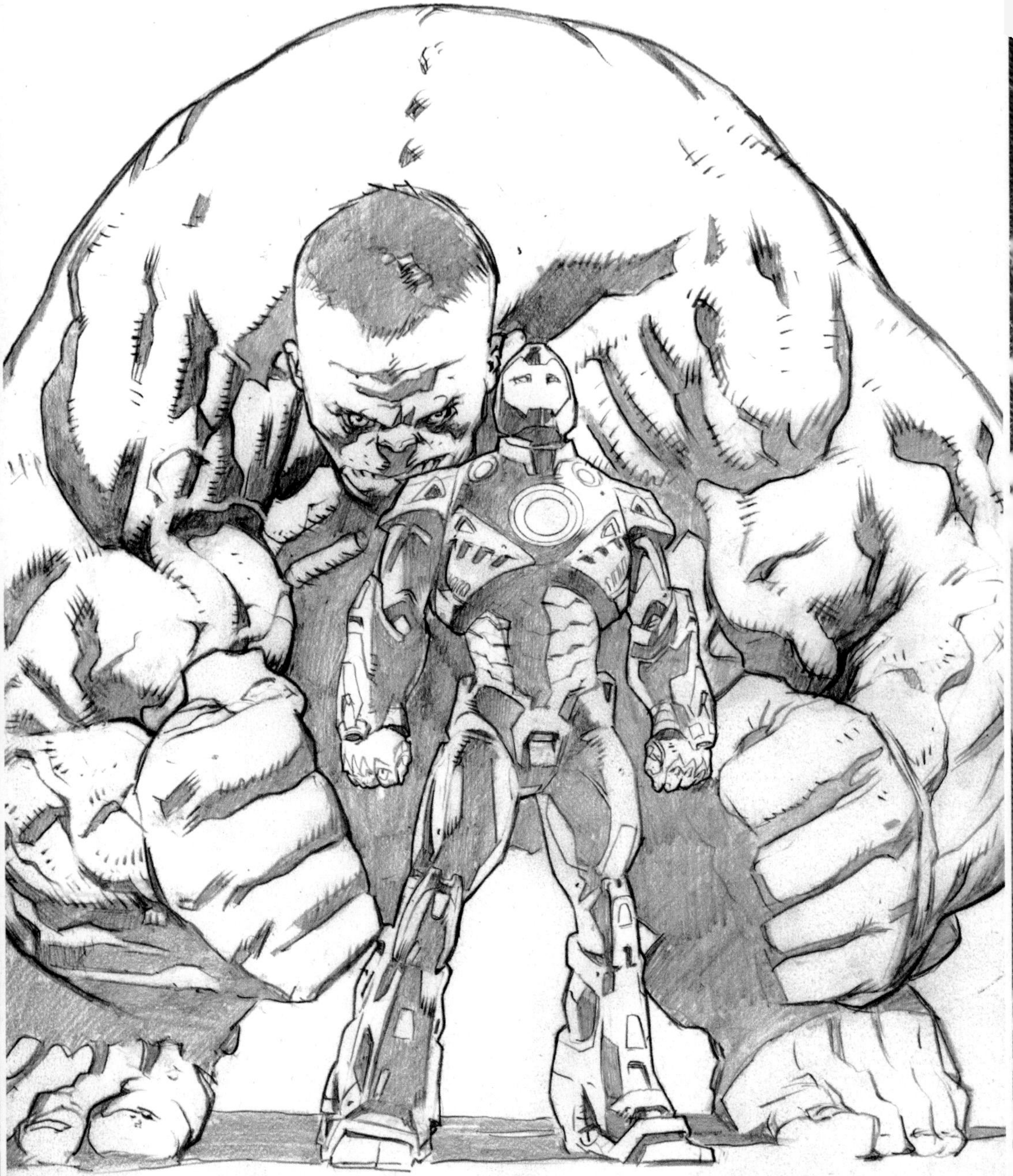
carynord '07

PORTFOLIO REVIEW

What happens when you get better after having a nuclear bomb dropped on you? If you're the Hulk, you go smash the person responsible: Tony Stark. From the mind of writer Warren Ellis and brought to powerful life by Cary Nord, comes the fight of the century, Ultimate Iron Man vs. Ultimate Hulk locked in a battle of wills...and fists... as they find who is the ULTIMATE HUMAN.

We sat down with artist Cary Nord and editor Bill Rosemann to get their take on the players involved and what it takes to bring together the two most powerful, and misunderstood, men in the Ultimate Universe!

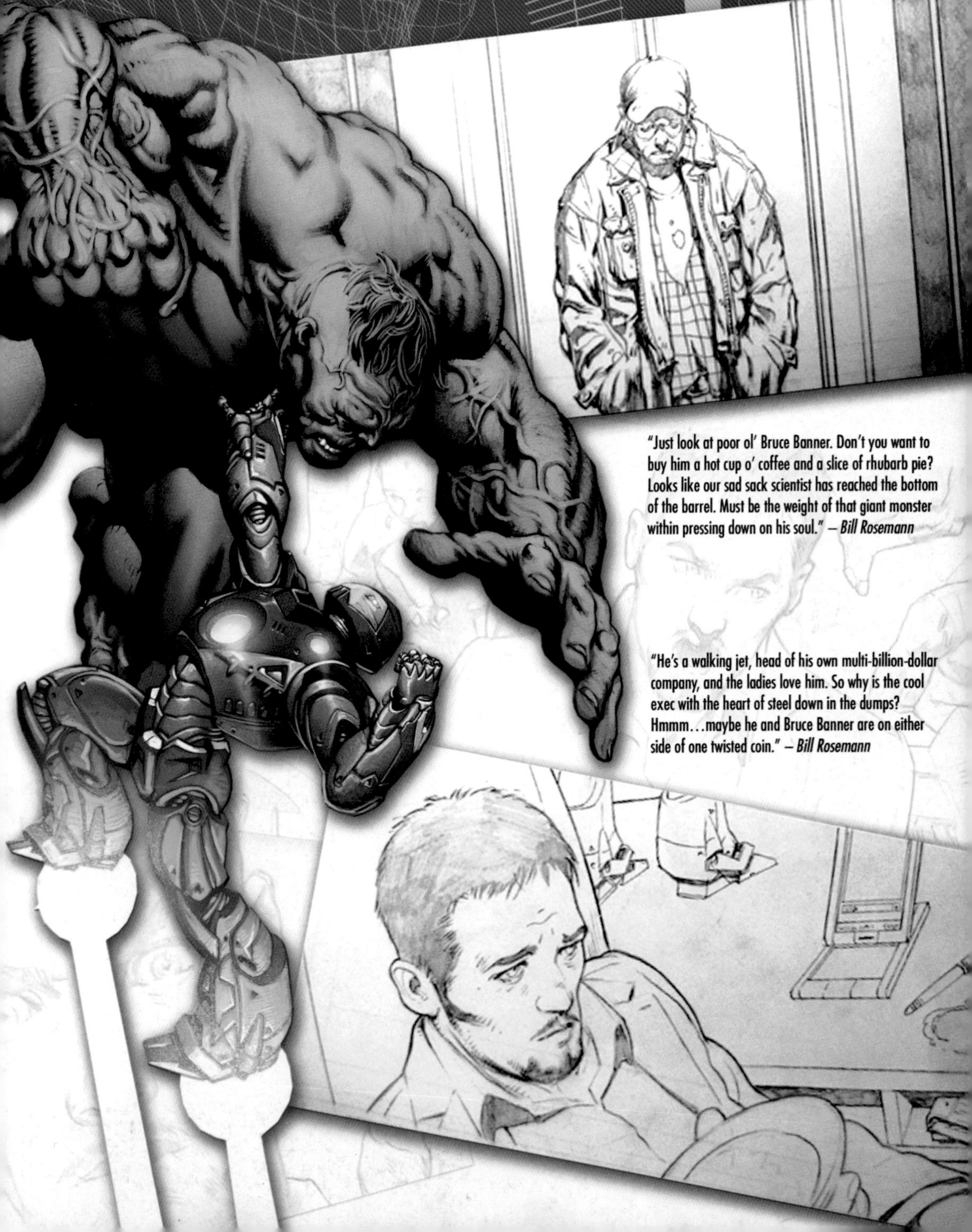

"Just look at poor ol' Bruce Banner. Don't you want to buy him a hot cup o' coffee and a slice of rhubarb pie? Looks like our sad sack scientist has reached the bottom of the barrel. Must be the weight of that giant monster within pressing down on his soul." *– Bill Rosemann*

"He's a walking jet, head of his own multi-billion-dollar company, and the ladies love him. So why is the cool exec with the heart of steel down in the dumps? Hmmm...maybe he and Bruce Banner are on either side of one twisted coin." *– Bill Rosemann*

"After coming from the barbarian world of the Conan series, drawing a man in high-tech armor has been both challenging and interesting, but I have to say, I get the most enjoyment out of drawing Hulk. He's just raw power and aggression and it's easy to lose yourself in that." – *Cary Nord*

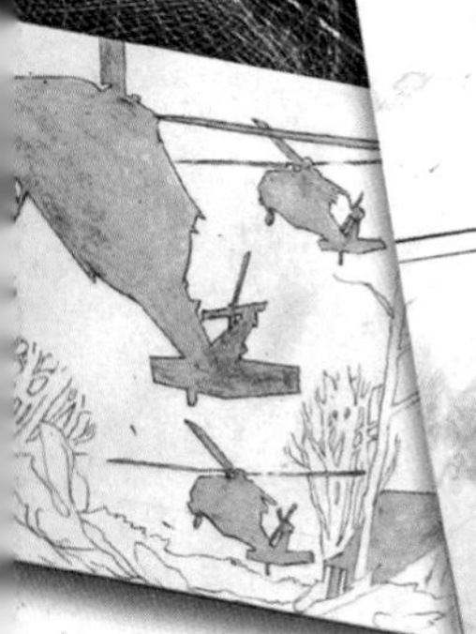

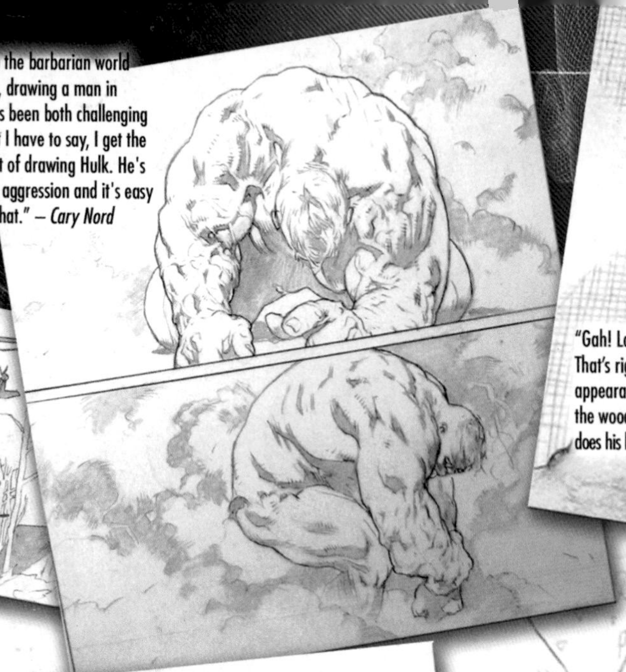

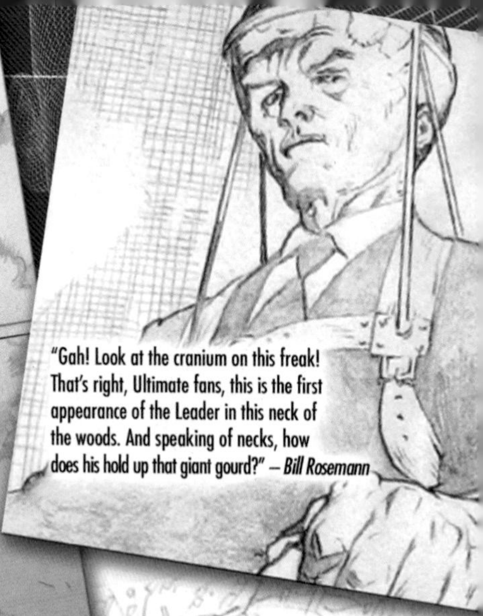

"Gah! Look at the cranium on this freak! That's right, Ultimate fans, this is the first appearance of the Leader in this neck of the woods. And speaking of necks, how does his hold up that giant gourd?" – *Bill Rosemann*

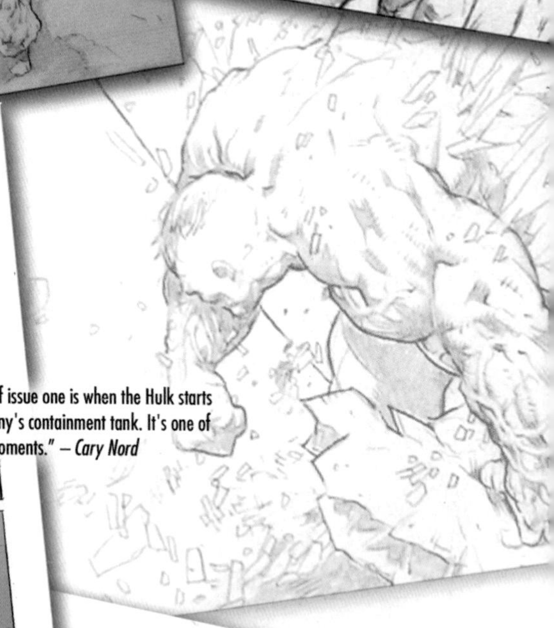

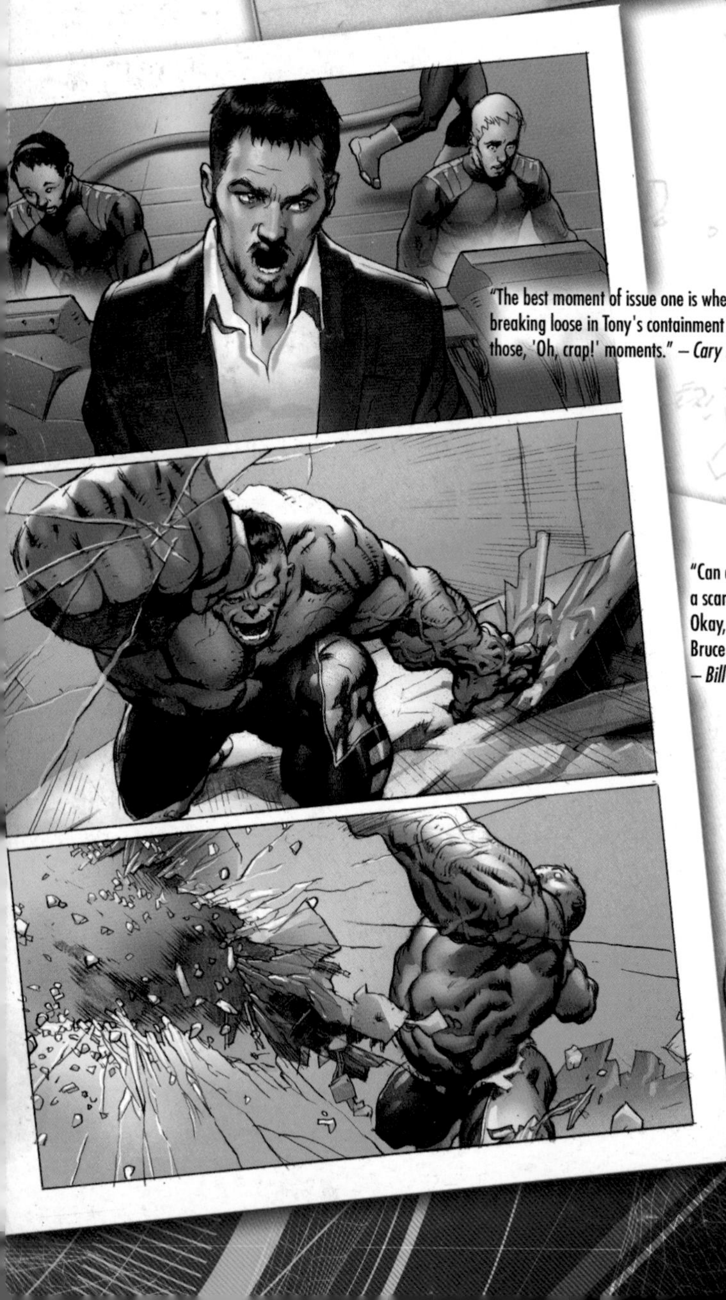

"The best moment of issue one is when the Hulk starts breaking loose in Tony's containment tank. It's one of those, 'Oh, crap!' moments." – *Cary Nord*

"Can artist Cary Nord draw a scary gray goliath or what? Okay, who went and made Bruce Banner angry?"
– *Bill Rosemann*

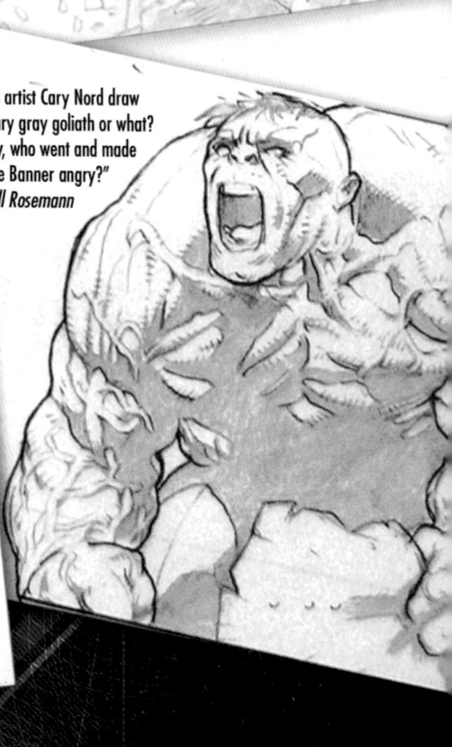